MARCHING OVER AFRICA

MARCHING OVER AFRICA

Letters from Victorian Soldiers

FRANK EMERY

We're foot–slog–slog, slog–sloggin' over Africa!
Foot–foot–foot–foot–sloggin' over Africa –
(Boots–boots–boots–boots, movin' up and down again!)
There's no discharge in the war!

'Boots', Rudyard Kipling

HODDER AND STOUGHTON
LONDON SYDNEY AUCKLAND TORONTO

British Library Cataloguing in Publication Data
Emery, Frank
Marching over Africa: letters from Victorian soldiers.
  1. Africa—Colonization—History
  2. Great Britain—History, Military—19th century
  3. Africa—History, Military
  I. Emery, Frank
  960'.23   DT32

  ISBN 0 340 38291 0

Contents

Acknowledgments

My warmest thanks are due to Dr. G. K. Woodgate, St. Peter's College, Oxford, for allowing me to use the diaries and letters of Major-General Sir Edward Woodgate; to Major Robert Smith, Curator of the Regimental Museum (The South Wales Borderers and Monmouthshire Regiment), The Barracks, Brecon, for permission to quote from letters in his charge; to the County Archivists of the Gloucestershire Records Office and the County of Hereford and Worcester Record Office, and to Mr. David Vaisey, Keeper of Western Manuscripts, Bodleian Library, Oxford, for their consent to quote from letters in collections deposited with them; to Major Edward Green, Regimental Headquarters, The Staffordshire Regiment (The Prince of Wales's), Wellington Barracks, Lichfield, for permission to include the letter from Colour-Sergeant Anthony Booth, VC; to the staff of the British Library Newspaper Library, Colindale, for their assistance; to the Revd. R. H. Lloyd, Christ Church, Oxford, to Mr. Tony Lee, and to Mr. Norman Holme, Regimental Museum, 23rd Royal Welch Fusiliers, Caernarfon Castle, for help with the illustrations; and to Miss Colleen McMillan for her skilful typing.

I am also grateful to editors of journals in whose pages some of the African campaigns were discussed in recent years: *Natalia*, 8, 1978, pages 54–60; *Natalia*, 11, 1981, pages 16–26; *History Today*, 31, June 1981, pages 26–31; *The Transvaal War, 1881* (Victorian Military Society Centenary Publication), 1981; *South African Military History Journal*, 5, 1982, pages 163–71; *The Royal Engineers Journal*, 96, 1982, pages 33–9.

Maps and Illustrations

Credits

Page 34, Dr. G. K. Woodgate, St. Peter's College, Oxford;
page 43, *Illustrated London News*, 6 December 1873; page 48,
from *From Midshipman to Field Marshal* by Sir Evelyn
Wood, (John Murray, 1906); page 53, Regimental Archives,
The 24th Regiment (South Wales Borderers), The Barracks,
Brecon; page 55, from *On Active Service* by William Whitelock
Lloyd, (Chapman & Hall, 1890); page 77, *The Graphic*, 28 July
1879; pages 92, and 121, Gloucestershire Records Office,
D.1233, D.873, C. 110; pages 148, 151 and 162, *Punch*, 23
September 1882, 14 February 1885, 23 April 1898.

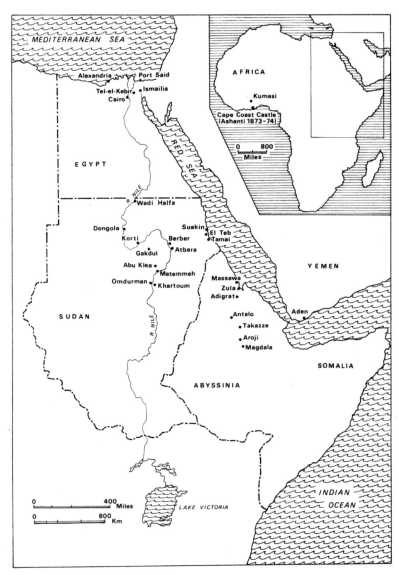

Campaigns in Abyssinia, Ashanti, the Sudan and Egypt

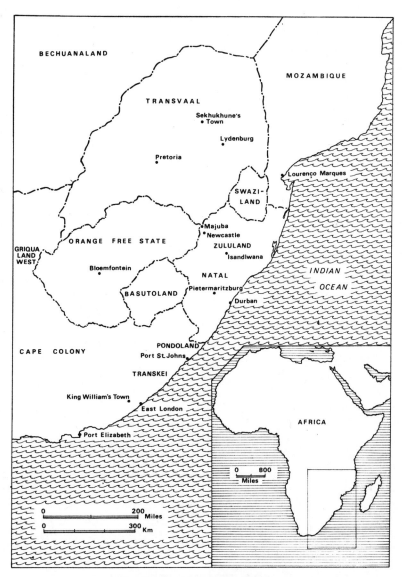

South-east Africa in the 1870s

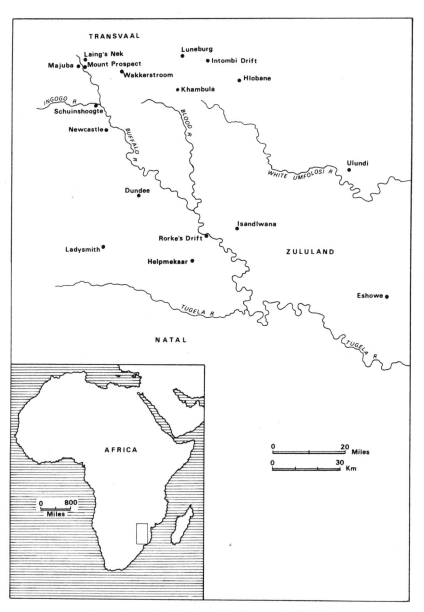

Campaigns in Zululand and the Transvaal, 1879–81

PREFACE

There is no shortage of books dealing with the military side of British imperial history in the Victorian period. Brian Bond has edited an excellent survey of the many wars that afflicted the Queen's long reign, *Victorian Military Campaigns* (Hutchinson, 1967), including the Crimean War, the Indian Mutiny, and the South African War of 1899–1902. Other but lesser engagements, both to the east and west of Suez, figure in Byron Farwell's view of *Queen Victoria's Little Wars* (Allen Lane, 1973), or in I. F. W. Beckett's more pictorial record, *Victoria's Wars* (Shire Publications, 1974). Individual campaigns or spheres of successive actions are well covered in such titles as *The Opium Wars of China* by Edgar Holt (Putnam, 1964), A. Swinson's *North West Frontier* (Hutchinson, 1967), or Darrell Bates, *The Abyssinian Difficulty: the Emperor Theodorus and the Magdala Campaign, 1867–68* (Oxford University Press, 1979).

Occasionally the authors make use of quotations from letters written by soldiers who were involved in the imperial ventures, but not to any great extent in comparison with the mainstream of source material from official reports and correspondence, published works, or newspaper coverage. Few realise the abundance of Victorian soldiers' letters that may be used to depict the harsh business of imperial action. Their potential was suggested in my book *The Red Soldier: Letters from the Zulu War* (Hodder and Stoughton, 1977). Now I wish to continue the exercise by bringing together a wider range of letters from the wars in all parts of Africa, beginning with a campaign against the Emperor Theodorus in what was then called Abyssinia (1868), and running on in time to the defeat of the Khalifa at Omdurman (1898). During those thirty years a series of major confrontations arose with the Asante (Ashanti) in West Africa; with the Xhosa, Pedi, Sotho and Zulu nations in southern Africa; with Egyptian loyalists in 1882; and a protracted war was fought with the Mahdist leaders of the Sudan. Nor were these confrontations in every case matters of British policy threatening an indigenous black power: in 1880–81 a brief but vicious war erupted between Britain and white opponents, the Boer or Afrikaner republicans of the Transvaal and Orange Free State. Worse was to follow between these white adversaries in 1899.

13

The nature and value of soldiers' letters is assessed in the opening chapter. All that needs to be said here is that they offer personal insights of military events, great or small, that cannot be found elsewhere. Collectively they yield a perspective of common experience gained at first hand in Africa. They were written at a time when intervention against native polities, land-grabbing, exercising influence, and punitive actions were all part of Britain's role as the most powerful of all the imperial states. They reveal what it was like to be there, and how things happened in the turmoil of active service. Perception under stress is the keynote, and wherever possible I have used letters from private soldiers or non-commissioned officers. This widens the social background of authorship, and brings unexpected credit to the ordinary soldier for his powers of expression.

Perception of African campaigning, or even of the nature of warfare itself, was to some degree conditioned by the writers' social status in Victorian Britain. The best introduction to this aspect of things is a recent book by L. H. Gann and Peter Duignan, *The Rulers of British Africa, 1870–1914* (Croom Helm, 1978). Their chapter on 'The Army' (pages 71–101) outlines the character of the imperial regiments and corps that served in Africa, with all their strengths and peculiarities. In their following chapter, 'Military Organization and Campaigns' (pages 102–53), not much is said of the purely imperial episodes in which the regular 'redcoat' soldiers took part, save for the Ashanti campaign (1873–4) and the Boer War (1899–1902). Instead there is full discussion of the part played by military units raised from Africans and colonists, as in Nigeria or Rhodesia. Even so, the analysis touches on many of the themes mentioned in soldiers' letters, such as the systematic destruction of villages, crops and livestock, or the employment of African auxiliaries to reinforce the British troops.

African service dominated the military careers of many men. Edward Woodgate first went there in 1868 when he served in the mountains of Ethiopia, and we learn something of that from his journal; within five years he was back to bush fighting in the equatorial forests of 'Ashantiland' in West Africa; in 1878 he began a strenuous involvement in the Zulu War; twenty years later he was back with the West African Regiment in Sierra Leone; in 1899, as a knighted general, Woodgate took a command in the South African War, and there died of wounds received at Spioenkop. He went five times to Africa, and by his third sailing he wryly tells his sister Nell (in May 1878), 'I am going on the warpath again, to the Cape this time. I shall soon begin to know my way about Africa.'

The African warpath is a recurrent theme throughout the letters, drawing men of all ranks into action where, if they were fortunate and survived, they would find military advancement. Sir Garnet Wolseley did well as a general in Ashanti, South Africa and Egypt, but less successfully in the attempt to rescue Gordon at Khartoum. As the most professional of soldiers, he had no doubts as to the rightness of a military initiative in gaining national prestige, views shared by many in the African armies. He applauded the appointment of Evelyn Wood, one of the toughest of British commanders, to the Transvaal during the first war against the Boers. 'I envy you the good fortune of being once more upon the warpath,' Wolseley writes from the War Office in 1881, 'the only path upon which it is worth travelling in these degenerate days of cant, puffed-up philosophical cosmopolitanism, and maudlin humanitarianism.' Whatever he had in mind there, he makes plain his ideal view of imperial force-of-arms. 'I know that wherever you go,' he assures Wood, 'you will do well and maintain our national reputation for hard straight hitting and gentle humanity of a manly nature.' The soldiers' letters will reveal plenty of the former, perhaps less than one would wish of the latter.

At this time military letters were not subject to censorship, although problems could arise when inaccurate or critical letters appeared in the press. During his campaigns against the French armies Wellington deplored the ignorance shown by some writers, 'and the indiscretion with which those letters are published', but he did not favour censorship. The more cautious correspondent was able to avoid such difficulties, as with a lieutenant of the 43rd Light Infantry writing to his brother from the Pyrenees in 1813: 'Allow me to request that none of my letters may appear in the newspapers.'[1] Criticism of the generals was always likely to creep into the letters, nor was this peculiar to the British army. From the picturesque setting of the American West and its Indian wars, a captain of the 7th Cavalry tells his wife how 'General Custer is very injudicious in his administration, and spares no effort to render himself generally obnoxious. I have utterly lost all the little confidence I ever had in his ability as an officer.'[2] Such things were best kept in the bosom of the family.

Letters presented in this book, especially when they appeared in

1. Michael Glover (ed.), *A Gentleman Volunteer. The Letters of George Hennell from the Peninsular War, 1812–13* (London: Heinemann, 1979), pages 122–3.
2. Robert M. Utley (ed.), *Life in Custer's Cavalry. Diaries and letters of Albert and Jennie Barnitz, 1867–1868* (New Haven and London: Yale University Press, 1977), page 50.

newspapers, are more or less free of such criticisms. The ordinary man was loyally disposed towards his commanders, but his revelation of the darker sides of warfare could arouse strong emotions at home. Young officers with a healthy self-interest in promotion asked their families not to publish the letters when they gave vent to their feelings. If there was nothing controversial in what they wrote the soldiers relished seeing their narratives appear in print. The scale of all this grew as the century went on, and when the South African War broke out in 1899 it was probable there would be vast numbers of letters available for publication. Not everyone approved of the trend. It really raised for the first time the question of censorship. Early in the war Sir E. N. Bennett thought it disgraceful that English newspapers should print letters from soldiers at the front criticising their leaders. 'Publicity of this sort strikes at the root of military discipline and common fairness,' he said, 'for the public can scarcely expect a British General to reply in the public press to the letter of a private serving under him.'[3]

Bennett was a sharp observer who had covered the Sudan campaign as a war correspondent in 1898. At the outset of the Boer War he served as a medical orderly in South Africa, and he has some significant things to say about his comrades. He pays tribute to their level of interest in issues of all kinds. 'As a Tommy myself I had some unique opportunities of learning what they talked about and how they talked, and certainly the subjects discussed sometimes covered a very big field.' They also disliked Kipling. In their sing-songs around the camp fires the choice ran to patriotic songs and sentimental ballads, 'but seldom, I am glad to say, to that wearisome doggerel *The Absent-Minded Beggar*. The more intelligent of them heartily dislike the manner in which they are represented in Mr. Kipling's poems, as foul-mouthed, godless and utterly careless of their duties to wives and children.'[4] Perhaps there Bennett was airing his prejudices, but the quality of the letters in this book may surprise anyone with a Kipling-inspired image of the Victorian soldiery.

FRANK EMERY

St. Peter's College,
Oxford.
August 1985

3. Ernest Nathaniel Bennett, *With Methuen's Column on an ambulance train* (London, 1900), page 126.
4. *Ibid.*, page 54.

ONE

'From the Seat of War':

VICTORIAN SOLDIERS' LETTERS

'I spent the evening, as usual on the eve of a battle, in writing a letter to my parents. This done, I retired to rest, and slept soundly.' The battle was Gujerat, fought by a British army in the Punjab during the Second Sikh War of 1848–49. The writer was a private soldier, Robert Waterfield, whose *Memoirs* cover his military service from 1842 to 1857 and give a classic pen-picture of his experiences in the Victorian ranks. Only now is it becoming clear that many others followed Waterfield's pattern of correspondence. Their writings (leaving aside those of their officers for the moment) are a largely untapped source of information, hidden away in regimental museums, record offices, or family collections. Occasionally they appear in print in the military journals. Very few were published in book form: Sergeant Timothy Gowing's letters from the Crimean War may be read in his *Voice from the Ranks* (1883), which he described modestly as a record of facts, not as an attempt at fine writing.

By far the most productive archive, however, is to be found in the columns of Victorian newspapers, national and local. It was common practice for soldiers' letters to be submitted for publication by whoever received them, and editors gladly accepted the best of them as first-hand reportage of events in the news. They appeared regularly in such provincial papers as the *Western Morning News*, the *Birmingham Daily Gazette*, the *Sheffield Daily Telegraph*, and the *Oxford Chronicle*. On a general level there is common ground between the letters and Kipling's *Barrack-Room Ballads*, where he brought into focus the British rankers, 'this fellowship of professional fighters, who rejected the proprieties and inhibitions of Victorian society', as a recent editor of the *Ballads*, Professor Charles Carrington, puts it. At the very least, letters could be the raw stuff from which to distil the soldier's hazards, what he thought of his officers and the enemy, what he talked about before and after going into battle.

It is not easy to determine the letter-writing potential of the non-commissioned officers and the rank and file of the British army during the nineteenth century. Perhaps because most of the regulars were recruited from the labouring masses in town and country, there is a common assumption that they were inarticulate and illiterate. This view is certainly contradicted in individual cases as early as the campaigns of the 1840s and 1850s, but what we really want are proportional figures on the broadest possible scale. The only usable statistics have to be drawn from military sources, and they are probably not as disinterested as we would wish them to be. Nevertheless, they claim that forty-three per cent of private soldiers and non-commissioned officers could read and write by 1878. In addition, forty-eight per cent had the kind of educational standard, geared though it was to the modest demands of the fourth-class army certificate, that enabled them to draft a letter. Whatever the gains from progress in elementary education in the nation as a whole, particularly after the 1870 Act, it is clear that serious attempts were being made to improve educational services within the army.

Soldiers had to attend school for five hours each week, although the effectiveness of this provision varied from regiment to regiment according to the commanding officers' enthusiasm in such matters. Promotion to corporal, however, required a third-class certificate of education, and letters from NCOs are proportionally more plentiful than from the private soldiers. Writing from Natal, in 1878, a private of the 24th Regiment (who was killed at Isandlwana at the outset of the Zulu War) sent his mother news of a lance-corporal comrade: 'hope he will get on, but he is a very poor scholar, that is a great drawback to him in the service'. As a sample group we may take the men of the 24th who fought with such desperate zeal at Rorke's Drift. The personal records of sixty-five of them survive in sufficient detail to show that thirty-eight were awarded certificates of education during their army service, twenty gaining a third-class certificate or better. Thus fifty-eight per cent of the group were well able to write letters home about their part in defending the mission station, and quite a number of those have survived.

By the 1870s, then, it is reasonable to estimate that at least half of the NCOs and private soldiers were capable of writing letters from active service, if opportunity allowed. The circumstances of a particular campaign were also a determinant of how many letters were sent off. Archibald Forbes, the war correspondent, insisted that he had never seen so much letter-writing done by troops in the field as he saw in Zululand; there was little else for them to do when off duty. As to the extent to which the editors of local newspapers might have changed whatever came into their hands for publication, it goes without saying they would have tidied up spelling, improved grammar and punctuation, and possibly corrected the proper names appearing in their raw copy. Some of the letters required such cosmetic treatment, but their substance and content would appear unchanged. After all, only letters that were reasonably well-written and had something worth reading in them would be taken for publication. They represent the best sample in which the editors had least to do in the way of interference between writer and general reader.

Although this book is concerned solely with Africa, perhaps we should introduce it against a wider perspective. Letters come to light from some of the earliest campaigns of Victoria's reign. The pitched battles against the Sikhs in 1845–46 saw British armies in action on that scale for the first time since Waterloo, a generation previously. Most of the generals in command in the Punjab were veterans of the Peninsular fighting with the French, but very few of the ordinary soldiers had gone through a baptism of fire. The nature of the engagements they experienced in these Sikh Wars was of the old military order, with set-piece manoeuvres of infantry regiments, much use of the prestigious cavalry, and short-range bombardments by muzzle-loading field artillery. So the soldiers' letters are full of such traditional scenes, as in the description penned by Private Edward Milton of the 3rd Light Dragoons. He charged with his regiment against the Sikh gun-batteries at Mudki on 19 December 1845, and again two days later at Ferozeshuhur:

> Just before we reached the guns, they opened a dreadful shower of grape-shot upon us, when my poor horse which had carried me in triumph at Mudki at this moment was cut in halves by a cannon shot. After the fall, and during the time I was fighting my way on foot, I got slightly wounded on the thigh and knee, but I managed to possess myself of another horse whose rider had fallen in defence of his country. The battle continued without ceasing the whole of the night, and such a night I never spent – the groans of the poor wounded and dying draw a sigh from me while I relate it. Poor unfortunate sufferers, some without limbs, begging for mercy's sake not to be left alone, but we were compelled not to notice their entreaties.

His style is inflated with conventional phrases; the point about 'fallen in defence of his country' is scarcely true of British forward policy in the Punjab, but he does paint an effective word-picture of that kind of battle because the style seems to fit the scene.

Surveyed through the whole period of Victorian warfare, the letters also reflect the changing nature of military action and deployment. The Crimean War was something of a watershed in this respect. On the one hand, it is possible to echo and repeat Milton's account of a dash at the guns by sabre-wielding horsemen: Sergeant Clifford Mitchell attacked at Balaklava with the 13th Light Dragoons, 'one of the most murderous charges on record', as he described it in a letter to his brother. But the Crimea also showed a foretaste of more static struggles involving large numbers of infantry fighting from trenches and redoubts, with the attrition of massive bombardments by the heavy guns.

Plenty of letters were written from the Crimea, and some appeared in the national dailies, the local weeklies, and in reviews such as the *Weekly News and Chronicle*, which carried in 1854–55 a regular feature of 'Scenes at the Front, culled from private correspondence'. Private Joseph Coulter, for instance, not yet eighteen years of age, fought with the Scots Fusilier Guards at Inkerman, and was wounded five times in that hand-to-hand mêlée. He described it all in a letter from the hospital at Scutari, and how he crawled away to safety ('I never got timorous till then'), adding that 'If it had not been for my uncle Robert being here I would have been a dead man'. More usually the soldier's name was not given at this time, perhaps wisely, because many of them were as critical of military mismanagement as William Russell's outspoken dispatches to *The Times*.

One cavalryman of the Heavy Brigade explained how he was too cold in his tent amid the winter snow to write more, 'not having the power to hold my pen any longer'. He said there was no sign of the long-awaited huts that would keep out the cutting wind they called the Cossack North-easter: 'speaking my mind, I think we are in a fix, and the authorities don't know what to do'. Personal hardships were commonplace. Sergeant Bargus of the 63rd Regiment at Inkerman had 'fought all day without any food, and in the evening I got a bit of bread from a dead Russian officer, and it served me till the next day'. A corporal of the 19th gave his parents a wry account of conditions at the siege of Sebastopol in January 1855:

We [the Light Division] have still the post of honour in front, and which, you may believe me, we would consider it an honour to be deprived of, as the duties are most onerous and harassing, particularly as we are very badly fed and, I was going to say, without a rag scarcely to cover us; but that would be wrong, as we have nothing but rags upon us. I am now, with the exception of some bread, nearly fifty hours without food; it is that, and the chilly damp weather, lying under tents, instead of snug wooden huts like the French, that creates fevers, dysentery, diarrhoea, and causes such a frightful mortality.

Letters naturally reflect the character of the campaign from which they were written, especially as to the balance between general and particular observations. Nowhere is this better seen than in soldiers' comment during the 'Great Rebellion' or Mutiny of 1857–58 in India. There the insurrection reached beyond the purely military orbit and impinged on a British civilian population. Atrocities on a deeper scale than elsewhere in the Victorian experience were to provoke some harsh responses from the troops. Few letters fail to include a general awareness of these incidents, which filled the soldiers with the sense of being part of an avenging host. William Saddler, a sergeant in the 14th Light Dragoons, told his father about some notorious events:

The insurgents have killed 132 European families that were on the road to Calcutta. At Cawnpore they were going down the river in boats; they stopped them and jammed them up, and fired grape and canister at them, and afterwards what they did not kill they cut to pieces with swords; since that they have killed some 500 men, women, and children. At Delhi they took some European children, and threw them up in the air and caught them on the point of their bayonets as they fell.

After his regiment charged a body of rebel sepoys at Aurangabad, it seemed natural for Saddler to report that the prisoners were tried by court martial: 'we shot six and blowed [*sic*] four away from the guns, and hung one'. He found his duties 'most confounded hard', but did not care so long as 'we can have revenge for what these savages have done to those who have kept them from slavery and starvation' – a nice piece of moral justification from a man in the Victorian ranks. Saddler's figure for the Cawnpore casualties is reasonably near the mark, for there were 630 civilians present when they were first besieged by the sepoys; allowing four persons per family for those killed after surrendering on 25 June 1857, the total would work out at 528. Not that one should expect the soldiers' letters to be invariably accurate in matters of statistics: they had a natural tendency to exaggerate the numbers of the enemy confronting them in battle, and of those put out of action.

Political and moral arguments at home about the rights and wrongs of interventionist wars, the criticism of what were seen by some as unjustified, costly, and badly-organised campaigns in support of policies to which they were opposed, all had some measure of reflection in the letters. For the editors of Liberal newspapers who wrote against the Zulu War it was tempting to publish letters that put the conduct of operations in the worst possible light. Thus the appearance of letters telling how wounded Zulus were killed out of hand, after the British victories at Khambula and Ulundi, sparked off a volume of public protest from such bodies as the Aborigines' Protection Society. There was reaction at a local level, too, as when one of the Oxford newspapers printed a letter from Private Thomas Jackson of the 58th Regiment, who had worked as a compositor in the city before joining up. He recorded how the attacking Zulus at Ulundi were shelled by the big guns, 'which they did not seem to relish, as it made them jump about in a very lively manner, much amusement being caused by their antics'. Afterwards the troops planted the Union Jack over Cetshwayo's royal kraal or *umusi* at Ulundi, burned down all the houses, and marched away as the bands played 'Rule Britannia' and 'Three Cheers for the Red, White, and Blue'. The following week there appeared a sharp letter of complaint about Jackson's 'cruel flippancy' over the death 'of his fellow-creatures, with whom he had no quarrel'. A year later, unabashed, he was home again in Oxford, reading a paper on 'The Boers and the Zulus' to his lodge of the Order of Good Templars.

Sometimes the soldiers hit back at their critics. Sergeant Harry Thomas took part in the British invasion of Afghanistan with the 25th Regiment, and when writing in April 1879 he was at Landi Kotal, deeply involved in mountain warfare. He defended the soldier's rôle as best he could:

You must know, dear father, that everything that goes out of the camp, if only for a quarter of a mile, has to be escorted by an armed party, camels grazing, bullocks for water, men of regiments making roads through the country, etc. Convoys escorting food for the expedition from place to place are fired upon, and it is surprising to read, in the few papers we get, about bishops, ministers, and others making mention of the cruelties they say are practised upon the Afghans up the Khyber Pass, and at different places. If these people could be made to traverse through these mountains from month to month's end, and know not the moment they would be cruelly butchered (not shot), they would not sympathise so much with these savages. We who are among them know everything concerning their savagery.

Not infrequently the soldiers comment on the background or causes of war, generally accepting it as a *fait accompli*, endorsing the official view of the rightness of British commitment. Occasionally they venture a more profound debate on the broader issues, as in the letter written by Corporal George Howe to his brother in Sheffield. He served in the Royal Engineers, a corps whose reputation for being the army's intellectuals is certainly borne out by his writings from the Anglo-Boer War of 1880–81. Howe had already written some remarkable letters about his experiences during the Zulu War, but by March 1881 he was in a more demanding situation after three successive British defeats at Laing's Nek, Ingogo, and (heaviest of all) at Majuba. As he wrote, the Gladstone administration was negotiating for peace and planning to grant the Transvaal Boers their independence, albeit under British suzerainty. There is a prophetic ring to the corporal's somewhat rhetorical analysis:

If peace was made now, it would not last, but by-and-by the Boers would be in arms again, and we would have to fight the whole miserable war again. I am no advocate for war. God forbid! But now, when we have drawn the sword, it will never do to sheath it with dishonour. I would be as glad as the next one – as the most enthusiastic peace-at-any-price follower – to hear of peace being declared; but let us have peace with honour; no patched-up treaty; no crying peace, peace, when there is no peace. Much as this war is to be deplored, now we have entered upon it it would be cheaper to go, if needs be, to the bitter end. It might have been avoided if some of our bigwigs had not been led by the nose, and duped into the belief that it was only a few of the worst characters who were crying for Republicanism. I count the Boers as much as our Scottish Covenanters, with this difference: one fought for liberty of conscience, the Boers from a dislike to, and liberty from, a foreign yoke.

At another level, the letters often take us with the individual soldiers directly to the sharp end of battle, behind the official dispatches to the realities of dangerous encounter. Another corporal of Engineers throws a rare spotlight on the Sudan campaign of 1882–85, rare, that is, from the viewpoint of the ordinary soldiers. Plenty has been written about the politics and strategies of Wolseley's unsuccessful effort to rescue Gordon from Khartoum, but soldiers' letters are peculiarly rare. The reason must lie in the appalling hardships of sand, thirst, heat, disease, and sheer distance. Paper, ink, or pencils had little appeal for the troops, who were struggling for survival against the environment and lack of supplies as much as against the Mahdist forces who opposed them so tenaciously. There was little spare time for correspondence, and as soon as the fighting was broken off they were quickly evacuated from the Sudan because of threatening Russian military moves in Central Asia.

Scarcity value therefore attaches to a letter by Corporal F. W. Bennett, who was caught up in the battle of Tofrek on 22 March 1885. Sixteen of his immediate comrades were killed when the Sudanese attacked the British camp behind its protecting enclosure of thorn trees or *zareba*:

> No Company of Engineers has lost so many since the Crimea, and may God grant that no other will share the same fate. Many of our poor fellows were killed while running to get their arms, they being at work cutting down trees, bush, etc., when the alarm was given, and however the rest reached the square will ever remain a mystery. Our men tried to escape in the bush when they found their retreat was cut off, but were brutally stabbed. After that was seen, very few of the enemy's wounded stood much chance. Soon squares were formed and eventually one square, and up went a good British cheer. The first thing was to kill all the camels of our own, as this was the only possible chance of saving ourselves. After another lapse of a few seconds we opened fire on all sides. On came these brave rebels, time after time, only to meet certain death, and after two hours' hard fighting, hundreds of them were lying dead close up to the *zareba*.

Tofrek was the last encounter of the campaign, followed by the withdrawal of British forces from the Sudan and then by more than a decade of stalemate. When fresh intervention came it was sealed and settled in a military sense by the crushing defeat of the Khalifa at Omdurman. A soldier who fought there on 2 September 1898 wrote about it to his brother at home, and his depiction of the onset of battle is proof enough of the graphic style that makes the best of the letters so memorable. He was Sergeant Thomas Christian of the Seaforth Highlanders:

When daylight made things clear, we saw as far as sight reached the great plain covered with white jebba-clad Dervishes, banners flying and drums beating – a splended sight! We were ordered to kneel down, but could see through the *zareba* as they came on. It looked as if the whole of Africa was coming at us, for their front extended for miles. When they advanced to about 2,000 yards the guns opened on them, and they commenced a terrific fire, but we heard no familiar whistle of their bullets yet. When they came to 1,300 yards we fixed bayonets and rose, firing section volleys, each volley aiming just below a flag. Each time a flag fell, up it came again, and we heard them all singing.

Repeatedly during the many conflicts between the Victorian army and a non-European enemy, the fighting had to be conducted along informal and unfamiliar lines. Text-book tactics were discarded, and the need for a modified approach was painfully recognised. When facing the Xhosa people in the Cape during the late 1870s, for example, the value of mounted infantry soon became clear, using volunteers drawn from the ranks of line battalions. Again in the Zulu War the British high command was forced by disastrous defeats to envisage the enemy as though they were cavalry, and to adopt the obsolete formula of drawing up the British troops in laager and open square. By this means they eventually defeated the Zulus at Ulundi, and the square was retained for much bloody fighting in the Sudan after 1882. Even with such responses, there was always the risk in these 'little wars' that unorthodox tactics by a more mobile or desperate foe would throw the British formations into confusion.

What happened then was the kind of action called 'a soldier's battle', in which there was little or no scope for command. Small groups of men knew only what was happening in their immediate vicinity. It was every man for himself, and a picture of what went on is most likely to emerge from the personal writings of soldiers who were pitchforked into chaotic battle. The classic setting for minor but deadly skirmishes of this genre was the North-West Frontier of India, where a mountainous terrain and the surprise attack by Afridi and other tribesmen caused immense difficulties for isolated parties of troops. Such was the fate of two companies of the 2nd Oxfordshire Light Infantry caught on the hop near the Khyber Pass in the last days of 1897. A private soldier who went through it described this incident of the 'Frontier War' for the benefit of a comrade who had returned to England:

On the 30th December we were covering party, out in small picquets covering the Sappers and Miners destroying the enemy's villages. About two o'clock p.m. the Sappers returned to camp, and as soon as the big guns had got nearly to camp the enemy swarmed down on our small picquets in hundreds and, Jack, then came the time for the old 52nd to show their metal – they did it and no mistake. We tried to retire, and then the shots fell thick and deadly. Corporal Bell of your company was shot dead, he being the first to fall. Colonel Plowden went to fetch him in and he got shot in the stomach, so he had hard lines; also Lt. Owen got shot in the forearm, and the enemy kept creeping up. So we were forced to retire into the village, as it was getting dark, and it was useless to stop in small numbers. We all got in the village the best way we could. Men were falling wounded on all sides. We held on to the village until help arrived, but had we tried to get home there would not have been a single man alive to tell the tale.

Shortly afterwards, an early letter from the Second Anglo–Boer War drew comparison with the Frontier: writing from Ladysmith in October 1899, a corporal of the 19th Hussars told how the Boers 'get into the hills much like the Afridis, and take a devil of a lot of shifting, and are remarkably good shots'. For the next few years such a huge British army was in the field in South Africa that the yield of letters is predictably high, indeed many weekly newspapers had a regular feature of 'Letters from the Front'. Collectively they offer a first-hand panorama of all phases of campaigning against the elusive Boers. By then some of the soldiers were quite accustomed to seeing their letters published in the papers, and even wrote to the editors on their own account. Those from the 'Black Week' of British disasters in December 1899 are particularly vivid due to the scale and severity of the battles. Lance-Corporal W. E. Wicks of the Black Watch survived the decimation of the Highland regiments at Magersfontein:

We had to lie till about 3 p.m., when we made another three successive dashes, but failed. By this time the guns had blown up the enemy's trenches and some of us got in and gave them the skewer, but had to fly for our lives on a flank party coming up. Of the awful sights and privation I won't speak, only I must say that we had no water for 32 hours, and dozens died through want, wounded of course. I got through with my helmet knocked off, two bullets through the kilt, and one through my spats. Do what you like with this letter, it is all the truth.

Phrases like 'gave them the skewer' (for a bayonet attack) add some edge to the style of the letters, reflecting the soldier's personality as well as his experience. We see it with the guardsman at Inkerman (1854) who declares that 'Had I stood up I should have been killed a dozen times, as the Irishman said'. 'I felt during the day as if I had a hot iron going into my head,' says a rifleman besieging Delhi in the searing heat of July 1857. A soldier marches into Afghanistan (1878) 'without a covering but for the bright frosty sky and twinkling stars, as light-hearted as if we were children at home for our holidays'. Another who helped in the relief of Ladysmith says, 'That is just what I would like, to stick a couple of Boers on the end of my bayonet like a bit of toast, I'd teach them to fire into our hospitals and ambulances.' By their letters the Victorian rank-and-file cease to be a mute and anonymous body of men marching past in scarlet or khaki columns.

What of their officers in this respect? In exploring the African campaigns through soldiers' letters, it would be absurd and short-sighted to ignore them. As a group, and as might be expected, most officers were sufficiently well educated, motivated and leisured to write letters often and regularly to their families and friends. We can take for granted that they had the ability, if not always the inclination, to write about their war experience. Many had benefitted from going to one of the English public schools founded in the 1850s and 1860s, as the Victorian middle classes grew in affluence and bought education for their sons. The point can be substantiated if we look at the education record of sixty British officers who had the misfortune to be killed in action, or who died from other causes during the Zulu War of 1879. No fewer than forty-six had been at public schools: ten were Old Etonians, four went to Rugby, four to Cheltenham. Of the other fourteen, all the Gunners and Engineers had entered the Royal Military Academy at Woolwich, thereby elevating the standard of educational achievement enjoyed by the whole group. Indeed, school magazines such as *The Marlburian* or *The Cheltonian* are sprinkled with letters from young officers who had left school a few years previously. Nor should we forget that ten per cent of this Zulu War sample of officer casualties had been at university. Four of them were killed on the same day at Isandlwana: Vereker was at Oxford, Melvill at Cambridge, Cavaye was an Edinburgh graduate, and Surgeon-Major Shepherd had trained at Aberdeen University.

Compared with other spheres of warfare, for instance the Peninsular War of Wellington's army or the various campaigns in

India mounted against the Sikhs, the rebellious sepoys in 1857–58, or the Pathan tribesmen of the North-West Frontier, not many officers' letters or journals have been published from the African field of operations. There can be no doubt they exist, however, nor is their quality in question: a classic proof of this appears in the correspondence of Major Arthur Harness (1838–1927) of the Royal Artillery, which has been impeccably edited by Sonia Clarke.[1] Educated at Carshalton School, he then entered the Royal Military Academy, Sandhurst, in 1853. Harness was awarded a brevet Lieutenant-Colonelcy for his services when commanding N/5 Battery of field artillery during the Cape frontier war of 1878. He moved to Natal to join the British invasion of Zululand, where he became a key figure in the critical phase of troop movements at Isandlwana, on 22 January 1879. Harness's letters not only throw light (though more would be welcome) on that dismal episode, they are also the essence of personal and public communication, as felt by a regular letter-writer at the seat of war.

Charles Ernest Commeline is representative of the younger officers of junior commissioned rank who were such prolific writers. He was born into an old Gloucester family in 1856, his father being managing director of the Gloucestershire Banking Company. After his schooling at Cheltenham College, he was commissioned into the Royal Engineers in 1875. When we meet him he was a subaltern in the 5th Field Company, and had landed at Durban on 4 January 1879 after a month's voyage from home. Commeline's description of the awful conditions through which the company made its way to the front line of the Zulu War is already in print.[2] His fellow subalterns with 5th Field Company in South Africa were J. R. M. Chard and R. Da C. Porter. By the time we begin to read the letter of 31 January 1879 Chard had gone ahead to join the column with which Lord Chelmsford led the invasion of Zululand, and, indeed, had already won his Victoria Cross. From the Helpmekaar base camp on the Natal side of the Buffalo, we hear Commeline's account of the shattering events of 22–23 January at Isandlwana and Rorke's Drift. Incidentally, he celebrated his twenty-third birthday in the midst of all this furore, on 24 January.

1. Sonia Clarke, *Invasion of Zululand, 1879* (Johannesburg: Breathurst Press, 1979).
2. Frank Emery, *The Red Soldier: Letters from the Zulu War, 1879* (London: Hodder and Stoughton, 1977), pages 56–60.

Long before this reaches you you will no doubt have heard of the terrible disaster which happened to our little Army on the 22nd inst and in which I think there can be little doubt that but for our numerous delays on the march all our Company would have been involved. We have lost 800 white men besides a large number of natives and not a single Officer who was not mounted escaped from the field [i.e., at Isandlwana]. The 24th Regt lost 6 whole companies with the exception of five men and the whole of the Rocket Battery was destroyed. All the Engineers present were killed, viz Col Durnford, Lieut MacDowel, and the four men of my Company who were sent on ahead of us with Chard.

I daresay you will see many accounts of the affair in the newspapers but as I have heard all about it from several of the few survivors who are with us here, and also from many who were with the general at the time and saw the field of slaughter that night, I may as well give a short account of it. Lord Chelmsford had crossed the Buffalo at Rorke's Drift and advanced a day's march into Zululand, pitching camp some 9 miles beyond the river. Several reconnaissances had been made by the Mounted Corps during the week before and the enemy were not supposed to be in any considerable force, although they had been seen about on the hills. The following morning a body of Zulus with a large herd of cattle were seen on the hills near the camp, and the General leaving the 6 companies of the 24th and 2 guns and some Mounted Police to guard the camp left with the remainder of his force, some 1,200 strong, to pursue the enemy. Shortly after he had gone Col. Durnford came in with his Native Contingent and the Rocket Battery, and suddenly enormous numbers of Zulus appeared on the hills on three sides of the camp. The latter was not intrenched in any way and was very badly placed to resist an attack, lying on a low piece of ground from which the only line of retreat lay between two hillocks. The enemy made their usual dispositions for attack, which consist of encircling the opposing force and then advancing from all sides at a given signal. When all was ready great lines of skirmishers advanced from the main body and came pouring down on the camp. Our men formed line in front of it and kept up a tremendous fire, the Zulus falling by hundreds. Still on they came like ants, as a man fell another taking his place, in perfect silence. They came on in five lines of skirmishers by rushes in the most approved modern European style, towards the end all lying down at the flash of the guns which had mown them down in rows.

Our native contingent soon bolted and our men's ammunition becoming exhausted they had to retreat into camp to get more, but there was not time, for the Zulus were amongst them and the butchery began. Our poor fellows then turned and tried to escape but except 20 men of the 30 Mounted Police, and several other mounted officers and men, none got away, all being assegaied. The whole affair lasted little more than an hour. The General was only 15 miles distant and could see that fighting was going on, but of course could render no assistance. When he got the news of what had occurred he at once gave orders for a retreat on the camp, deciding to sleep there and cut his way across the river next morning if possible, though his chance seemed a small one.

In fact the army was saved from utter annihilation by the brilliant defence of the little mission house at Rorke's Drift at which Chard of our Company was the Senior Officer. He had with him Bromhead of the 24th Regt and his Company of 100 men and Dr. Russell,[3] when at 4 o'clock in the afternoon they saw a great force of Zulus coming down on them. These had been detached from the main army as soon as it was seen our poor fellows were done for, doubtless with the intention of destroying the detachment at the Drift and the pontoons for crossing the river, thus cutting off the General's retreat. The fighting was most desperate, lasting till 4 o'clock next morning, and the Zulus probably lost over 1,000 men, 367 bodies being counted in the enclosure of the house.

They were twice repelled at the point of the bayonet, their advance being blocked by the dead bodies of their killed. Our fellows only lost 13, most of whom were sick men lying in a hospital close by, which the Zulus fired just as it was growing dark, thus probably saving the remainder by the sacrifice of these few, as the light from the fire enabled our fellows to use their rifles on the masses of the enemy with terrible effect. One gallant old soldier of the 24th probably saved them again. He observed a Zulu on the opposite hill light a torch and rush down to apply it to the thatch of the Mission house at a retired corner. The soldier leant out of the window and fired at the man at 5 yds. distance and missed him, but loaded again and shot him through the head just as the thatch had given signs of taking fire. The Zulu was found afterwards dead with his torch gone out, but raised to the thatch.

Probably no more desperate and brilliant defence of a post has ever been chronicled among the many gallant deeds of British soldiers than the defence of Rorke's Drift. Its consequences must also be most important, as the General was enabled to bring his little force back over the river, and such a disastrous repulse must in some way have restored our prestige in the eyes of the Zulus. In the two affairs they probably lost between 3,000 and 4,000 men,

---

3. Russell is wrong: he means Surgeon J. H. Reynolds, Medical Officer to the 2/24th Regiment, who won the Victoria Cross for his part in the defence of Rorke's Drift.

though we know nothing for certain. And now here we are bottled up between this camp and Rorke's Drift, some 800 men at each place, not strong enough to advance and with no orders to retreat, until I suppose we get reinforcements from Home. The Zulus if they please can march on Maritzburg[4] or Durban as there is not a soldier to bar their way.

This Helpmekaar is a funny place. It consisted when we arrived of a row of corrugated iron stores surrounded by a wall of waggons piled above and below with sacks. We Engineers have been hard at work superintending the throwing up of a strong earthwork all round which is to supersede the waggon laager. The stores contain ammunition, commissariat stores and sacks of oats and mealies [Indian corn]. During the day the men live outside the laager, a good many tents having sprung up all round, but at night all sleep inside round the parapets ready for an attack. We Officers sleep in one of the sack stores, spreading our rugs on the sacks and making ourselves as comfortable as we can. I have not taken off my clothes for a night since the 22nd, and am not likely to do so for many nights to come.

Commeline served throughout the Zulu campaign down to the battle of Ulundi, on 4 July 1879, which he described in one of his letters. Ulundi was not to be the last bit of hot action experienced by Commeline in 1879. By November he was in the thick of the fighting that crushed Sekhukhune, the hostile leader of the Pedi people. That was in the Transvaal, and he stayed on to work at various garrisons there throughout 1880. By the end of the year the First Anglo-Boer War had broken out, and Commeline was trapped in Pretoria when the Boers besieged it. He was then serving with 2nd Field Company, Royal Engineers, and together they suffered many privations before the conflict petered out after Majuba. At the close of 1881 he was posted to Pietermaritzburg, and there he remained for two years, his duties in Natal being enlivened by such incidents as joining the escort for politicians who met Cetshwayo, the deposed Zulu king, on his return from exile in 1883.

In these later phases of his five-year stint in South Africa, just as he had during the Zulu War itself, Commeline wrote letters to his father on a dutifully regular basis. Nor should we forget the discomforts under which he wrote these letters. As he observed (15 May 1879), 'I have not written to Cheltenham for a long time, but

4. Pietermaritzburg, the colonial capital of Natal.

31

letter-writing is often very difficult, one's knees or a biscuit box frequently doing duty for a table, and now candles are exhausted so one cannot write after dark.' They are full of interest, and we shall read extracts from some of them on another occasion (pages 90–6).

Commeline died in 1928, after long retirement, as a Colonel of Engineers, and one can only speculate as to how many officers like him enhanced their bold young lives by writing about the ups and downs of African campaigning. We shall meet another of them, P. S. Marling, in Egypt and the Sudan during the 1880s.

Two

'I Am Writing Under Great Difficulties':

The Campaigns in Abyssinia and Ashantiland

The brief but spectacular campaign in Abyssinia (or Ethiopia, as we now know it) got under way after Queen Victoria declared war on the Emperor Theodorus, in a speech delivered on 19 November 1867. The circumstances that provoked this expedition are explained wonderfully well by Sir Darrell Bates.[1] There is something unreal about the despatch of a force of 64,000 men to the landing place at Annesley Bay, just to the south of Massawa on the Red Sea. Of these, nearly 15,000 were combatant troops drawn from British and Indian regiments, including a Naval Brigade. About 36,000 transport animals were needed, camels and elephants among them, to cope with the difficult operation of supporting the force as it climbed inland among the Ethiopian gorges and mountains. Sir Robert Napier's command went ashore during January 1868; by early April it had reached the Delanta plateau, and an engagement with Theodorus' army took place at Aroji on 10 April. The royal stronghold of Magdala was captured on 13 April, followed by Theodorus' suicide; a few days later the British force started to retrace its painful progress to the coast. Total casualties amounted to two killed and twenty-seven wounded on the British side, almost bloodless by African standards.

Among those present at the first clash of arms at Aroji (he called it 'Arrogui') was Edward Woodgate, a young ensign serving with the 4th Foot, The King's Own Royal (Lancaster) Regiment. His account of it, written in his diary under Good Friday (10 April), runs as follows:

> We marched at daybreak down to the Bashilo which we reached about 8, and crossed it without boots or socks as there was plenty of water in it. We expected to halt there and go reconnoitring up

1. Darrell Bates, *The Abyssinian Difficulty: The Emperor Theodorus and the Magdala Campaign, 1867–68* (Oxford University Press, 1979).

33

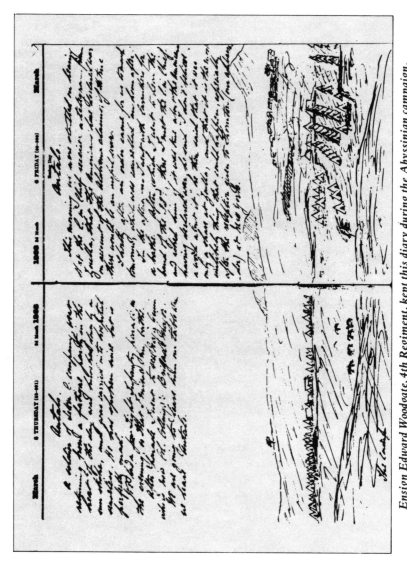

Ensign Edward Woodgate, 4th Regiment, kept this diary during the Abyssinian campaign.

the road, but instead the Brigade was divided, and the Artillery, Naval Brigade, and Baggage went up the road, while the Infantry climbed the hills to the right. Thinking we were going to halt the men did not fill their water-bottles, as the river was muddy, and consequently we had no water with us all day and were fearfully thirsty, and the hill was very steep. I was never so thirsty before. We reached the top at about 4 p.m. about two miles from Fala hill.

We had just piled arms and were lying down when a gun was fired from Fala; I thought at first that it was for bravado when two more shots were fired; these first shots of Theodorus' were received with a cheer from the men, and all at once we saw Abyssinians swarming down the hill by thousands, apparently to attack us. The men fell in again without their kits, and we marched down to meet them on a flat piece of ground between our hill and Selassie and Fala. On the way down there we met the Naval Brigade coming up to get into position, soon after they opened fire with their rockets; at about the same time Penn's battery who were on a hill just above the road also opened fire. We went down on to the plateau, followed by the Baluchis and Bombay sappers; the first two companies that got there extended as skirmishers, and advancing met about 3,000 of the enemy, they commenced firing, advancing; when 200 yards distant the fire was returned, both advancing until they were about 80 yards apart, when the Abyssinians turned and ran.

In the meantime I was with the colour party with the reserve, but the companies in support being sent off to the left to reinforce the companies on Baggage Guard, so the companies in reserve became supports and we came close up to the skirmishers. I was so thirsty that when a shower came I sucked the water out of the colour. Coming after the skirmishers we passed some 6 or 8 dead and wounded Abyssinians lying close together, soon after the skirmishers halted, and we came up with them. The mob of Abyssinians had retreated to the foot of the hill, about 1,000 yards distant, but a good many remained skulking in bushes near us, from where they wounded several of our men. Sergeant Creedon was shot through the leg, and Kirby of my company through the arm, giving him a compound fracture. The guns at the top of the hill kept up a fire, but could not be depressed enough, and most of the shot went over us; one however struck the ground close to us as I was talking to a sergeant. About this time the colour party was ordered to join the Baluchis. By feigning to retreat and then kneeling down so as to be out of sight, the Abyssinians were induced to advance again, they were allowed to come well within range, and then our men reopened fire and drove them back again.

The Baluchis were ordered to fire but fired so much into the air that they were stopped. In the meantime, Abyssinians who attacked the Baggage Guard were driven into a ravine where they were crowded together, and slaughtered by hundreds by our men, the Punjabis and the Artillery, who sent shells into the middle of them. There was a squadron of the 3rd Light Cavalry on the ground, but had no opportunity of charging. There were some beautiful shots made by some of our men, who picked off the chiefs as they rode about 500 or 600 yards off. There was one man behind a bush on the hill, who had fired two or three shots at us, when a sergeant of the colour party quickly knelt down and shot him dead, he was 500 yards off.

Theodorus was said to be riding about the field and a great number of shots were fired at a man supposed to be him, but without hitting him. During a lull in the firing I saw Speedy riding out to the front, and challenging Theodorus to come out and fight.[2] It is the custom of the country for two opposing kings to ride out in front of their armies and fight hand to hand. At nightfall the enemy all retired up the hill where we were too tired to follow them. We then marched back and got the kits from where we left them, and then marched down to a hill below Aroji (where we had been fighting). On the way down I and a lot of men missed our way in the dark, and went on the plateau of Aroji where we heard a great deal of talking in our front; it was the natives looking for their wounded relations and friends.

Coming to where the camp was I passed some officers of the Punjabis, who offered me some dinner which I accepted, and was never in my life more thankful for a glass of water. From them I learnt that Roberts had been wounded, he was on Baggage Guard with his company and got shot through the left elbow. I did not stay long there as I expected to find something for me at our camp, and so I went there but found absolutely nothing, as all our baggage had been left in a ravine below. I shared a waterproof sheet and blanket with a sergeant; about the middle of the night some men found some water near, which was very acceptable. The chief of Theodorus' vanguard was one of the first wounded and offered to give us any information he could if taken care of; he said that the guns at the top of the hill were being worked by Europeans, which turned out to be untrue.

The fighting at Aroji, thus described by Woodgate who was at the forefront of it, was the sharpest of the entire campaign. Napier's troops buried 560 Abyssinians, but it is estimated that 700 of the emperor's men were killed and about 1,500 wounded, a price

2. Captain Charles Speedy was a British officer and traveller who had spent much time in Abyssinia, and was attached to General Napier's staff.

executed by the breech-loading Snider rifles of the British infantry as much as by the shells and rockets. On Easter Monday, 13 April, the fortress stronghold at Magdala was stormed against only slight opposition and with little loss. Woodgate's regiment was not involved, most of the action falling to the 33rd Foot, but the entries in his diary for 14–17 April give a good idea of how things came to an end, 'Before Magdala'.

We have great difficulty in getting water, especially now that all the people who have been turned out of Theodorus' camp go to our wells; before breakfast I went down the gully to the west of the camp, where I found a little good water and had a wash. All trophies and loot of every kind has to be given up to be sold by public auction, the proceeds of which to be given as prize money to the soldiers and sepoys.

In the morning (15 April) we marched back to Magdala to exchange places with the 33rd who have been looting the place to such an extent that they cannot be kept there. I was put on guard over the magazine, arsenal and treasury, consisting of an enclosed space in which gunpowder of all kinds, from Hall's sporting down to the government ammunition, was scattered all over the place. In one shed it was full of Abyssinian manuscripts, two or three were full of firestocks and pistols, almost all flint or match-locks, another contained a set of church bells, and the rest, some five or six, contained odds and ends of all kinds, glasses, china ware, English and Brussels carpets, carpenters' tools of the finest make, part of photographic apparatus, two broken harmoniums, etc., besides a large quantity of croziers, mitres, censers and crosses. Most of this was loot that had been brought from Gondar and partly from Debra Tabor. I also saw fine breech-loading cartridges and gun cases from which the guns had been looted, there was hardly a box in the place which had not been broken into and rifled. Among other things were two suits of chain armour. All these things were to be sold by auction soon, and the proceeds to go as prize money.

Magdala is a fearful place for fleas which grow to an enormous size, last night although on an iron bedstead I could hardly sleep a wink, people pick them out of their trousers by dozens; the worse places for them are the huts into which I will not venture. The place is also horribly dirty and full of horrible smells of dead animals which lie along the road up from Aroji, the place where we fought on Good Friday. The Gallas, who lie south of Magdala, have become very troublesome, looting everything that they can get hold of. Several are prisoners in the hands of our Quarter Guard, given over by the 33rd, one of them in trying to escape

37

was shot and his body thrown over the cliff. I intended today (16 April) to have visited Fala and Selassie, but my boots wanted mending so much that I had to stop at home while they were resoled. Theodorus was buried on Tuesday (14 April) in the verandah of the chapel, which is a little square building just like many others that we have seen.

Our company was ordered (17 April) to escort the booty to the Bashilo, accordingly we left Magdala with it at about 2 o'clock. In the road I met Bagenal of the 45th whom I knew at Sandhurst. An hour or two after I left with the rear of the Baggage the rest of the brigade cleared out, and Magdala was set on fire. The regiment went down to the old camping ground of the 2nd Brigade. I did not get to the Bashilo until nearly 8 o'clock. I was anything but glad to find most of the natives out of Magdala there, especially as they had brought their fleas with them. As soon as I had had some dinner I went to the river for a bathe.

Woodgate's account of the return march of four hundred miles shows that it was by no means devoid of incident. By 14 May the King's Own had reached Antalo, the mid-point of their journey.

In the morning the 45th, Penn's battery, and the 10th Bombay Native Infantry marched away. We paraded and the regiment was photographed at the ruined village near the camp. I was on a district Court Martial to try a man of the 33rd.

Rassam gave a dinner, to which he asked us all, in Abyssinian style.[3] The dishes consisted of boiled ribs of beef and a sort of curry, with country bread and *tej* (a kind of honey beer or mead); he also had some Abyssinian chiefs who ate raw beef, flavoured with a sort of chutney made of chilis and onions. The raw piece of meat is held by a servant so that the guests can cut at it as they like, they use no forks, but take their meat in the palm of the left hand to cut it. Theodorus' son was there, waited upon by a eunuch who cut up his meat for him. He is a very small boy about 6 or 7 years old.[4]

I gave our butler Francis a sound thrashing, he is usually rather impudent, and today he cheeked me beyond all bearing. I wrote to my mother and to Grace, who asked me in her last letter to send her some of Theodorus' hair, so I enclosed a piece of hair off a woman in the bazaar.

3. Hormuzd Rassam was a British civil servant and agent who played a key role in negotiations with the Emperor Theodorus before and during the campaign.
4. The Prince Alamayu was brought to England under Queen Victoria's patronage, and eventually went to the Royal Military Academy at Sandhurst; he was only nineteen years old when he died in 1879.

It was not all a matter of feasting and personal dilemmas, because as they neared the Suru Pass, on the last leg to the coast, Woodgate was faced with the dangers of a hostile country. Under 29 May he writes:

> Having to make a double march we started at 2 o'clock in the morning, and reached Undul Wells, 18 miles from Baragudi, at about 9. It appears that a murder was committed here yesterday evening. A man named Doveton, in the intelligence department, started from here yesterday afternoon accompanied by two native followers, for Upper Suru; when about three miles from here he was attacked by a party of Shohos. Both the native followers were killed, he was left for dead. He was not found until this morning, when he was brought back to camp, he had two spear thrusts through the body, besides one hand and one foot cut off. The news of the affair was telegraphed to Sir R. Napier. Doveton died soon after we came in. We half expected to get an order to make a raid into the hill to revenge his death, but no order came, and at 3 p.m. we marched again for Upper Suru, which we reached some time after dark, very tired, the pass is very hot, especially when the breeze is shut out by the hills.

On 2 June 1868 Woodgate was steaming homewards from Annesley Bay, aboard the S.S. *England*. His future military career was to take him back to Africa for active service on four more occasions, including the Ashanti campaign in 1873 and the Zulu War in 1878–9. His remains lie there to this day in the tree-shaded churchyard at St. John's, Mooi river, in Natal. During the disastrous early stages of the South African war, as Major-General Sir Edward Woodgate, he led a British force to attack and hold Spioenkop: there, on the morning of 24 January 1900, he was fatally wounded by a Boer marksman.

So far as his experiences in Abyssinia are concerned, it is clear from Woodgate's diary that he wrote several letters to his family at home. Even so, relatively few soldiers' letters from that campaign can be traced. Among these are two from an officer whose name is not recorded, painting a picture of the arduous conditions under which the march to Magdala took place. Napier's advance force of 700 troops covered the 130 miles from Buya to Lat in ten days' forced marching through the mountains. He then ordered a drastic reduction of personal baggage so as to increase mobility still further. It was to be limited to what a man or his horse could carry, little more than a greatcoat, blanket and groundsheet: no camp beds were allowed. All this comes to light in the letter written at Lat on 24 March 1868:

> I scribble you a few lines from here, where we arrived this morning after a series of forced marches over the most mountainous country I have ever been in – awful marches up mountains so steep it was almost impossible to ride. I climbed over most on foot to save my horse, as did most of us, over precipices and drops of thousands of feet in depth. The scenery is beautiful but the fatigue great. We could not go on farther today as our animals are quite done up. We are allowed to take nothing with us but our bedding strapped on one of our horses. I have a cork mattress and a couple of blankets, and in them I wrap up two shirts, two pairs of socks, a toothbrush, a piece of soap and a towel, and that is all. Food we trust to getting on the road from the commissariat people, but I believe it will only be biscuits and tea.
>
> We ought to be opposite Magdala in six days, and I hope we shall have licked those fellows before that; of course, they can't hold out against us for any time. We have crossed five high ranges of mountains during the last three days, sometimes on paths only two feet wide; but I have quite lost any uneasiness in looking over these places. I am writing under great difficulties, for I have such a lot of work to do here today, and my tent is inundated with men asking for information and orders of all kinds. We are very badly off for food. Goats killed and eaten half-an-hour afterwards are not nice, and we have no liquor of any kind; we shall get a little rum today, I hope. The water is not nice without something to qualify it. Old campaigners of the Crimea, Indian Mutiny, and China say nothing ever came up to the fatigue and privations of this. I certainly have experienced nothing like it, but I am glad to say I have not had fever since Adigrat, so it suits me apparently.

A few days later he wrote again from Dildi, after more strenuous marching had brought the advancing troops within sixty miles of Magdala:

> We march on tomorrow, and as I may not have another opportunity of writing (for we have long marches before us over frightful country, and very hard work to undergo) until I reach Magdala and all this is over, I send a few lines from this. We have had terrible marches from Lat. We came on here, 28 miles at one stretch over three very high ranges of mountains. No road. I walked 20 out of the 28 miles to save my horse, for he could not carry me up the steep sides of the hills. On top of one range we got

into a thunderstorm, hail and rain, drenched to the skin. We arrived at our camping ground just at dark, having started at six in the morning. Had nothing up, and slept on the bare ground, which was very rocky and stony.

It is to me a marvel I am not down with fever, but thank God I am not. Sir Charles Staveley [commanding the spearhead of the British force] is very bad with sciatica; he has to be carried on the march, also one of his aides-de-camp. It rains every day. I think I bear it all very well, and it suits my constitution. It is very hard work, the poor animals suffer and die. I think Theodorus will have one rub at us. He intends, he says, to oppose us in a difficult pass there is, and to make a night attack on our camp on another occasion. I fear he won't like his reception if he does. There is no firewood or grass at the place we go to, so we have to cut it, and carry it with us on the march.

On the threshold of battle with Theodorus and within three days' march from Magdala, a staff officer (also not named) wrote a letter home on 9 April: although he did not know it, the battle at Aroji was to be fought the following day.

I snatch a few moments to write you a line or two. As usual I'm up to my eyes in work, we marched in here yesterday with a large brigade. The commander-in-chief is three miles ahead of us with the other brigade. We halt tomorrow and then go on to Magdala, where Theodorus evidently means to give us an opportunity of licking him, for he means to fight. I expect our affair will come off on Sunday – the better the day, the better the deed. We have a tremendous precipice to go down, and then up another before we come to the Delanta Plain, but thanks to the king there is a road.

We are living in the roughest fashion; we have no sugar, no milk, no butter, no flour, no bread, no liquor of any kind – nothing but water, we get tea though, and drink it without its usual accompaniments, but we don't get much of it. We eat biscuits, which are like dog biscuits broken up into hard bits, a labour to masticate; and tough beef killed just before being taken. When they brought our ration of it this morning the muscles were still twitching, this sounds odd but I assure you it is perfectly true, my servant called the ADC to look at it. I'm sorry to say all sporting is to be discontinued from this date as no guns must be fired, being calculated to mislead and alarm the picquets, so no more ducks for dinner. I've got nothing but the clothes I stand up in, one change of shirting and one pair of socks.

The thermometer at the top of the Tacazze Pass went down to 19 degrees and once water was all frozen; this was at night. In the middle of the day the sun takes the skin off your nose. You would be amused to see us all with sore noses and hands. If you get a slight wound from a thorn or anything here, it turns into a bad festering sore, there are a great number of men in this way. Beyond the Bashilo river I hear we are to go on without tents. I expect Theodorus will oppose us at the Bashilo.

In the strictest military sense, there is a certain similarity between events in Abyssinia and the next campaign that was set in West Africa, generally known as the Ashanti War of 1873–74. A British expeditionary force was sent ashore at an inhospitable spot on the African coast; although much smaller in numbers and equipment than that used in Abyssinia, it was a mixed army of regiments of the line and West Indian troops; it was commanded by a famous general; it had to strike inland through 150 miles of difficult and hostile terrain, where equatorial rain forest and swamps took the place of the mountains of Ethiopia; its destination was the stronghold of an African national leader, which was duly seized and burned to the ground. The action lasted only a couple of months, and perhaps because of the peculiar circumstances under which it took place, the yield of soldiers' letters from it is again very slender.

The political background, on the other hand, was quite different. British motivation to act in Abyssinia was a compound of the broad strategy of maintaining a sphere of interest in Egypt and the Red Sea, together with the specific aim of releasing British subjects being held as hostages by the Emperor Theodorus. By contrast, the Ashanti campaign belongs in the much more familiar and recurrent context of punitive expeditions designed to disrupt African societies, directly or indirectly, and thus leading to the eventual imposition of protectorates, annexations, and colonial control. It was much more in the mainstream of the kind of military interventions in Africa that became (to liberal opinion, at any rate) distressingly common as the nineteenth century ran into its last quarter. Some of them, including the Ashanti business, seem to have happened fortuitously.

A Select Committee on the West African Settlements in 1865 had recommended that Britain should withdraw at some future date from the burdens of maintaining those unprofitable footholds, except for Sierra Leone. The abolition of domestic slavery wherever the Union Jack flew had destroyed an institution vital to the local economies, and the continuing British presence at the old-established trading ports brought with it an involvement in local

THE ILLUSTRATED LONDON NEWS

REGISTERED AT THE GENERAL POST-OFFICE FOR TRANSMISSION ABROAD.

No. 1788.—VOL. LXIII. SATURDAY, DECEMBER 6, 1873. WITH EXTRA SUPPLEMENT | SIXPENCE. BY POST, 6½d.

OFFICERS AND MEN OF THE 23RD FUSILIERS IN THEIR ORDINARY UNIFORM AND AS EQUIPPED FOR THE GOLD COAST.

The expedition to Ashanti in 1873 was equipped by Wolseley with a special grey kit of serge smock-frocks and trousers, with long sailors' boots. Here some of the 23rd Royal Welch Fusiliers are wearing it, alongside comrades in their usual uniform.

politics. Such was the case on the Gold Coast by the middle of 1873, when the 'loyal' Fanti at the coastal towns were threatened by the powerful Asante (Ashanti). It was thought needful to check the expansionism of Kofi Kalkali, head of the Asante empire (the Asantehene). To this end the punitive expedition was mounted against the Asante, with an in-built probability of an extension of British indirect influence inland from the coast, as the natural cohesion of the country was undermined.

Command of the operations was given to no less a national hero than Major-General Sir Garnet Wolseley. It was to be his first, but by no means his last, taste of taking the imperial hammer to an African people. Wolseley arrived at Cape Coast Castle as early as 2 October 1873, but a great deal of preliminary staff work had to be done before any sort of strike could be made against Kofi's inland capital at Kumasi. Eventually he achieved all that extremely well, and after the arrival of three British battalions in December a move could be made. The column (for that was what it had to be, following a road hacked out of the jungle by pioneers and engineers) set off on 5 January 1874 and reached Kumasi one month later, after a constant struggle against disease and ambush by the Asante warriors, many of them armed with rather ancient firearms.

The immediate gain from so much effort and expense was not great, but it served as the first effective move in what might be termed 'the softening-up' of the Asante. Further military activity was to follow in 1890; after a bloodless campaign in 1896 the Asante accepted a British protectorate and Resident; when the Governor demanded, in 1900, the symbolic golden stool ('the soul of the nation') from the exiled Asantehene, he was besieged in Kumasi as the Asante went to war for the last time. Their territory was annexed in 1901 and became merged in the colony of the Gold Coast, reaching inland for 400 miles and containing two million Africans: we know it today as Ghana.

On the transport ship that berthed at Cape Coast Castle on 16 December 1873, bringing the 42nd Royal Highlanders (Black Watch), was George Pomeroy Colley. At that stage of his career a colonel attached to Wolseley's staff for special duties, Colley was destined for rapid promotion as a brilliant administrator within a modernising British army. He served in southern Africa on three further occasions: at the last, as Major-General Sir George Pomeroy Colley, he commanded the imperial forces during the First Anglo-Boer War of 1880–81. Late in February 1881 he led a British force to the summit of Majuba mountain, where he was shot dead by the

Boers in the total defeat of his demoralised command. When we encounter him in a letter written to his sister on 29 January 1874, however, Colley was on top of his job, the demanding business of organising the transport of supplies for the British column already advancing on Kumasi. The logistics were that 3,000 troops required no fewer than 9,000 African bearers to carry their essentials of life: animal-drawn wheeled transport was ruled out by the exigencies of the forested environment. Colley's chief problem to start with was the way his corps of bearers constantly deserted their posts:

> Three days of very hard work in the sun, followed by sleepless nights while I was personally taking measures to prevent desertions, brought me down and for a few days I was laid up with fever, but I carried on my work all the time. I made my plans for re-forming my transports, and started to visit the deserting tribes. The first day I was obliged to walk a few miles in consequence of the badness of the road, and I was very nearly done for, but the fever was off me; the next day I had gained strength and before the week was out I was walking 20 miles a day, and had to leave my companions, having knocked them up.
>
> Our week's raid was an interesting and a successful one. We surprised several villages at night, surrounding them and taking all the inhabitants prisoners; frightened the chiefs thoroughly and fined one of the kings, who immediately paid up in a bag of gold dust; and after seven days' absence reappeared with all the men of the tribe so thoroughly organised and so well in hand that I have not had a desertion among them since. I went to the Prah river a few days afterwards to see Sir Garnet and make the arrangements for the final advance. My reception was most cordial and flattering, and I know that none of the headquarter staff blame me for the first failure; they know I was put under a crumbling house which nothing could then save.

With things moving along smoothly, Colonel Colley was nevertheless caught up in the main battle at Amoaful on 31 January, and in the running fights to keep the road open. He tells of all this in a letter of 7 February, after seeing the sights of Kofi's charnel house at Kumasi, and as he was superintending the convoys of wounded soldiers and bearers now being taken back to the coast.

> The next day [2 February] bad news from the rear, of convoys interrupted and fired upon, took me back all the way to Fommanah. On arrival there I found it closely attacked and had to

fight my way in with my escort. On taking command I found the Ashantis attacking all round in considerable force; the position a long, straggling village with no defences, and the stores at one end and hospital at the other – very awkward to hold. The attack continued for about four hours, and even after it had ceased, when we sent down a party for water we were received with a volley. Captain North and Captain Duncan, two of my transport officers, were wounded, also several convalescents, European and West Indian.

I had only a few hours of daylight in Kumasi, and not ten minutes to spare. I ran hurriedly through the king's palace, and the general impression that and everything left on me was of the most horrible charnel-house one could conceive. Drums hung with skulls and smeared with blood, stools clotted with blood as if smeared afresh after each sacrifice, impaled bodies – unbearable stench of human sacrifices and victims in every direction. I was never so glad to get out of a place again.

Wolseley's most vigorous and able field commander was Lieutenant-Colonel Evelyn Wood, VC. His contribution was to raise and train a regiment of local levies, known as Wood's Irregulars, kept in hand by a team of specially selected young officers. One of them was Edward Woodgate, whose experiences in Abyssinia we have just shared. In Wood's return of the number of days' duty done between 2 October 1873 and 28 February 1874, it is shown that Woodgate was 150 days on the regimental strength, 125 days effective and twenty-five days sick: a note says that he 'did more night work than anyone'. Another, Lieutenant T. A. Eyre of the 90th Light Infantry (Wood's own regiment) was mortally wounded in action, and Wood wrote two sensitive letters of sympathy to members of his family. The first, to his widowed mother, is dated 6 February 1874 from (somewhat boldly) 'Agemum, Africa':

My dear Lady Eyre,

It is with intense pain I have to announce to you that your gallant boy is dead, shot through the body when showing a grand example to his men, who were unsteady from the close proximity of the Ashantis. Though I was within 40 yards of him I was so busy in directing the men that I did not notice his being hit until I was told. Going to him the doctor took off his rings, and passed them to me. I stooped down and kissed him, when he said waving his hand to me 'Give my love to my Mother and say my last prayer is for her.' This was about 7½ a.m. on the 4th February.

Having seen him carried out of fire I did not see him again for

46

two hours when we had gained the village of Ordasu, and as the Ashantis had surrounded us Dr. Mosse brought him into the village, where he spoke to me and asked me to get the cot or hammock lifted off the ground. I did so, but did not speak to him as he had been given opiates and Dr. Turton who first saw him and passed the rings to me had given me an additional message to you, 'that he was plucky to the last'. This I was to let you know. Poor boy, he need not have added this.

Often and often have I tried to mitigate the risks of war, knowing how you must suffer should he fall. About 1 o'clock having just returned from placing some men to keep down the Ashanti fire which was closing on the village, I saw Thomas Arthur's servants in tears and so learnt that the bravest and most thorough gentleman of my acquaintance was no more. Before we left the village I fastened up the body, kissed his poor face once more for you, and buried him, carefully covering his grave with dried leaves so that it might not be discovered; as I repassed the spot yesterday I looked at the spot and I feel confident that it is not likely to be noticed.

I have not been to bed for four nights and have been out in drenching rain, so excuse this incoherent but well meant letter. Dr. Mosse cut off some of Arthur's hair for you. I will arrange about his things. We mutually desired each other that the survivor should forbid a sale. Lt. Wauchope and Lt. Douglas were close to Arthur when he was hit.

I cannot express to you how I suffer for your sufferings. All consolation in such moments is vain save that from on High, but later I hope your grief may be lessened by the reflection that your brave son did as his gallant father would have been content to do, leading soldiers to victory.

A week later Wood wrote the second letter from 'Moinsey, Africa':

Poor Arthur Eyre used to tell me that an Aunt constantly wrote to him, and I believe it was you. I do not like to write more to Lady Eyre than I can help for I can well imagine my name will have a painful ring in her mind as long as life lasts. May God help and console her.

I ever strove, sometimes enough to anger the lad, to shield him from the dangers of this horrid war. I cannot describe to you how Arthur's memory is ever present to me. I enclose a note I wrote after being wounded on the 31st January which will best explain the terms on which we lived and the right I have to share in your grief.

Yesterday I destroyed all his letters save this note. As the

47

Regimental books were in his tin box I had to force it open, and I disliked the idea of the possibility of others reading lines intended for himself alone. If I live to reach England I will forward all his property. In case I am killed, in a bag in my desk are his eye-glass, watch, chain, and various small articles he wore the day he was killed. That he rests in Heaven is the prayer of his late affectionate friend, Evelyn Wood.

In his autobiography Wood includes a sketch of himself attending to the wounded Eyre, although he describes the incident in only the barest outline – an example of how letters can add so much detail to other sources.[5] Wood himself was wounded in the Ashanti campaign, but recovered to serve again in Africa on several occasions: in 1878 in Cape Colony, 1879 in Zululand, 1881 in the Transvaal, and 1882–85 in Egypt and the Sudan. Throughout his experience he was a tireless and unrelenting leader of the troops he commanded, nowhere more so that in South Africa. He was described by Bishop Colenso, with some justification, as 'that man of blood'.

It would be a pity to leave Ashanti without hearing a voice from

Lt. Col. Evelyn Wood, VC, attending to one of his young officers, Lt. T.A Eyre, who was mortally wounded in action against the Ashanti, 4 February 1873.

5. Sir Evelyn Wood, *From Midshipman to Field Marshal* (London: Murray, 1906), volume 1, pages 279–80.

the ranks of those who fought there. For this we can turn to Private George Gilham of the 2nd Rifle Brigade, who joined the army at Canterbury in 1870. After serving with his regiment for a few years in Ireland, he found himself under orders to sail for West Africa with Wolseley's expeditionary force. Gilham landed at Cape Coast Castle on the first day of 1874; after he and his comrades were issued with pipes and tobacco to reduce the risk of catching tropical diseases, they set off at once inland along the forest tracks. Daily marches of about ten miles took them to the Prah river, separating Fanti territory from the Asante.

There they stayed for a fortnight to await the arrival of the rest of their battalion, then on 21 January made for Kumasi across the pontoon bridges built by the Royal Engineers. After climbing the Adansi Hills – 'We were disappointed in the view,' says Gilham, 'for we could see nothing but tree-tops' – the British force of some 2,000 men fought the main engagement of the campaign at Amoaful on 31 January. Skirmishers fell back after meeting a sharp fire from the Asante, and Gilham takes up the story of what happened next, catching the peculiar quality of combat in thick forest.

> Upon this we received the order 'Chinstraps down, open out, and push on through the jungle'. I was one of the leading four of the front company, and as our skirmishers came in I noticed one with the bones of his arm broken by slugs from the enemy's muskets. We cut our way right and left into the jungle with our cutlasses, lying down in the underwood, standing behind trees for cover, pegging in where we could, and forming a semi-circle to the front; but the foliage was so dense that it was like being in a net, and the farther we went the thicker it seemed to get, so that I don't believe we advanced a hundred yards during the whole of the fight.
>
> The enemy were all armed with flintlock muskets, and they fired at us with rough bits of lead, old nails, pebbles, and rusty iron, which at first passed over our heads and showed us that the enemy were on a slope below us, whereupon we fired low and did terrible execution among them, although we could only catch sight of them here and there. They outflanked us on several occasions, but we changed front, first on one side and then on the other, so that we were always ready for them. We had not been long in action before a slug crashed into the breast of a marine on my right hand, poor fellow, I shall never forget how he fell back and curled up in his agony. Directly afterwards a man belonging to the Naval Brigade was hit in the shoulder and went down like a

49

log. The doctors were continually passing up and down behind us, and two came along just afterwards and cut the slug from the marine's chest, but could not get at the bullet that hit the sailor. Both men were carried to the rear to the sick-tent, which the Engineers had hastily erected.

A small field-gun which was got into position did good work among the enemy, as did also the rockets sent among them, and no doubt astonished them. When at last they retreated we went after them as well as we could, and we found they had dragged their dead into heaps. Pressing on beyond their dead, and driving the fugitives before us, we captured their village, Amoaful. We rested here that night, but were alarmed once by the enemy making an attack upon our sick and baggage, however we drove them off and heard no more of them. Our losses in the fight, in killed and wounded, were Naval Brigade, 29; 42nd Highlanders, 114; Rifle Brigade, 23; Royal Welch Fusiliers, 53. On the following day we continued our march towards Kumasi, and drove the natives from several villages through which we passed.[6]

Gilham says that Wolseley refused an Ashanti request for a few days' truce because he wanted to finish the campaign and leave before the rainy season broke. After taking Kumasi and blowing up the royal palace on 6 February, the troops returned to the coast in half the time it had taken them to advance, despite the wounded they carried with them. As Gilham says, 'we had left parties of the two West India Regiments at each stopping-place on the way up, so that the road was open to us all the way back, and we burnt each village as we came to it, and so left nothing behind us but smouldering ruins. At last we arrived at Cape Coast Castle and re-embarked on the *Himalaya* on 21 February, arriving at Portsmouth on 26 March. Four days later we were reviewed by the Queen at Windsor.' By the standards of African campaigning it had been an extraordinarily brief and efficient exercise of arms.

6. *Told from the Ranks: Recollections of service during the Queen's reign by privates and non-commissioned officers of the British army*, collected by E. Milton Small (London, 1897), pages 76–86.

THREE

'It was Indeed a Slaughter':

WARFARE IN THE CAPE COLONY AND ZULULAND, 1877–79

At the very same time when Wood was wounded on 31 January 1874 ('an Ashanti lying close to me shot the head of a nail into my chest immediately over the region of the heart'), Sir Bartle Frere was pointing an imperial finger towards southern Africa. Over the next few years the policies advocated by Frere were to instigate an explosive series of war situations in South Africa. He had already enjoyed an impressive career in India as a proconsul of Empire; now, in a speech that inaugurated the African Section of the Society of Arts (30 January 1874) he argued for a more active British exploitation of resources in Africa. In particular, Frere thought Britain should interest herself in that 'temperate' region running from the equatorial forests southwards to the Cape. Potentially it was fertile, healthy and accessible to world markets; it also had diamonds, gold, and (a great asset to Frere's mind) the coalfields stretching down to Natal, which could provide fuel for steamships in the Indian Ocean, and for railways in the future.

All these attractions acted together to inspire a new process that Frere termed 'a welding together the loose elements of a great South African Empire'.[1] As early as January 1874, then, Frere went on public record in favour of a policy of confederation, which was to be championed by Lord Carnarvon, the Colonial Secretary who entered office in Disraeli's government in 1874. Frere was to champion the confederation of British colonies and Boer republics, together with native African territories of various kinds, even in the face of serious opposition. It became with him a dogma of successful advancement of 'civilised' over 'savage' values and precepts. Eventually, besides half-a-dozen armed conflicts of varying

1. Frank Emery, '"South Africa's best friend": Sir Bartle Frere at the Cape, 1877–80', *Theoria*, LXIII, 1984, page 27.

severity that were sparked off in the interests of confederation, it brought personal disaster for Frere. Nevertheless, he began well enough after he went out in 1877 as Governor of the Cape Colony. The eastern frontier of the colony had experienced a long series of what were then called 'Kaffir Wars' against the indigenous Xhosa nations, the ninth and the last of which was directed by Frere. He successfully closed the frontier after a campaign in 1877–78 waged against the Ngaika ('Gaika') and Gcaleka ('Galeka') people. The fighting centred on what is now the Transkei, mostly a scrambling sequence of patrols, skirmishes and ambushes in tangled bush, with very few confrontations in open battle.

For most of the British troops engaged, therefore, there was a minimum of martial achievement to write home about. So much is clear from a letter composed when the war was over: Griffith Griffiths was a private soldier in the Second Battalion, 24th Regiment, who wrote to his father, mother and sisters at their home near Swansea. It comes from 'Perie Bush, April 17th, 1878', and in its original version must have been typical of many that tried to convey the flavour of service in foreign parts to the people at home. Here it is, with the idiosyncrasies of spelling and punctuation smoothed out; the battalion had sailed from England aboard the *Himalaya*, and when it reached Cape Town the young soldiers were described as 'stout, healthy, well-built lads, with plenty of beef in their muscles, and as likely fellows as could be found to turn into soldiers of the best type'.

> I have had a chance once more to write you a few lines to let you all know that I am safe and healthy at present, and I hope that you are all the same. Dear father and mother, I hope that we shall meet once more if the Lord please. I am in a strange country but I have plenty of friends who are all four jolly Welshmen together, not living very far from one another. The reason that I did not write sooner, I have had no chance. We went on board the ship the first of February and we sailed on the second of the same date, and we reached Madeira in five days, but we did not stop there at all. We stopped at Simons Bay one night and a day, and then we sailed on to East London.
>
> We stopped at East London one night and then we marched up the country a few miles, and we went with the train about 40 miles to King William's Town. We stopped there two nights, no train farther, and marched then on 13th March across the River Buffalo, and to a place they call Perie Bush. Here I have all wonders, every sort of birds, monkeys, and one particular thing I

Perie Bush April 17th 1878

Dear Father and Mother and sisters
I have had a chance once more to write to you a
few lines to let you now all that I ham safe and
healthy at preasant and I hope that you are all the same
Dear father and mother I hope that whe shall meet once
more if the Lord pleace I ham in a strange country
but I got plenty of friends who are all 4 Jolly Welsman
together not liveing very fare from one another to the
reason that I did not write sooner I have had no
chance whe whent on board the Ship on the first of
Fiebruary and whe sail out on the second of the same
and whe reach Madera in 5 days but whe did not stop
there at all whe stop Simons Bay one night and a day
and then whe sail on to East London in the
38 days that whas on the 10th of March and I was
not thinking nathing about Llangyfalach faer then

*Letter written to his parents at Clydach, near Swansea, by Pvt. Griffith
Griffiths, 2/24th Regiment, while serving in the Ninth Frontier War, Cape
Province, South Africa, 1878. By trade an engine driver, he enlisted at Cardiff
early in 1877, aged twenty. During his twelve years' service, almost all of it
overseas, he achieved the Army Certificate of Education, 4th Class.*

have noticed is a grasshopper, it is so big as a blackbird, wonderful size, and you can see a butterfly so big as any of the black martin birds that build in Hebron Chapel. There are millions of goats here, bullocks, and nothing to be seen very pretty . . . I get plenty to eat here, you can buy a sheep for five shillings, good one too, I can say now that I have pulled oranges from the tree without asking anybody. So now I must conclude with my kind love to you all many times, give my kind love to little Sally if she is alive and let me know how she is coming on. I am going on sentry now, I will write every week if I can, this morning I had the paper and stamp.

Thanks to the army reforms begun by Cardwell the 2/24th Regiment, based at Brecon, was in 1874 full of Welsh recruits like Griffiths. So too were the more recent members of the 1st Battalion, 24th Foot: in 1881 these battalions were to form the South Wales Borderers. The 1/24th had served in South Africa since 1875 and bore the brunt of the bush fighting with the Xhosa. Among those who enlisted as regular soldiers in June 1875 was a group of young men from Pontypool, an industrial town where the iron-works were hit by recession and unemployment. Their military career is mirrored in the letters of 610 Private George Morris, who took the shilling after serving in the Royal Monmouthshire Militia. After sailing out to join the 1/24th at the Cape in August 1877 he was detached for duty with the gunners, and wrote a rather complaining letter to his father in March 1878:

For the last four months I have been unable to procure either stamp, pen, ink or paper. I have been nearly all over Africa and have not known what it has been to sleep in a bed for that time. My clothes are worn to rags and I have not a boot to my feet, and God knows when I shall get any. I have drawn no pay since the 16th of January, and don't know when I shall; when I do I will surely send you some money . . . We get nothing only a little tobacco and soap . . . I am getting this paper and stamp from a Volunteer captain, or God knows when I should be able to write.

I am attached to the 22nd Brigade, Royal Artillery, in charge of the rocket apparatus, and have not seen my own Regiment since Christmas last [1877]. I have great difficulty in getting letters as they follow my corps about and they keep them until they know where I am. I only got your letter dated 22nd December on the 27th February, I got one from Maggie the same time, they have been all over the colony. The 2/24th are here, there is one company about 50 miles from this station. I have not had the pleasure of seeing any of them yet. I believe part of them were engaged the day after they landed, they are fighting now at a place called Perie Bush with about 8,000 Kaffirs.

This [Fort Wellington] was during the last war a small mud fort, but there is very little trace of it remaining now. There is no house within 20 miles, it is up in the table lands about 60 miles from the coast. It is on the top of a hill, we have about two miles to go for water. God knows I have had enough of campaigning this last few months; the weather has been very bad and wet, and many of our poor fellows have died from dysentery.

Six months later, when the Ninth Frontier War had come to an end, George Morris was still in the eastern Cape, but in the relative comfort and civilisation of King William's Town. It was by far the biggest and most important place in that part of Africa, but even so it had a population of only two to three thousand. A more ordered life had allowed George to arrange with his paymaster that ten shillings would be sent home to his parents each month. He was thus able to keep his promise to help them financially, meagre though his soldier's pay was at one shilling a day. His hopes of returning home were growing weaker each day with rumours of a fresh campaign for the 1/24th in another part of South Africa: 'but

Sketches of military life on active service in the eastern Cape, South Africa, 1878, drawn by Lt. W.W. Lloyd, 1/24th Regiment.

now I am greatly afraid we are going to Natal'. The death of his father overshadows a letter to his widowed mother (25 October 1878) while still at 'King':

> I am so anxious to hear from you and how you are going on by your poor self. How I wish I was once more at home with you. You must feel so isolated by your poor self . . . I should very much like to have a *Free Press* now and then, or a *Weekly Mail*. If you could manage to send me one occasionally, it would not matter to me about them being old. I saw a *Monmouthshire Merlin* with one of my comrades one day, and I then thought how nice it was to have a home paper . . . I am thinking of stopping it out here with the 2nd Battalion until I have my term of service in; then when I come home I shall be a free man. What do you think of it? . . . I cannot have but very little money when I come home as it is, unless we have some prize money; they say we will get some . . . I suppose you see by the papers that we are to have a medal for the late war. They are doing a little fighting in Natal now; if it is not soon over we shall have to go there. Do Alfred Jones' people know of his death?

Local newspapers like the *Monmouthshire Merlin* were much in demand by the Welsh soldiers of the 24th, being a welcome link with home. George Morris evidently thought it a good idea to stay overseas with the Second Battalion, which had only just arrived in South Africa and could expect to remain there or at some other foreign station for some time, unlike the veterans of the 1/24th who had been overseas for twelve years. By serving out his five years with the colours in the Cape or Natal he could share in the prize money obtained by selling captured cattle. Alfred Jones was one of seven soldiers of the 2/24th who died of sickness in the closing winter months of the war. By early November, as the summer heat began to build up, Morris was among the garrison of Fort Glamorgan, near the port of East London, and already looking ahead to a fresh campaign.

> It is a fine healthy station but it is very quiet, no life whatever. It is on the sea side, and you know how fond I am of the sea, I have a swim nearly every morning, and I think it does me an infinite amount of good . . . How are things looking in Pontypool? I am much afraid that it will be some time before I shall see it again. We are under orders to proceed to Natal, and it is thought we shall have some hard fighting up there, as there are not sufficient troops

to properly rout the rebels, as they are 20 or 30,000 strong and in an awkward country, and there is a great difficulty in getting at them . . . I shall very possibly see Charlie Long when we go to Natal. I believe he is a lance-corporal, hope he will get on, only he is very poor scholar, that is a great drawback to him in the service. I saw young Harry Smith one day on the line of march, poor boy he cried when he saw me, they have had a good deal of knocking about out here.

George Morris did indeed sail and march away to the borders of Natal and the Zulu kingdom. He continued to write letters to his mother, the last coming from Rorke's Drift on 10 January 1879, filled with premonition about the impending conflict. Twelve days later he was killed in action at Isandlwana when his regiment was annihilated by the Zulu, including most of the Pontypool comrades he mentions in his letters. Eventually his mother received £10.00 from the War Office, thanks to the care with which he had arranged for deductions from his soldier's pay. Before considering the special case of the Zulu War in more detail (special because of the many letters it generated), we must look at a closely-related campaign taking place not far away in the eastern Transvaal. For years the Pedi people under their astute leader Sekhukhune had been suffering repeated encroachments on their territory by the Transvaal Boers, who wished to farm it for themselves. The Pedi turned to armed opposition in 1876 and defeated a Boer commando; this development in frontier unrest was one of the reasons why Britain annexed the Transvaal in 1877.

In an attempt to subdue Sekhukhune military posts were set up as bases for volunteer units and troops from the British garrison of the Transvaal, commanded by Colonel H. Rowlands, VC. When the Cape fighting came to an end in June 1878 there followed a massive movement of imperial forces from the Transkei to Natal. Some of these were ordered to press still further on the line of march, continuing into the Transvaal to reinforce Rowlands. Among them was the Frontier Light Horse, a hard-bitten corps of mounted mercenaries in charge of Redvers Buller, then a major. He was shortly to win a Victoria Cross during the Zulu War, a fearsome reputation as commander of irregulars and as a combative general in the Sudan, but was fated to finish his career with a tarnished image during the Second Anglo-Boer War. The prevailing impression Buller created was that of a dour, brooding personality, but it is certainly not true of him in a letter to his close friend, Evelyn Wood, written from the abortive show of force against Sekhukhune. He even launches into verse, as a sort of overture, but the theme is vintage Buller in its uncompromising criticism of Rowlands, his commander. It is dated 22 October 1878, at Lydenburg in the Transvaal:

Oh for one hour of Wolseley bright,
Or well-trained Wood to lead the fight,
And quit us of this Rowlands wight,
Who does not understand it quite,
To smash this Sekhukhune.

There, do not be conceited, though the combination of two such poets as Sir Walter Scott and Major Buller in an ode praising you may well cause your appreciative self to blush. No, I do not wish to be rude, but still as a sort of relief to pent feeling you must allow me just once to say Damn that Rowlands. There, I am better now, a little better. Fancy, here I have been for a month, what have done? Nothing, what has anybody done? nothing. Yes we have, though, we have let the Kaffirs get cheeky, and now we are bolting.

Between you and me, my dear, and please keep it dark, Rowlands is quite useless, he cannot make up his mind to do anything, sitting on his behind in his position, and Harvey unfortunately is worse, much worse than useless, for he possesses the same faults as Rowlands and to an aggravated degree. As I wrote to Crealock today I *even* (!) wish you had been here. Joking apart, I do wish you had. I feel sure we should have tried to do something, and usually to try means to do, but this idiot don't try, damn him, sits on his behind, that's his form, but I had rather be cursed by someone who would do something.

We have had nearly 500 horsemen at Fort Burgers for a month, what have we done? I have done two patrols and both those I had to invent and ask leave to go. Now, just as he has made up his mind to bolt and give up, he has been persuaded to do what I suggested three weeks ago, and the cause of this wrathful letter is that I am out of it. Hard case. B. bullies R. for three weeks to attack Umsuti's Kraal; R. cannot make up his mind; R. sends B. away because his horses are dying and then makes up his mind to attack; B. is consequently out of the fight. What should B. do? Answer adjudged correct, curse R.! And I have done it, my dear E, I can tell you. I have written him such a letter that I fully expect he will change his mind again, and send me an order to rejoin him.

How are your horses, how is War Game, well I hope? I have lost 46 up to date and expect to lose some more before I get out of this. Poor brutes, I cannot bear to see or even think of them. It seems hard that there should be no cure for such a sickness. I had

one charming patrol all down along the eastern slopes of the
Drakensberg, went out through Kruger's Post, Pilgrims Rest,
Macmac and McLaughlins, then down the berg and along under
the berg northwards for four days, up the berg again and back. It
took in ten days and we only had rations for five, but luckily we
took enough cattle to live on; still, meat alone without salt or
groceries is hard food. The country is too lovely, and we rode
through marshes inhabited by buffalo and giraffe, and my heart
burned for a hunt. I shall certainly try a month there when this
cruel war is over. Let me know the news, are we to fight the Zulu?
I leave in two days' time for Newcastle, so please address your
answer there.

For the next six months Buller was more embroiled than most in
the Zulu War, and, somewhat ironically, he had already left South
Africa when British troops returned to confront Sekhukhune. That
came at the end of 1879, but at least he had the consolation of
knowing that it was Wolseley, named in the first line of his 'ode' to
Wood, who finally captured the leader of the Pedi. In due course we
shall read a few letters describing how that took place, including
one from Sir Garnet himself, but the focus now turns inevitably to
the conflict against Cetshwayo kaMpande, King of the Zulu. The
circumstances leading to the outbreak of the Zulu War in January
1879 are a subject of intensive research by historians, and there is
plenty to read on the 'causes' of this deplorable war, especially in
books and articles written since its centenary in 1979. Whatever the
order in which one places the profound factors underlying it, it
must be admitted that war need not have taken place at all, had it not
been for the determination of Sir Bartle Frere (as High Commis-
sioner for South Africa) to force it upon the Zulu. So much was said
openly by his critics at the time, for instance by Lady Florence Dixie
after Cetshwayo had been captured. She was hoping (in vain) to
persuade Evelyn Wood to share her views: 'I am not going to argue
with you about poor Cetshwayo, in rendering assistance to the king
you would be but doing justice to a man who has received at our
hands the grossest injustice and who in his dreary captivity is
suffering for the ambition and cupidity of Sir Bartle Frere.'

We have already had an introduction to the opening phases of this
war in the letter written by Lieutenant Charles Commeline, RE
(page 29). Now to sample some others we may turn to the *Sheffield
Daily Telegraph*, which had a surprisingly full coverage of the war
(as well as other African campaigns) from its own 'Official Correspondents' with the three main columns that invaded Zululand on

11 January 1879. One suspects they were officers with local connections who initially had their letters published, and who were then paid for regular contributions. Of the private letters that appeared in the paper, an informative series came from the pen of Corporal George Howe who also served in that most literate of all the army corps, the Royal Engineers. He depicts the full impact of military events at a personal level or small-unit level, something that cannot be readily derived from other sources, especially for those on the sidelines of major engagements. How otherwise, for instance, can we specify the degree of alarm engendered by news of the disaster at Isandlwana on 22 January, and fears of a massive invasion of Natal by the victorious Zulu army?

The sappers of 5th Field Company, Royal Engineers, were caught in this uncertainty while still moving up to the front. They marched from Greytown on 21 January, and had gone only a few miles further on the 22nd 'when we met a mounted messenger with a note, "Push on for Mooi river; rumours of a reverse". That was all we could learn. Push on we did, we almost ran. We got to Mooi River about one. All we could learn there was that the camp had been captured, and every man was cut off.' This party of sappers was only sixty strong and faced an unpleasant dilemma: should they go back to Greytown, which they thought would be attacked, or should they dig in where they were? Corporal Howe gives the answer:

> About a hundred yards from the river where we had first crossed stood the house of a settler. We took possession of this. Along one side and down towards the river we drew up the waggons in line. On the other two sides we threw up a shelter trench. We were hard at work until dusk, when we broke our fast. At night we turned into the trenches . . . The eyes were coming out of our heads with trying to pierce the gloom. About twelve a Dutchman came in, and said he had seen the enemy. Hour after hour we stood, but no enemy. The least noise brought the rifle to the ready. We all knew we had to deal with an enemy who did not know what mercy was, and should have to fight to the bitter end. I took one cartridge and put it in my breast, determining if it came to the worst to blow out my own brains rather than fall into their hands. At last day broke, and never did we welcome it with such joy.

By 5 a.m. Howe and his comrades were marching bravely on; after covering twelve miles they were about to pitch camp when a messenger arrived with the news that thirty waggons filled with ammunition stood undefended at Sand Spruit. So on they had to go until 10 p.m. On 24 January they built a makeshift fort at Sand Spruit. Four days later they marched to Helpmekaar, and so on to Rorke's Drift. There they had to help in the construction of another and much stronger fortification, as the entire British army recoiled upon its bases and dug in. It was the same story the length of the front, from Wood's emergency laager at Khambula, to the entrenched settlements and supply posts, to Helpmekaar, and to the coastal column, with Pearson's force bottled up at Eshowe and others on the defensive at Fort Tenedos. The Zulu gibe that the red soldiers had been changed into antbears in their holes was well justified. Fear of renewed attack runs through the soldiers' letters after Isandlwana, succeeded by the extreme caution that their commanding general took so long to throw off.

They also bring into focus the appalling conditions under which the men lived in these congested strongpoints. February saw Rorke's Drift turned into a hellish place as hundreds of rain-drenched soldiers, under the shaken command of Colonel Glyn, packed themselves without shelter into the old fortifications, emerging each day to work on the new fort there. As Corporal Howe described it, 'To guard from surprise, we fall in and stand to our arms until daybreak. When we can see the coast clear we march out and pile arms, and then go to work. We work till 5 p.m. At six the bugle sounds and we all go into fort. We are not allowed to take off our things, but lie down in them, our rifles near our sides. We have no tents, we have a rug and take the open air. Sunday we have a church parade at nine, and go to work at ten.' A sergeant of the 2/24th records their forlorn and verminous plight: 'It is not safe to get a drink of water without our rifles at present. We have lost all our tents and cooking utensils, we have only what we stand up in. The Zulus destroyed everything belonging to us. We are literally in rags and will soon be carried about, for we are getting plenty of companions and can't keep them away. You would laugh to see the regiment, some with no boots, some with their jackets and trousers patched with sheepskins and all kinds of things.' By 14 February he had not taken off his clothes or pouches since the day of Isandlwana, three weeks before.

Eventually, after a delay of four months during which reinforcements were awaited and fresh strategy worked out, the British columns embarked on a second invasion of Zululand. They were aimed at Ulundi where Cetshwayo had his royal residence, and the letters capture the full flavour of their day-to-day movements. Even then the fates seemed to be against the imperial commander, Lord Chelmsford, because at the very outset all the old fears were revived when the Prince Imperial of France, Louis Napoleon, who was attached to the British forces, was killed on 1 June. The effect was shattering for the newly-arrived battalions that numbered many young, half-trained soldiers in their ranks. Nerves were stretched to straining point, as witnessed by a series of panic situations where the troops fired by mistake on their own comrades.

First among the victims of this circumstance were 5th Field Company, Royal Engineers, then attached to Wood's redoubtable Flying Column. On 5 June Wood's advance guard ran into Zulu opposition at the Ipoko river, and suffered casualties; as he wished to camp there to wait for supplies to come up, he decided to fight. First he detached the Engineers and sent them back to Newdigate's column, in laager with hundreds of waggons about eight miles to the rear. The sappers were to build a strongpoint for defending the store depot, so when they arrived on 6 June they pitched their tents on site and began work, well outside Newdigate's laager. About ten p.m. they were awakened by shots and dived into the protection of the walls, only two feet high, on which they had just begun working.

They heard the outlying picquets fire three volleys, saw them retreat, and persuaded them to shelter within the walls. At once they all came under heavy fire from Newdigate's laager. Corporal Howe relates the story of what happened next in this dangerous and farcical situation:

> 'Good heavens, they are taking us for the enemy. Under cover at once!' cried Chard, the hero of Rorke's Drift. It was not safe to move. The buglers sounded the cease fire. Our men got over the wall to rush on the laager when they, taking us for a rush of Zulus, poured another volley into us. Back we had to go helter-skelter over the wall. Men jumped on to one another and were lying huddled in hopeless confusion, whilst shot was pouring into us like hail. Before it ceased five Engineers (including a sergeant and two corporals) had been wounded. Next morning we found the stones on the wall covered with lead and bullet marks. The artillery told us they were just going to fire when they heard our bugle sound. If they had, not one of us would have escaped.

Such was the disastrous origin of Fort Newdigate, better known to the troops as Fort Funk. Similar false alarms ruffled the columns as they continued their slow advance, and the artillery did in fact fire in one of the worse incidents just before Ulundi. Among other things, it was to deal with such lapses of soldierly conduct that Chelmsford encouraged the flogging of offenders; over 500 floggings were administered during the campaign at a time when it was otherwise little used as an army punishment, and indeed it was abolished in 1881, Chelmsford speaking in the House of Lords for its retention.

Again, the letters are useful because they were written consistently throughout the war in all its stages, not simply after the main battles. Long periods of relative inactivity were at least as likely to be punctuated by soldiers writing home. Few wars can have reached their climax after such a long stalemate – not a pitched battle for three long months, between the last shot at Gingindlovu (2 April) and the final encounter near Ulundi on 3–4 July. Once Chelmsford had emerged from his comatose state with the advance begun on 31 May, the Zulus were subjected to severe destructive action, particularly in the path of Wood's and Newdigate's columns. The spotlight of international publicity directed at the Prince Imperial's death may have diverted attention from what was in effect indirect warfare on a civilian population – the systematic burning of homesteads, destruction of crops and stored mealies, driving away of cattle. The letters, however, are full of it.

Among the mounted volunteers serving with Wood was Baker's Horse, raised in Port Elizabeth and district; from their yellow facings they were known as the 'Canaries' and, for other reasons, as 'Baker's Boozers'. A trooper of this unit took part in a sortie against three military kraals, late in June. All the mounted troops of both Wood's and Newdigate's commands were involved, 600 strong, but the Zulu impi opposing them was scared off by the big guns, no doubt remembering their costly lesson at Khambula, and did not fight. Instead (to quote the trooper), 'the expedition returned having succeeded in destroying three kraals, and over 3,000 huts must have been consumed that day, with large quantities of grain stored in the different kraals'. Native levies were regularly employed on this kind of punitive work. As early as 6 June, Corporal Howe of the Engineers said, 'We are burning all the kraals we come to.' Just after Ulundi, he was complaining of the winter cold, adding, 'How the Zulus will manage I don't know, we burnt about 20,000 huts. I feel for the poor women and children.'

Indeed, it may be claimed for the letters that they are able to shed light on otherwise unknown or obscure incidents and situations within the whole campaign. Two examples from Isandlwana present themselves; at the time, men who returned with Chelmsford to the devastated camp late on 22 January were reluctant to publicise the various ways in which the British dead were mutilated. It became a highly emotive question. Captain Penn Symons, 24th Regiment, in his detailed reconstruction of the battle, steers clear of it. He does say that many bodies were found tied by the hands and feet with strips of rawhide, and he acknowledged the Zulu practice of disembowelment. But he stopped there; 'further details', he says, 'would be too sickening'. Some of the soldiers who saw those sights, however, did not hesitate to describe them, and there is general agreement as between a number of writers; one hopes their relatives at home were not too squeamish. Again, one particular batch of letters could be usefully informative, namely those from men who returned to Isandlwana in May, as the first burial party. Their findings reveal something of the closing moments of that struggle. Thus we read in one from a man in the 17th Lancers: 'I enclose you a card of four of diamonds which lay close to the colonel of the 24th [i.e. Lt. Col. Pulleine]. They had evidently been playing cards, for a whole pack was kicked about, lots of music, too, I picked up.'

The best instance of revelation by letter comes from the battle of Khambula. There, instead of Chelmsford and Durnford we have Wood and Buller fighting deliberately on ground of their own choice, with four field-guns and two line battalions. On the Zulu side once again an impi of 24,000 warriors came on the attack, full of confidence after a string of successes, armed with the Martini-Henry rifles they had captured at Isandlwana and the Intombi Drift. The morale of the British could not have been lower, not only because of the reverses they had suffered since January, but also because of the disastrous failure the previous day. On 28 March a carefully-planned attempt to storm the Zulu fastness of Hlobane Mountain came amiss, and Wood's volunteer horsemen were severely mauled at the Devil's Pass and on the lower slopes. So when the Zulu horns began to extend early on the afternoon of 29 March, the Imperial lion was in poor shape.

Four hours later, after inspiring leadership by Wood, desperate firing by all defenders of the two laagers and fort, with more than one tense moment when the Zulus were about to burst in, the enemy broke. It made Khambula the turning-point of the whole campaign. The soldiers felt it at the time; they were glad to have saved their skins, and thirsty for revenge. Only the letters of men who took part in the grim success of the British pursuit can convey something of the carnage that took place. One was written the next day by Friedrich Schermbrücker, the elderly commander of a corps of German volunteers and their sons, known as the Kaffrarian Vanguard. After manning the north-west face of the laager during the battle, these Cape volunteers (whose horses were already saddled and tied to the picket-rope) raced out after the retreating Zulus.

I took the extreme right [he says], Colonel Buller led the centre, and Colonel Russell with mounted infantry took the left. For fully seven miles I chased two columns of the enemy. They fairly ran like bucks, but I was after them like the whirlwind and shooting incessantly into the thick column, which could have not been less than 5,000 strong. They became exhausted and shooting them down would have taken too much time; so we took the assegais from the dead men, and rushed among the living ones, stabbing them right and left with fearful revenge for the misfortunes of the 28th [i.e. at Hlobane]. No quarter was given.

About fifty of his men kept up with their fiery Commandant, who claims they killed 300 Zulus before dusk and a heavy mist fell at 6.30 p.m. His own losses were light, one man killed, another wounded, fourteen horses killed; the white horse he was riding 'got a bullet across his right ear' and nearly threw him. Buller he saw 'like a tiger drunk with blood, and, no doubt, the vivid recollection of the cruel manner in which the Zulus destroyed part of his forces on the 28th increased his war fury. Schermbrücker believed that Khambula 'finished the Zulu war, and I am proud of the part my men have taken in it'. Given that he was unaware of the further defeat of the Zulus at Gingindlovu and the subsequent relief of Eshowe, it was a shrewd judgment.

Writing on the same day, an officer of Wood's Swazi Irregulars adds further proof of the vulnerability of the Zulus in retreat after a lost fight.

Towards the end of the pursuit [he says], they were so tired and exhausted that they couldn't move out of a walk, some scarcely looked round and seemed to wish to die without seeing the shot fired. Some turned round and walked to meet their death without offering resistance, some threw themselves down on their faces and waited for their despatch by assegai or bullet, some got into antbear holes, reeds or long grass and tried to evade detection, but very few succeeded in this. It was indeed a slaughter.

The infantrymen saw nothing of all this, but they were jubilant at the crushing effect of their shot and shell. As Private Brett, one of the defenders, told his sister, the Zulus 'did me out of my dinner, but we did a good many of them out of their tea'. It is a shame no war artist was there to witness Khambula and record it. Other merciless pursuits, though not as bloody as that on 29 March, were to follow the Zulu defeats at Gingindlovu and Ulundi. They bring into the open the utmost savagery with which total war was being waged by the British and Zulu armies alike.

These, then, are the gains from using soldiers' letters – they reveal the pressures and predicaments of war as experienced by individuals and small units; the conditions under which they lived, worked, and fought; they have immediacy and a determinable time-context; they come from all phases of the war, active and passive; they illuminate little-known episodes and tell us of unsuspected ones. There is also the pleasure of appreciating the style in which they were written, sometimes terse and matter-of-fact, sometimes remarkably eloquent and vigorous pieces of composition. Consider this opening by a soldier of the 80th Regiment, written on 6 April: 'Dear Sister and Brother, death has been very busy gathering his harvest in this country, counting his victims by tens of thousands, without respect of race or colour. With the advent of the New Year, war in all its horrors has been let loose upon South Africa, and still the storm rages.' A little flowery for some tastes, perhaps, but a far cry from the picture of Tommy Atkins so often drawn by Kipling.

Naturally the letters cannot always be accepted at face value. Soldiers then, as later, were tempted to inflate the number of the enemy facing them, and the numbers killed by them in battle. They exaggerated the dangers and discomforts of active service to impress their loved ones at home. There is at least one letter from a soldier who claimed he had fought at Rorke's Drift, whereas (despite the question-marks that still exist on that muster-roll) the probability is that he was many miles away when the fight took place. Even so, we have various independent sources against which the letters can be checked, and the letters are so numerous that they can be cross-checked with each other. The chief determinant of variance lay in the military status of the letter-writers. Differences of rank tend to show: officers write longer letters and in more general terms than other ranks, although the gulf does not seem to have been as deep as it was in the First World War. One of them, Major Alfred Walker of the 99th, even wrote a charmingly-phrased letter to his young daughter, telling her about the battle at Gingindlovu: afterwards, 'The long grass outside was full of dead Zulus. I was very glad to turn round and go back to the laager. I thought how glad my little darling would be to know that I was quite safe and unhurt. Tell mamma that on the day of the battle the General promoted me on the field.'

Differences between the functioning arms of the imperial forces may also show in the letters; the most expressive would be associated with the skills of the Engineers, Artillery, Army Service Corps, Medical Service, but the Cavalry and Infantry certainly do not seem to be far behind. More penetrating differences might be expected between the professionals of the British army and the volunteer units that fought so bravely with them. Even there we should expect variance between the mercenaries of units like the Frontier Light Horse, and the truly colonial-born soldiers from the Cape or the Natal Carbineers, for whom the war was a domestic matter and whose knowledge of the country and their enemy was so much more intimate.

For a variety of reasons, the Zulu War fired the public imagination more completely than any other African campaign up to that time. To fill out the picture we shall range over a brief selection of letters from particular incidents, beginning with one from a survivor of what was from the British standpoint a total and shocking disaster. Students of the battle of Isandlwana are familiar with the letters written by four of the officers who managed by great good fortune to survive that devastating day – Cochrane, Curling, Gardner and Smith-Dorrien. Taken together with their submissions to the half-hearted Court of Inquiry held at Helpmekaar on 27 January 1879, (and that of Essex, the other officer who survived), these letters are a major source of information as to how the fight took place. Letters from ordinary soldiers, as distinct from officers, however, even though considerably more of them came through, are very rare indeed. Two may be introduced here.

The first is fragmentary, written by Sergeant-Major Thomas Sharp who had 'given up baking and gone to the front, as it is a better paying thing at present, but more dangerous'. That is fair comment on his day's work at Isandlwana, where he went into action with the Natal Native Contingent, probably with Nourse's company of the 1st Battalion, 1st Regiment. 'We advanced about a mile,' says Sharp, 'threw out skirmishers, and commenced banging away; the more we fired and killed, the stronger they seemed to appear [i.e. the Zulu left horn]. At last we had to retire on the Regulars who were fighting in another direction.' As the British defence crumbled, Sharp caught a horse and managed to ride away to safety.

The other letter is much more important and informative. Its author was 1387 Driver Elias Tucker, who served with N Battery, 5th Brigade of the Royal Artillery. He wrote it from Helpmekaar on 28 January 1879, less than a week after he had fought with the two 7-pounder guns left behind by Chelmsford to defend his camp at Isandlwana. It went to his parents at Plymouth, telling them what he had been through and that he was safe; they in turn passed it on to the editor of *The Western Morning News*, who published it in that newspaper on 28 March 1879. There is no reason to doubt the authenticity of Tucker's account of his experience. He would scarcely have been tempted to fabricate his story of being one of the handful of survivors of an historic battle. Others were to do that, but much later in time and certainly not in a private letter. A more positive point in his favour is that (as his letter reveals) he was acting as manservant or batman to Lieutenant H. T. Curling, one of his battery's officers. Curling was with the guns at Isandlwana and survived the battle; his servant would have been in the camp with him, rather than out with Chelmsford and the rest of the battery, and may even have had a better chance than most of securing a horse on which to make his escape.

The battery was raised originally (as K/11) at Devonport on 1 February 1871. Tucker attested, at the age of twenty-two, on 3 February 1871, so he was probably one of several young men from Plymouth who enlisted in the unit. This again would be a discouragement to him to spin a yarn in his letter home. He left the army by purchase towards the end of 1881, before completing his engagement, so his discharge papers do not survive to throw an indisputable light on his presence at Isandlwana: Tucker's name does not appear in the list of survivors of N/5th suggested by Major P. E. Abbott in his article, 'N Battery, 5th Brigade, Royal Artillery at Isandlwana, 22nd January 1879' (*Journal of the Society for Army Historical Research*, LVI, 1978, pages 95–111). But as Major Abbott is at pains to point out, it is impossible to make a watertight, indisputable list of the artillerymen who escaped. Certainty is attached to only three men: Curling, Driver James Burchall and Driver Edward Price.

It seems most likely that Curling and eight of his men survived. The evidence comes from a reliable NCO of N/5th, Sergeant W. E. Warren, who wrote a long letter from Helpmekaar, part of which is published in *The Red Soldier*. Warren says (in the continuation of his letter) that having been out with Chelmsford and returning to Isandlwana after the battle, he reached Helpmekaar on 24 January. There 'we found nine of our men who had escaped, and they gave us an account so far as they were able, poor fellows'. Warren's total figures of the casualties corroborate those of Curling: one captain (Stuart Smith), sixty-one NCO's and men, twenty-four horses, and he adds thirty mules and seven mule owners. It is a pity Tucker does not name more survivors, but as it is his testimony clears up the identity of the sergeant who escaped, John Costellow; Curling gave the name of 216 Sergeant William Edwards, but he was killed. Another discovery is the appearance among the survivors of 665 Gunner William Green, who was not among those listed by Major Abbott. Obviously, there is still scope for tracking down the three artillerymen remaining if we accept the names of Curling, Costellow, Burchall, Green, Price and Tucker as being among the nine.

As with many of the ordinary soldiers' letters, it is too much to expect that their facts as to numbers, times and so on will be absolutely accurate. Tucker is reasonably near the mark in respect of the relative numbers of combatants on the British and Zulu sides at Isandlwana. He is wildly off target with his 12,000 Zulu casualties, but that could be a misprint in the newspaper for 2,000, much nearer the mark. Soldiers like to exaggerate the strength and discomfiture of their foes. Nor is it likely that the British 'held the field' until as late as 3 p.m., but his other details make sense, e.g. there was a detachment of the 1/13th Light Infantry at Helpmekaar on that day, marching up country to join Evelyn Wood's column on the Blood river. All in all, Tucker's observations are worth reading, for instance his remark that the firing of the 24th was 'cutting roads through them', and it has the unique quality of being the only one of its kind so far known. It runs as follows:

> Dear Father and Mother. It gives me great pleasure to think that I am alive to write to you. We have a severe cutting up on the 22nd of January. Lord Chelmsford went out with the column about three o'clock in the morning; he went about 15 miles from camp to attack the Zulus – to Isinlonana or the Lion's Mane [Silutshana?]. They left 2 guns and 65 artillery, 5 companies of the 24th Regiment, in all about five hundred men. The Zulus watched the column out of the camp, and then attacked the camp: they came into camp by thousands, about seventeen thousand Zulus. They came on the camp like wild beasts, which they are.
>
> We played well on them with the two guns, and the infantry

fought well, cutting roads through them. We held the field from half past eleven in the morning until three o'clock in the day. We killed twelve thousand Zulus, but they were too strong for us. They came right around us, and massacred every one; there are only twelve left to tell the tale. Out of sixty-five artillery only four remain, and I am one of the four – Sergeant Costellow, Lieutenant Curling (that's my master) and myself and Gunner Green. We four had a horse each, and we charged right through the Zulus and cut our way out. I was in my shirt sleeves carrying ammunition to the guns.

We lost everything in camp; they burnt everything that would burn. All our waggons and carts we had for ammunition they filled up with dead white men. They cut everyone up, and took his heart and laid it on his breast, and put his right hand in where they took his heart from, and put all the skulls up in a heap. I expect you will see the massacre in the papers before you receive this. I could not write before. We rode a hard gallop from the time we cut our way out of camp until four next morning, and we found ourselves in sight of Helpmekaar, and that gave us fresh strength, hoping to find some help there; but when we got there, there were only six men on guard belonging to the 13th Regiment. We frightened them out of their lives. There is only one store in Helpmekaar, and that was filled up with stacks of corn. We got that out and barricaded all the doors, and cut some loopholes through the sides and ends to fire through. We were afraid they would attack us here, but they have not been.

Dear Mother, still there is hope for us, for our relief came this morning. A lot of Engineers and the 4th (King's Own) Regiment marched in here; we gave them three hearty cheers. Dear Mother, I must now conclude, as they are sending out a mounted orderly tonight, and I want these few lines to go with him. I have not received any letters from England since October. The Zulus have taken possession of all the houses on the road and burnt them down. Please to drop a few lines to London to Tim and my sister to let them know that I am living and well, for I cannot get paper to write on. I gave a shilling for this envelope and paper, and it is cheap at that. We cannot get paper or envelopes for love or money here in the midst of a wilderness and savages. Please to give my kind love to all inquiring friends and tell them all that I am alive and well, only a slight wound on the back of the hand. So, good-bye, and God bless you all. They have sent to England for more troops, and we shall pay the Zulus out for this yet.

Just as the military nerves were beginning to calm down after this experience, unprecedented as it was, they were upset once more by a reverse that in some ways was like a miniature Isandlwana. In the early hours of 12 March 1879 an entire company of soldiers belonging to the 80th Foot (Staffordshire Volunteers) was surprised at a drift on the Intombi river. The Zulu killed all but a handful of those who were on the east bank of the flooded river; they were there as an armed guard for a convoy of waggons coming down country, filled with stores for Wood's command. Many of the soldiers were speared to death in their tents before they could dress and arm themselves. Clearly the 80th had not yet learnt the essential first rule of service in Zulu territory – have plenty of sentries or piquets stationed well out from any defensive position. Yet even the Intombi affair had a gleam of redemption, because it was distinguished by the fighting retreat of that section of the company posted on the west bank of the river. Pursued by the jubilant Zulu, this party managed to extricate itself and live to fight another day, commanded with flair and determination by the author of our next letter. He was awarded the Victoria Cross for what he did, and it was one of the best-deserved of the twenty-nine VCs won during this brief but intensive war.

Anthony Booth is the epitome of the long-serving Victorian regular soldier. He was born at Nottingham, and at the age of eighteen (his trade given as 'tailor') he enlisted in the 80th in 1864. Quite early in his military career he was promoted to the rank of corporal, and he possessed the 2nd Class Certificate of Army Education, both pointers to his abilities. The first seven years he spent on garrison duties at home and in Ireland, during which time he married Lucy O'Brien. In 1871 he re-engaged for 'such time as shall complete a total service of 21 years', and then embarked on what proved to be eight years of duty overseas. This took Booth to Singapore and Hong Kong, where he saw some action against the forces of the Sultan of Perak, and, more fatefully, to Natal in 1877. The 80th arrived to share in what had been hitherto the colonial garrison's rather humdrum routine, but the recent annexation by Britain of the Boer republic of the Transvaal had sparked off new tensions. There had to be a military presence in the Transvaal, and some of Booth's regiment went at once to build a fort at Newcastle, on the northern border of Natal. It coincided with Anthony Trollope's journeyings through South Africa, and the novelist writes of seeing men of the 80th on the march, and of enjoying a few bottles of Bass in the officers' mess-tent.

Sterner duties lay ahead of the 80th in 1878 when they became involved in the abortive demonstrations of strength against

Sekhukhune of the Pedi. No doubt Booth served his initiation to African bush fighting against an elusive foe in the closing months of 1878. Early in the new year he was drawn, along with his regimental comrades, into the fresh prospect of an even more demanding campaign against the Zulu in that difficult terrain where the Transvaal, Natal, and the territory disputed with Zululand all marched together. Such was the background of the incident in which Booth was to play such a spectacular role. One feature of it was that the commissioned officer present, Lieutenant Harward, left Sergeant Booth in the lurch by galloping off to the safety of Luneburg: he was court-martialled for this disgraceful piece of conduct, and Booth draws attention to it in his letter.

After the Zulu War was over, he returned to England in 1880, and served another eight years with the 80th as Colour-Sergeant. Then in 1888 he transferred to the 1st Volunteer Battalion, South Staffordshire Regiment, where he was instructor until his final discharge from the army on 30 April 1898. By then he had a continuous record of service to Her Majesty of 33 years and 182 days; few could have celebrated the Old Queen's diamond jubilee with more fervour. The photograph of Anthony Booth and his family was taken at about this time, showing that his four sons were all soldiers in his old line regiment. The veteran himself sits in a basket chair, wearing the crimson sash of a colour-sergeant and the insignia of an instructor of musketry. His Victoria Cross, worn with his campaign medals, is proof of the coolness and marksmanship he had shown in a desperate situation twenty years earlier, and we can read about this in his own words.

My dear wife and children,
You must please excuse me not answering your last letter that I received about eight days since. I know you will all be thankful for the most miraculous escape I have had, and I know you and our children will be proud of your husband and father when you will see in the papers the account of the battle at Intombi River. We left Luneburg on the morning of 7 March to escort a convoy of waggons, about some 24 in number. We arrived at the Intombi River, some six miles from Luneburg on the road to Derby, about 11 a.m. The river was very high and we could not cross it only on a raft that me and Mr. Lindop [Lt. A. H. Lindop] and some of the men constructed, the rain coming down heavens hard, which continued for four days successively. I was acting Quarter-Master Sergeant for the 103 men, Captain Moriarty, Lieut. Johnson,

Lieut. Lindop, and Doctor Cobbin, also a lot of volunteers and nigger drivers. In all that was engaged in the battle was 154 officers, men, etc.; only about 41 men and some niggers arrived at Luneburg to tell the tale.

Mr. Lindop had gone to Luneburg the night before the battle, also Lieut. Johnson, and one man, Lieut. Harward, came out to relieve them. About 4.30 a.m. on 12 March 1879 I was awoke by hearing a shot fired in the direction of the mountains. I should have told you we were under Mbelini's Cave, a notorious chieftain. Lieut. Harward called for me and told me to alarm the camp on the other side of the river – for there was me and Lieut. Harward and 33 men on one side of the river, the remainder on the other side. I called out for the sentry on the other side to alarm the camp; he did not answer me, but a man named Tucker came to the riverside and I told him to tell Captain Moriarty that a shot had been fired, and to alarm the camp. He sent word back that the men were to get dressed but to remain in their tents. I was in the commissariat waggon taking charge of the goods, I went in the waggon again and lit my pipe and looked at my watch, it was quarter to 5 a.m. I put on my ammunition belt, and me and another man was smoking in the waggon when about 5 o'clock I heard another shot fired, and someone shout 'Sergeant Johnson'.

I looked out of the waggon, and I shall never forget the sight I saw. The day was just breaking and there was about 5,000 Zulus on the other side. They were close to the tents and shouted their war-cry, 'Zu Zu'. They fired a volley into us on this side of the river, then they commenced assegaing the men as they lay in the tents. I rallied my party by the waggons and poured heavy fire into them as fast as we could, some of the men coming out from the other side of the river and coming across to us. Crawford was one of them, he was the only man out of his tent that got across alive. Captain Moriarty and Doctor Cobbin was murdered in their tents, and most of the men also.

I commanded the party on this side as *Lieut.* Harward saddled his horse and galloped away, leaving us to do the best we could. When I saw all our men across, about 15 in number, all as naked as they was born, I sent them on in front and we retired firing. There was hundreds of the Kaffirs crossing the river to try and cut us off, but we made good our retreat to a mission station, and expected to be outflanked there, but we fought our way to within a mile of Luneburg. The distance we had to run and fight was nearly five miles, so you will have a guess how we were situated. We arrived at Luneburg about 15 minutes past 7 o'clock, losing nine on my side, and 46 on the other side was buried, and all the remainder was assegaied in the river.

A party went out to bury them on the same day, but they have been and taken them up again (I mean the Kaffirs) and skinned them. So we are ordered out again to go and bury them, we go directly, I am one of them. [Booth then lists the names of the forty-one killed, and another twenty-one who were missing, 'they must have been killed in the river']. I am acting Pay Sergeant of a company now. There was a parade, and I and my small party was complimented on the bravery we exhibited in saving as many lives as we did, and bringing them in with such little loss of life on my side. I am mentioned in dispatches to the General and to Colonel Wood, there is also a letter sent to the editor of the *Natal Argus*, I will send you one when I get it.

Now, dear wife, I hope you and our children are all well. I hope Lucy is better and that she was not so far gone as you thought. Remember me to all enquiring friends. With fondest love to you and all the chicks, trusting God to spare me from all evil and grant me life to see you all again, I remain your loving husband, A. Booth.

Sixty-two officers and men were killed at the Intombi, placing it next after Isandlwana as the most serious loss to regular troops during the entire Zulu War. Despite this, it is still one of the least known episodes of the war, so perhaps it is worth our while to sample another rare letter from someone else who survived it. Private Henry Jones of the 80th wrote on 13 March, the day after it all happened, to friends at Claybrook in Leicester, describing how he had gone to the drift with Captain Moriarty's column on 5 March. His narrative is shot through with immediacy of close combat: he was on the other side of the river from Sergeant Booth, and was one of a handful of men who made their escape independently of Booth's rearguard action.

When we arrived at the river we found it swollen very much from the recent heavy rains so that no waggons could cross it, it being about 10 feet deep in the centre and over 100 yards wide. The whole of the waggons were on the other side awaiting us, and we set to and made a rough kind of raft to take us over. On the morning of the 6th Capt. Moriarty ordered the A Company and 13 men of E Company with three mounted orderlies (Fisher, Tucker, and myself) to cross the river and camp. There we waited day after day for the river to fall until the morning of the 12th – a morning never to be forgotten by any of those who escaped back to Luneburg.

About 2 a.m. it began to rain very hard and continued until 4 when it ceased and a very thick fog came down the hills on each side of us. About this time one of the sentries reported hearing a shot, but a long distance off, so we took very little notice of it. Most of us lay down again thinking to get another hour's sleep. But we had not been down long when one of the most frightful yells that ever issued from human throats alarmed the whole camp. We instantly sprang up, seized the first rifle we could get, rushed to the waggons and poured volley after volley into the approaching Kaffirs, numbering some thousands. They must have crept upon our sentries unawares and murdered them before they could give alarm. After firing several volleys the Kaffirs broke cover and rushed the waggons.

Then commenced one of the most terrible hand-to-hand fights that has been known for years. But fight how we might we could have no chance, as the enemy at this time numbered over 4,000. We tried several times to reach the horses, but all to no purpose. All at once I heard a cry of 'We are surrounded', I looked around and saw to my horror that the Kaffirs had closed round us and cut us off from the river. Then the slaughter of our poor fellows commenced. I never thought I should live to write this, as death seemed to stare us in the face. How the few escaped that did is quite a miracle.

Jones says that with a group of about ten of his comrades he clubbed his rifle and tried to break out of the Zulu cordon:

By the time that we reached the river only four of us remained, Brownson, Fisher, Sergeant Sansome and myself. As soon as we reached it we threw in our rifles, the river ran so strong we could not take them with us. We then plunged in ourselves, followed by the Kaffirs. Brownson, after getting into the middle, was caught by the Kaffirs and speared. Fisher, Sansome and myself still kept together until we were within 25 yards from the side, when I had to dive underwater to escape three Kaffirs who were close to me. When I rose to the surface I saw that Fisher had reached the bank, but just at that time a Kaffir came beside me, grasped me by the throat by one hand and uplifted the other to assegai me. I caught his wrist and I drew my sheath knife and plunged it between his ribs up to the hilt.

I remember nothing more until I found myself clinging to the bank on the Luneburg side of the river. I scrambled up and there found Fisher and Sergeant Sansome kneeling down under cover, recovering their breath. I noticed several fellows at this time in front of me making for Luneburg. On looking down the river bank I noticed Kaffirs scrambling up in hundreds. We jumped up and commenced to run towards Luneburg. Before we had gone 20 yards the sergeant was shot through the back. After running a few miles we were compelled to stop and pull off our wet boots and trousers, as the Kaffirs were gaining on us. We then ran on until we came within two miles of Luneburg, when we were again compelled to stop and tear off our shirts to bind our bleeding feet; we then came on to Luneburg completely naked.

When we arrived here three of our company volunteered to go out with others, numbering in all 276 men. When they got in sight of the river they saw the enemy swarming up the hills. As they reached the waggons a frightful sight met their eyes, as the enemy had disembowelled all our poor fellows, and mutilated them so that you could not recognise one from the others. Everything that was on the waggons was thrown off and destroyed.

It is always encouraging when different letters serve to corroborate the same incident, and this can be done here. On 13 March an officer of the 80th, Lieutenant Edward Daubeney, wrote from Luneburg to his father, who was rector of Easington, near Northleach in Gloucestershire. His letter confirms the story told by Henry Jones and ends with a reference to Sergeant Booth's covering party.

A company of our regiment got awfully cut up yesterday, losing the captain and sixty men, and a civil surgeon who was with them was killed too. The way it happened was this: my company [Captain Anderson's] was sent out on escort duty to bring in a train of 20 ox waggons with provisions and ammunition from Derby. We got them as far as the river Intombi, five or six miles from here, but the river was swollen by heavy rain, and they could not be got over it, so as we had been out for a week, Captain Moriarty with his company and one subaltern Harward, was sent out to relieve us, and guard the waggons until the river went down enough to let them cross. The company consisted of 100 men, and 65 crossed the river, sending over their rifles and ammunition on a raft with Moriarty, while Harward stopped on this side with the remaining 35. The waggons were formed into a laager, in the shape of a horse-shoe, the ends resting on the river, and at night the oxen were brought into the space inside. They stayed there all right for two or three days, the river still too high to cross, and the day before yesterday, in the evening, Major Tucker rode out there, taking me and two other fellows with him, and we found them all right with no signs of Zulus anywhere. The next morning, about 5 o'clock, the alarm sounded, and we struck our tents and ran into the fort. We could see and hear firing on the track to the river, about a mile and a half away on the top of a hill – there was a horse dead-beat outside the fort, and soon after the Major came out of his tent with Harward, then a man came up the hill to the fort perfectly naked, and more men dropped in, some with clothes and some without, but all without their rifles and ammunition, and lastly a small body of about 30 men with their arms and accoutrements, who had been covering the retreat of the others.

Not long afterwards there came another reverse at the hands of the Zulu in this same northern sector of hostilities. Although the heavy casualties fell on units of volunteer mounted men and native auxiliaries, rather than on imperial soldiery, they were keenly felt in Wood's column to which they belonged. An assault had been planned on the mountain stronghold of Hlobane, partly as an act of retribution for the Intombi river affair, partly to capture the thousands of cattle kept by the Zulu on the flat summit of this precipitous bastion. Without going into detail here, the earlier stages of the operation went reasonably well, but the whole situation changed dramatically when Buller's force (then on the table-top of Hlobane) saw the main body of the Zulu army approaching in the distance. In the scramble of escape from this threat, the mounted troops were decimated both by local Zulu and by units of the main army. Evelyn Wood himself, who joined the assault after it was partly achieved, had to run for it.

We learn of this in a letter written by one of Wood's personal escort, Private Edmund Fowler of the 90th Light Infantry, of which Wood was colonel. Fowler won the Victoria Cross at Hlobane during the fire-fight that nearly cost Wood his life, and caused the deaths of his principal staff officer, Captain the Hon. Ronald Campbell (Coldstream Guards) and his interpreter, Captain Llewellyn Lloyd. The route used by Wood and his small party in ascending Hlobane took them directly beneath the sheer cliffs of its upper slopes. Rising in a series of rocky terraces, the foot of the cliffs is a jumble of huge slabs of rock fallen from above, perched one on the other, the gaps and crevices between them forming a kind of cave system. It is difficult enough to walk over this terrain on a peaceful morning at the present time, but on 28 March 1879 the caves offered perfect cover for the Zulu marksmen whose fire was very effective. Fowler won his VC in helping to combat this danger. His letter also refers to the battle that followed the next day, when the Zulu army made a full frontal assault on Wood's fortified camp at Khambula. In contrast with the sorry mess at Hlobane, that was a copy-book triumph for the British forces, and in effect Khambula sapped the Zulu of their military strength to such a degree that it was not recovered in the later stages of the war. Fowler writes in a plain but sharp style (on 9 April):

I shall remember all my life the 28th of last month, when I had a very narrow escape from an awful death. Many of my comrades were cut to pieces, and had it not been that a captain of the staff was killed, I should not have been able to send this to you. We left camp 500 men all told on the 27th, and camped out the first night in the open, not even taking the saddles off our horses. Before daybreak we started to climb the mountain [Hlobane], and then death came round on all sides. Men and horses fell thickly all round, and we could not see the face of a nigger to fire at, as they were in caves on all sides of us. Colonel Wood had a narrow escape as he had his horse shot under him. My horse was also shot under me.

We had a corps called Weatherley's Horse with us, and they were getting downhearted. Colonel Wood saw this, and ordered his escort to charge. We did so, led by a gallant officer of the Coldstreams, the Hon. Captain Campbell. Poor Campbell and I had just carried down Captain Lloyd, who was the Colonel's interpreter, and had been shot dead by my side. I saw Campbell turn around, his helmet flew off, and fell dead with the top of his head blown off. Then the colonel gave the word to retire and carry the dead and wounded with us, which we did. Under a very heavy fire we dug graves for the two staff officers on the mountainside, the colonel reading the service over them as if we were on parade. The dismal task over, we retired to the bottom of the hill.

The volunteers had not commenced to return then. After we had ridden about three miles we saw on our right front the whole of the Zulu army. The old man says 'Gallop for your lives, men', which we did, and a hard run we had of it for 25 miles. All the poor chaps that were left behind us were cut off and killed. We had a lucky escape, and when we reached camp [at Khambula] and told the news it caused a great sensation. We were in great suspense all that night, but they did not come.

Next morning they came in sight, to the number of about 30,000, making the air dark with the dust they raised as they came towards the camp. On they came, and down went our tents ready for action. When they came within half a mile of us all the horsemen rode out and opened the ball with them. We had a go-in for about ten minutes, when we had to run for it, and the big guns opened fire on them. Still on they came like a big rolling sea on all sides of us. But when they came within range of the Martini-Henry rifles it was awful to hear the fire we kept up, and the ground was soon black with their dead. They also kept up a good fire, which knocked a few of our men over.

The fight lasted five hours and a half, when they turned and fled in great disorder and out we went after them, and a great chase we had. They were done up, and stood for us to shoot them. We killed about 6,000 and they were buried outside the lines in big pits. It was an awful sight to see them. It took five days to bury the dead.

Fowler's estimate of the number of Zulu casualties must be halved to approximate to the true figure, and several other letters agree that it took three days to bury those killed close to the British position. The incident in which Fowler distinguished himself is described in Wood's account of the Hlobane disaster. Campbell charged into the cave with Lieutenant Lysons and four soldiers of Wood's escort, 'passing up a narrow passage only two feet wide, between rocks 12 feet high, for several yards. He was looking down into the cave when a Zulu fired, almost touching him, and he fell dead. Lieutenant Lysons and Private Fowler, undauntedly passing over the body, fired into the cave and the few Zulus in it disappeared through another opening.' There is also a sketch of how Campbell and Lloyd were buried under fire, reminiscent of Wood with the dying Arthur Eyre in Ashanti.[2]

Zulu casualties after the battle of Ulundi that ended the Anglo-Zulu war, 4 July 1879, drawn by the renowned war artist, C.E. Fripp, who includes himself in the picture.

2. Sir Evelyn Wood, *From Midshipman to Field Marshal*, (London: Murray, 1906), volume two, page 50.

It is well known that certain soldiers were allowed to take their wives and children with them on overseas service. Rarely do we hear much about them, but there is a letter from one soldier's wife, written at Cape Town on 3 March 1879. Her husband was with the force besieged by the Zulu at Eshowe, and the story she tells her sister is full of interest and pathos about the impact of war on a military family, especially the uncertainties that came after Isandlwana.

> It is with a heavy heart that I sit down to write to you. First I must tell you my poor Joe has gone to the war, he has been gone three months. I am sure by this time you have heard of the dreadful massacre of the 24th Regiment, there are 40 poor widows left, I do not know how many poor orphans. Now I must tell you about myself. We had to fly from Pietermaritzburg for safety. The Zulus are expected to cross the border into Natal, and if they did they would kill all before them. I never thought I should see such dreadful times. Before we left Pietermaritzburg we were afraid to lie down at night. Every evening we had our things put together ready, if the great gun fired, to fly to camp. Oh, the weary nights of watching I shall never forget. If we had stayed there much longer my hair would have gone grey. My two little children as I undressed them, I had to tie their things up into a bundle, ready to fly. The panic in the town was something dreadful, so the military authorities thought best to send us to Cape Town.
>
> Now we are safe, but our hearts are breaking for our poor men, they are so far away, on half rations now because it is not safe for to take them more provisions until reinforcements come from England, and God send them speedily or they will be starved out. What shall I ever do if I am left a widow? My poor dear Joe, you must pray earnestly, my dear sister, for God to spare him to his poor wife and little ones. When we left Maritzburg we had to travel three days and nights in bullock waggons, sixteen oxen to each waggon; you can fancy our terror, travelling through such a dangerous country. Had the Zulus come upon us everyone of us would have been killed, for we had three schoolmasters with us, about a hundred women, and double as many children. They could not spare men to go with us. If our poor men fall we shall be sent to our parishes.

Quite by chance, one company of Her Majesty's First Battalion, 24th Regiment of Foot managed to escape the holocaust that consumed their comrades at Isandlwana. We learn of this from a letter written by Private William McNulty to a friend at Wrexham, dated 17 February 1879 from 'St. John's River, Pondoland, S.E. Coast of Africa'. He belonged to B Company of the 1/24th and they were detached for special duties, while still in Cape Colony, on 12 August 1878. The purpose of this was a typical imperial move, the annexation of what might prove to be a useful harbour in the territory of the Mpondo people. Sir Bartle Frere was keen to achieve this on general principles, but more so if it would pre-empt the Germans from stepping into a territorial vacuum. It is interesting to hear from Private McNulty how it happened.

> My company was ordered to proceed by man-of-war to this place to take the river, which is a navigable and a splendid one, from the Pondos. We thought we should have hot work, and expected the Pondos would prevent us landing. They would have done so, for they were waiting for us to come by land, but instead of that we landed, along with General Lord Chelmsford, and hoisted the British flag and, when they found out that we had gained a footing they did not interfere with us, and now we have a fine fort built, and huts erected, and a regular little settlement formed, but we are expecting an attack from the Pondos as they are in a very unsettled state, and have got much more cheeky since the Zulus gained this victory over our troops. Anyhow, if they should pay us a visit, they will meet with a hot reception.

The Pondo did not attack.

Letters to their children are uncommon among the soldiers' writings, but have a special interest because of their blend of reporting the military essentials, local colour, and showing *rapport* with what the children are doing at home. We see this in a series of letters written by Lieutenant-Colonel Henry Fanshawe Davies (1837–1914), of the Grenadier Guards. Early in 1879 he found himself en route for Durban with a strong reinforcement of volunteers from other regiments, who were going out to rebuild the 1/24th Foot, shattered at Isandlwana. His earlier experience in the Royal Navy, which took him to Burma and the Crimea, served him in good stead when their transport ship, SS *Clyde*, struck a rock and sank on 3 April, just beyond the Cape of Good Hope. Thanks to his coolness and efficiency, not a single life was lost. Davies had two sons at Eton, just into their teens, and wrote to them regularly after he reached Natal and moved up to Zululand.

> Griffin's Farm, Natal, April 25th, 1879
> My dearest Harry,
> We are still marching up the country, tomorrow morning we go

to Estcourt when we shall have done just about half the distance between Durban and Dundee. You will find Estcourt marked in the maps. So far all has gone very well with us, the weather beautiful and we manage to live very well considering where we are. I am most flourishing, so are the horses; Taylor has got a touch of rheumatism in his knee, not much, and James has a blistered foot, with that exception they are well. I hope to buy a nice Natal horse at Ladysmith. If I go on the Staff I must have three.

Last night we dined at the inn at Weston on the Mooi river where we were waited on by a Kaffir whose only garment was a short flannel shirt, as it was a clean one I fancy he had put it on in our honour, in fact got himself up in his best. This is a most charming country, such fine hills and beautiful undulating grass country, all grass as far as the eye can reach. We see very few animals of any sort, there are deer but they avoid the road. Lots of dead oxen, at least the clean-picked bones, the Kaffirs eat the flesh directly and the vultures pick the bones. When we left Durban a terrier attached herself to us, and so far has stuck to us. The Kaffirs are such fine, muscular, well set-up fellows, they are very fond of buying soldiers' clothes, we often see one with nothing on but a tunic.

I am having pretty hard work, but I don't mind it. It is a great pleasure hearing from you dear boys so often. Up to this time I have written to you by every mail; but when once we advance into Zululand I can only write to Mamma, I am afraid, that you can understand. The postal arrangements will be very uncertain in all probability. We have only had two wet days since we left England. I am very sorry to hear of the accident to young Loder at Hawtreys, I suppose he is one of the twins. How did it happen? What sort of an Eleven will Eton have this year? I am glad Frank saw the wedding procession, I hope you went too. The days are hot but the nights are quite cold here, I fancy a little frost. I was sorry to hear that we had lost seven deer at Elmley.[3] The children seem to be riding vigorously.

For the first time this evening we laagered the waggons, that is formed them up so that we might get inside and defend ourselves. But I don't think there is any danger of meeting any enemies for some time. Everybody out here seems to approve of what I did at the wreck of the *Clyde*, I hope the people in England will think the same. Lord Chelmsford has published a general order on the subject, I have sent a copy of it to Mamma, so that you can see it.

3. Since 1875 Davies had leased the estate of Elmley Castle, lying under Bredon Hill in Worcestershire, from his aunt. He, his son, and grandson were successively lords of the manor down to 1982.

In a few weeks I suppose you will be at cricket, play as much as you can. I hope you both helped Mamma about everything during the holidays, and got on well with your dancing. Good-bye, my dear boys, I must go to bed as I have to get up at 4.30. Your affectionate father, H. F. Davies.

By 1 June 1879 he was playing his part with the force that had been amassed by Chelmsford for the final invasion of Zululand, although Davies was far from pleased with his defensive role. He wrote this letter on the day the Prince Imperial of France met his death on a forward reconnaissance.

Conference Hill. June 1, 1879.
My dear Harry,
I am still here and horribly disgusted, because I am left behind. The army is now advancing, and I have to take charge of this post which is just in the Transvaal. I have two companies of infantry and half the King's Dragoon Guards. I shall have to look after the communications, and take charge of the stores here. I don't like the post and I am very much disgusted at being left in the rear, and I am afraid I shall not have a fight.

There are, I believe, 6 to 8,000 Kaffirs about 20 miles in front of me, and no force between us. Of course they may come and attack me, and if so I shall only have about 200 men to oppose them in the forts, and about 200 cavalry to hover about their flanks, but as I have plenty of ammunition, I think we could give a good account of them. We may also have some little skirmishes with them at patrolling and cattle-lifting, which is part of the warfare in this country. We had three days' rain in the last week, but else the weather has been fine. James, Taylor and the horses are well; Limerick has had a bad mouth, called lampas, lately but it has been lanced and I hope he will soon be all right again.

If all goes well the war may be over in a month. But I think matters are uncertain how it will turn out and we may have difficulties. I think the Zulus will not oppose the main force much, but they will work round behind so as to cut off the supplies and perhaps attack such places as this. Lord Chelmsford has promised if possible to find a place farther to the front for me, but I have not much hope. I rather expected the English mail today but I have been disappointed. If we do not finish off the war this next month it will last another year, but it is quite a chance that I should stay out so long.

I shall be anxious to know how long it takes you to learn to swim, you must also learn to manage a boat. I hope that the Eton Eleven is good and will win the match this year. You will get this letter about a week before the match is played. Uncle Bye has promised to get places for you and to take you if possible. How I should like to see you all, I have been away just three months, it seems an age. I have done and seen so much, but at the same time the weeks go very quickly. I am glad to hear such a good account of you from your tutor. You will have to pay the postage on my letters but you must not let them charge you double, as I am on active service, they have no business to do so.

Perhaps we should leave the Zulu War with a brief glimpse of its most evocative clash of arms, the defence of the mission station at Rorke's Drift. It comes from a letter about the man in command at the Drift, rather than by him: John Chard was summoned to Balmoral Castle in October 1879 to tell his story, and a royal secretary describes what happened.

Chard has been here and left this morning. He explained the defence of Rorke's Drift to the Queen, Prince Leopold, the Grand Duke of Hesse, and Princess Beatrice in the Queen's private room, and did it all very clearly and modestly. After dinner he did likewise to us in the billiard room on the table, where store and hospital [the mission buildings] were books and boxes, and mealie-bags and biscuit tins [the breastworks] were billiard balls.

I gather from all I hear that Dalton was quite as much (if not more) of the presiding genius there, as himself. He conceived the idea of joining the two buildings with mealie-bags, etc. before Chard's arrival on the scene; tho' perhaps Chard would have done so, had he not found it in operation. The inner line, which was their great safeguard, was Chard's own idea, I fancy, and when they were deserted by so many of the defenders (natives, etc.) it was soon found that the first line of defence was too extended.

Bromhead (commanding B Company, 2/24th Regiment) had of course great influence over his own men, and kept them in their places or moved them about, controlled their fire with great judgment. Only one-and-a-half boxes of ammunition was left when morning came, besides what they had in their pouches. Chard made no complaint, but it seemed odd to me that he was not consulted as to the distribution of the Victoria Crosses [eleven defenders received the award, including Chard]. He is not a genius and not quick, but a quiet, plodding, dogged sort of fellow who will hold his own in most of the situations in which, as an Engineer officer, his lot may be cast.

84

FOUR

'We Have Just Had a Nice Little Campaign Here':

THE SOUTHERN FRONTIERS, 1879–81

Imperial warfare in southern Africa was marked by several differences from the course of events elsewhere in the continent. One important difference stems from the presence in the Cape Colony, Natal, and in the various fluctuating territories of the republican Boers of a white settler population of colonists and burghers. Although their towns, villages and farmsteads were scattered far and wide across the immense distances of veldt or valley, this white population was far more influential than its relatively small numbers would suggest. In the military sense their influence ran in various directions. Most obviously it meant that in times of conflict with black African nations, such as in the interminable series of frontier wars along the eastern Cape borders, the settlers formed themselves into volunteer units of mounted rifles. These fought alongside the red soldiers of the imperial garrison. Some of the colonial units were ephemeral and did not last beyond the immediate need of self-defence, whereas others like the Natal Carbineers persist as regular forces to the present day.

Another influence that quickened as time went on was the formation of units which were fully subsidised by the colonial governments as their own defence corps. So far did this trend go that by the 1870s the Cape Mounted Rifles and similar units fought their own campaigns, without the aid of imperial troops. It even led to tensions between the Cape Town administrators and the British general in command as to who should control what their combined forces did in the field. Nor should we forget the ultimate consequence of the European presence in southern Africa, where the Transvaal Boers in particular became rebellious opponents of the British government at home. The political tensions so produced became especially acute with the discovery of diamonds and gold in the region, and their profitable working after about 1870. Complex motives were bound into this situation which flared into serious armed struggle on two occasions. The First Anglo-Boer War of 1880–81 proved to be a mortifying experience for the British troops engaged in it. The second dragged on from 1899 to 1902, beyond the Victorian era, and with the savagery, intensity and weaponry displayed by two white powers it introduced a new dimension to African warfare at the very close of the nineteenth century.

The more usual flavour of what went on at the smaller scale of combat, where volunteer units of Cape colonists fought the Transkei Xhosa (and invariably helped themselves to as many of the Africans' cattle as they could) also appears in the occasional letter. One may be quoted, although it comes from as early as the Seventh Frontier War, long before the proper business of this book. It was written from the military camp at Uitenhage in the Cape, dated 16–17 June 1846.

> I mentioned in my last that the Kaffirs had stolen 300 head of cattle within half an hour of this place, and that Commandant du Toit of the Worcester Burghers had gone in pursuit. He was fortunate enough in overtaking the rascals at Pheasant Drift on the Sunday river, and shot all they saw, namely eleven, and recaptured the cattle. Du Toit behaved nobly, shooting two himself, but I regret that one of his men was killed by an assegai. One Kaffir got into the river and covered his head with reeds, young du Toit however shot him. An aide has just arrived from Grahamstown with a requisition to press all oxen and waggons to convey provisions from Algoa Bay to Grahamstown, as they are very badly off there. They have in consequence taken our oxen, and how long we shall remain here it is impossible to say.

Thirty years later, the troubled eastern borders of Cape Colony had been finally closed after a tense struggle during the Ninth Frontier War of 1877–78. But it was by no means the end of warfare in this part of Africa. Almost immediately the Cape Government found itself embroiled with the Sotho nation on its northern flank, in what became known as the Gun War. The mountain fastness of the Sotho, then generally known as Basutoland and now as Lesotho, had special status because it had been under the protection of Her Britannic Majesty since 1868. It was designed to protect their territory from attrition by the Boers of the Orange Free State. From 1872, however, when Cape Colony achieved its own 'responsible government', the administration of Basutoland was controlled from Cape Town, and after the defeat of the Transkei Xhosa in 1878 the Cape authorities began to pressurise the Sotho. One cause for concern was that the Sotho who had earned good money by working in the diamond fields were buying firearms on a large scale, but a deeper wish was to open some of the Sotho lands for white farmers. This was especially true of Quthing district, whose Sotho leader, Moorosi, was the first to defy Cape authority in 1879. His defeat only led to wider conflict, when Sotho hut taxes were increased, and under the Disarmament Act the Sotho were required to surrender their rifles. The Gun War then broke out: by September 1880 over 20,000 Sotho were in armed revolt, months of indecisive warfare followed, the Cape forces had to be withdrawn and the Sotho kept their guns.

While an imperial army was locked in bitter combat with the Zulu in 1879, therefore, the Cape had to conduct its own operations against the equally daunting Sotho, mobile on their mountain ponies and well armed with rifles as well as with their traditional battle-axes and assegais. In its way the fighting had much in common with the Zulu War, and certainly was just as fierce. The colonial units had to proceed slowly and carefully, nowhere more so than against the leadership of Moorosi. Making best use of the almost Alpine terrain, his stronghold on 'Moorosi's Mountain' became a symbol of Sotho resistance. Until it was finally stormed and taken, the colonial government was seen by Africans everywhere to be weak and ineffectual. When at last Moorosi fell the story was told by George Money, serving as an artilleryman with the Cape Mounted Rifles; on 21 December 1879 he wrote a letter to his parents at Woodstock, recounting his share in the taking of Moorosi's Mountain.

> I suppose you know by this time that the impregnable mountain has been taken by the Cape Mounted Rifles. On the night (or rather morn) of the 20th of November the camp was roused quietly, and the storming parties issued forth, attended by Tembookies bearing scaling ladders, at about 12.30 p.m. They were gone about an hour when Mr. Thomas, a Thembu leader, came rushing into camp with the rather startling news that there were traitors among his niggers, and he thought it quite possible that our *loyal* allies, armed with long rifles and bayonets, might attempt to sack the camp. Just after he arrived about 200 of these niggers were seen coming towards the camp, some of them went over the hills and about eighty of them squatted down about 200 yards off; we received the order 'with case shot, load'. One of the guns was laid on them. Number 3 had his lanyard under his belt and friction tube ready, had one of those nigger's guns gone off by

accident the whole lot would have been – well, slightly astonished. Luckily for them they thought better of it and walked away.

From then until daybreak we were building a redoubt of mealie-sacks; ours was rather a critical position that night, being only forty strong, armed with carbines only. The storming parties were served out with long rifles and bayonets that day. Much, as you may suppose, to the disgust of the Artillery, we were remaining in camp all this time. Just as the morning star arose we heard three shots fired from Moorosi's sentry at our principal storming party; not only this, but he rolled boulders and a bullock's hide full of stones on our men. This man evidently did not think it possible for our men to get up that part of the mountain, so he did not rouse his comrades. I forgot to tell you that the niggers carrying the scaling ladders had deserted our men long before this.

With great difficulty a 20ft ladder was placed against a perpendicular rock; when the men were on the top of this ladder they had another 20 feet of sloping rock to scramble up, again about ten more feet to climb up. Here Lieut. Sprenger distinguished himself; he bravely led the men on and received a shot from the nigger above, which took his forage cap off his head, then the nigger threw an assegai at him, which cut his coat; the men fired several shots at this nigger with no effect, eventually Mr. Sprenger brought him down with his revolver; the corpse in its descent fell among our men, nearly knocking one or two off. By this time the Basutos were thoroughly aroused and the fighting commenced; our men fixed bayonets and charged. The mountain was one sheet of flame for about an hour. We managed to put three shrapnels into them, after which it wasn't safe to fire.

The bullets came rattling into our camp, we had to get under cover; we begged and prayed to Colonel Bayly to let us go with the storming party, but he would not. At last some of our niggers, when they saw the firing had left our side of the mountain, rushed up to get at the spoil; then Colonel Bayly said, 'Let six men go and turn those niggers, if they won't come back fire on them.' No sooner had he said this than the whole lot of us jumped over the trench and wall, and away we went, Colonel Bayly yelling at us to come back, but of no avail. I only managed to get three shots at a nigger the whole time I was up there, at about 300 yards range.

About a week before the attack took place we received a mortar and 500 shells, and for three days and nights we were shelling the mountain. A redoubt had to be built for the mortar within 600 yards of the enemy's 'schanzes' [solid stone walls, loopholed and sited to cover all the paths up the mountain]. You may be surprised at the shortness of the range, this is easily explained, since the Colonial Government with their usual foresight sent us the wrong fuses for the mortar, we had to use 9 sec. Boxer Line fuse. We (the Artillery) sallied forth to build this redoubt, with a few niggers. No sooner did we get within range than they commenced peppering away at us. By Jove! I never saw men work so before in my life; we had that redoubt rigged up in less than twenty minutes; their fire was eventually stopped by our guns in camp. Our 12-pounder made some splendid shots. Colonel Bayly was heard to observe, 'Were those men Volunteers instead of Cape Mounted Rifles you would have seen them in camp long before this'; this was to Captain Giles, R.A.

The mountain is situated on the banks of the Orange river, so we had splendid bathing and fishing; I was, nevertheless, very glad to leave it, since we were always having dust storms, and living in indifferent tents we had little shelter from them. Moorosi and all his sons were killed but two, one of whom was captured, and the other, Doda, it is said escaped, but it is uncertain, I believe he was shot by the Fingoes while trying to escape; only two able-bodied men were made prisoners, very few escaped. One hundred and five dead niggers were counted on and about the mountain. I had almost forgotten the most important subject. On our way down from the mountain we were met at the gates of Queenstown by the Volunteer Band, who played us through the streets; banners and flags were flying, the people turned out and cheered us. When we arrived at the Town Hall a squad of the Queenstown Volunteer Rifles presented arms to us; we halted and they came to our front.

Captain Sprenger (promoted through bravery) received an address from the Mayor, we dismounted, handed over our horses to niggers, went into the Town Hall and had a regular feed; of course, we were considered a lot of etc., etc., and most of us got slightly inebriated before the dinner was well over. Can you wonder at it, after having been under the broiling sun for six hours and having all sorts of liquors forced upon us, French brandy, curaçao, champagne, sherry, beer, etc., all this on an almost empty stomach.

Evidently the personal hazards for such men were not confined to the battlefield. The celebrations at Queenstown were premature, because more severe fighting against the Sotho lay ahead for the Cape regiments, and it dragged on through 1880 and into the early months of 1881. It was a savage business on both sides. A sergeant of the Cape Mounted Rifles saw what had happened to one volunteer patrol on the way to relieve the garrison besieged at Mafeteng, when they were overwhelmed by Lerotholi's horsemen:

As I went towards the waggons, on the look-out for old friends, I came across a ghastly sight. Two waggons which had contained fresh meat for us were piled up with dead bodies of men, who by their uniforms were of the Cape Yeomanry regiments. They were lying in all positions, just as they had been hurriedly picked up and thrown on the first waggon which came along. It was a gruesome sight to look at. They had all been either battle-axed or assegaied, and were covered with gashes or stabs, in some cases half their heads were nearly cut off, and the jolting of the waggons caused these half-severed heads to open and shut as they moved along, and made many of us half-starved creatures very sick.[1]

Nor was Basutoland the only area of dispute with indigenous African forces at that time. As George Money was writing his letter about the defeat of Moorosi an even more ferocious encounter was taking place in the mountainous terrain of the Eastern Transvaal. Volunteer units were again taking part in it, but as minor elements alongside a sizeable field force of imperial British troops. Their objective was to crush the obdurate Sekhukhune, principal chief of the Pedi, who for more than three years had been in armed opposition first to the Boers and then to the British. Once the Zulu War had run its course by September 1879, it was decided to turn against him and bring him down. This must be seen as one among the many crises of the tense years between 1877 and 1881, characterised by 'disturbance, rebellion and war over a large part of the canvas of frontier South Africa'.[2] Reconnaissance of Sekhukhune's positions began at the end of August 1879, and it was reported that the task force required would have to be a strong one: 1,000 British infantry, four guns, 400 good volunteer cavalry, a detachment of Engineers to make roads, and 2,000 native levies. This report was accepted by Major-General Sir Garnet Wolseley, who arrived from Zululand to take command on September 27. Negotiations for a peaceful solution went on with the Pedi while supplies were being amassed, and by November a force of over 5,000 men was ready to make war.

Lieutenant Charles Commeline of the Royal Engineers kept his father well informed on how the campaign was turning out, and he wrote a magnificent account, almost a personal dispatch, of the final moves against Sekhukhune. By mid-November he was at Fort

1. H. V. Woon, *Twenty-five years' soldiering in South Africa*, (London: Andrew Melrose, 1909), page 145.
2. D. M. Schreuder, *The Scramble for Southern Africa*, (Cambridge University Press: 1980), page 62.

Oliphant, then marched out to build a new fort at Mapushela's Drift on the Oliphants river. It was tough going:

> As we advanced the bush became thicker and more troublesome to cut through, for roads of course there are none; the site selected for the fort and its neighbourhood close to the river had also to be cleared, a work of some magnitude. As far as work for the Royal Engineers goes the Zulu War was a joke to this one, which keeps MacGregor and myself employed from dawn till dark.[3] However, nothing could be more satisfactory as the Staff leave us to do our own work (and a good deal of theirs, too). Fort Albert Edward was finished on the 18th after two days' work, large numbers of men having been also employed in making the drifts practicable for the convoys of waggons bringing up supplies from the rear. The scenery round the fort was very fine, but the weather was intensely hot. The heat inside a bell-tent at midday is unbearable.

Here Commeline had to break off abruptly to go on what proved to be the successful assault on Sekhukhune's stronghold. He resumed the letter on 29 November while still at what he called (in this minefield of approximate spellings) Secocoeni Town, and first tells of the preliminary fighting:

> On the 22nd we marched up the Lulu Valley without water which was only obtained at our camp by digging holes in the sandy bottom of a stream, which filled up with brackish stuff pretty quickly. As usual we made a small fort next day while the mounted men and natives went out to attack Umgwan's Town, which was perched on the top of a hill some two miles off and looked quite inaccessible. The firing began about 9 a.m. on both flanks and from the camp we had a very good view, being able to trace the progress of the attack by the smoke rising from the various kraals set on fire, which approached gradually nearer the topmost kraal. About noon the latter was taken and the firing which had been very heavy became a mere exchange of shots. Sir Garnet Wolseley rode up at this time, returning to Fort Albert Edward soon after. It was just after this I was ordered to take some guncotton up to the caves for the purpose of destroying them, some men having been killed by the firing from them.

3. Lieutenant J. C. MacGregor, Royal Engineers, had served in the Zulu War, in charge of the line of telegraph and signal stations between Durban and Ulundi. He was in command of the sappers detached for duty against Sekhukhune. As a staff officer with Colley's force in the First Anglo-Boer War, he was killed in action in 1881 (see page 107).

Secocoeni Town
S. Africa
29. 11. 79
My dear Father
We have just re-
turned to camp after the attack and destruction of Secocoeni's
town. The battle began at 4.20 a.m.
lasting till 11.30 when the final
position was stormed. Our casualties
are not yet known but amount
to over 200. I am all right and
took part in the whole of it. A
post is waiting but I will write
by next mail at more length.
We hope to finish the business
without further fighting to any

Extent
Much love to all from
your affectionate son
Charles Commeline

Assault on Secocoeni Town — 29th Novr 1879

Savages &c.

Town

Left attack

Centre attack

Right attack

stream

Camp

Letter from Lt. Charles Commeline, Royal Engineers, to his father at Gloucester, written immediately after he took part in the capture of Sekhukhune's stronghold in November 1879, together with his sketch of the plan of attack.

A more awful place to assault it is hard to conceive and I was astonished at it having been taken with so little loss as some 20 killed. The mountain like most about here consisted of great masses of rock heaped one on another, and of course forming any number of caves into which the defenders retreat and from which they can fire unseen upon the attacking force. If they were good shots and had better weapons it would be impossible to advance against them. I found a party of men holding the top and proceeded to business, destroying the caves. A dropping fire was going on but we returned to camp without further casualties, meeting the native contingent returning to occupy the place for the night, driving before them a great herd of cattle and goats which they had captured.

Later that night sudden orders came for Commeline to go ahead and prepare a road for the British advance, leaving at dawn.

On the march we experienced no opposition though the natives yelled and shouted at us from the hills and fired a few harmless shots. On crossing a neck we saw Secocoeni Town with our glasses for the first time, lying along the foot of a range of hills. We camped about five miles short of Water Kop and threw up a shelter trench. At 12.30 p.m. the rest of the Advance Guard marched in consisting of two companies each of the 94th and 21st and some cavalry, and we all moved off together at 4.30 a.m. the next morning.

The troops found to their surprise that the Pedi were not in occupation of the Water Koppie, nor were they fired on very much; the explanation they favoured was that the enemy were keeping their ammunition for the main battle. Commeline was then within three miles of Sekhukhune's place, 'consisting of an immense number of little white round thatched huts. There were also several other towns or stadts perched about the neighbouring hills, their positions always being chosen with a view to defence.' He was busily road-making on the way ahead, as the warriors still held their fire, but 'making a great noise on the hills, blowing horns and chaffing our fellows'. Wolseley arrived on the scene and ordered the force to move within a mile of the town; another column of infantry and 8,000 Swazi fighting men were poised to attack simultaneously from the other side of the mountain on 28 November.

The troops fell in silently at 3 a.m., a cool cloudy night. All was quiet on the opposite hills and in the town the fires which had been numerous the previous evening were all extinguished. A slow march through the bush brought us in front of the town just as day had dawned and things were beginning to be seen pretty clearly. There were to be four separate attacks as shown in the enclosed rough sketch. The right consisted of irregular cavalry, the centre comprised the infantry and guns, the left the native contingent, while the other column attacked from the far side of the mountain. On the right front of the town there is a strong koppie known as the 'Fighting Kop' which commands the town and was Secocoeni's chief stronghold. It is simply an immense mass of great boulders 100 feet high and so honeycombed with caves as to be almost hollow. To add to its strength stone walls had been built in front of the numerous holes, and in good positions from behind which an effective and unseen fire could be kept up. This Koppie was to be taken by the centre attack, and as was expected gave us no end of trouble.

At 4.20 a.m. the six 6-pounder guns opened fire on the koppie, half the infantry being extended in skirmishing order between them and it, while the remainder lay down in reserve. We were near the guns and employed ourselves in making up guncotton charges in sandbags. A pretty brisk fire was at once opened on us from the koppie, though only two or three men were hit, and every puff of smoke from the rock brought a rattling fire from our skirmishers on to the hole from which it came. The niggers soon became rather more wary and their fire slackened. Meanwhile the guns were pounding away at the stone walls, making excellent practice, but their calibre was rather too light for the work, though they did a good deal of damage. Some of the shells burst right inside the caves and such was the hollowness of the hill smoke was seen to emerge from holes on the far side of it. Sir Garnet and his staff and Colonel Baker Russell remained with the guns, the latter having a horse shot under him. We were now much interested in the progress of the left attack, which became exciting, the natives rushing bravely across the open mealie-fields led by their mounted white officers, under a heavy fire from the stockades and the hills beyond.

The first rush was repulsed, but another was soon made of which the success was shown by smoke rising from the burning huts in the left of the town. At the same time the Swazis were seen against the skyline on the crest of the hills, advancing rapidly along them, and evidently having a hard fight among the rocks and caves. We could distinguish the red coats of the little infantry force in the thick of the fray, and before long the right rear of the town was also in flames. Meanwhile two companies of the 94th had been sent round to the right of the koppie, whom I accompanied with five of our men carrying guncotton. Here we lay down and kept up a fire on the caves for nearly an hour. The right attack had had heavy fighting but had been out of sight, also the Swazis had had a hot time of it on the other side of the mountain, losing a large number of men but from all accounts inflicting immense slaughter on the enemy. The doctors were now very busy, but the hills behind the town were swept clean of the enemy, and the town was in flames all along the line, the Fighting Koppie alone holding out.

It was now 11 o'clock and the troops of the centre attack were concentrated on the front and left of the Koppie for the final assault, in which the Swazis were also to join. We expected of course to lose heavily, the garrison being entirely hidden in the caves. At 11.30 a rocket went up and the troops rushed forward on our side. The sappers were up in the thick of it, and strange to say as we doubled over the open, though the bullets came very close no one fell, and the men were soon swarming up the rocks like bees. It is impossible to describe things as they were then, shots coming out of holes all round which killed two or three poor fellows, an officer of the Hussars falling back near where I was standing, shot in the mouth. The men fired down the holes and used their bayonets freely. Colonel Baker Russell was one of the first men on the top, to the great satisfaction of all who followed him.

Commeline then says that after a while most of the troops were ordered off the hill, leaving behind a couple of companies and the sappers, who were to drop explosives into the caves. He describes this with a rare, and only slight, expression of sympathy for the Pedi and a dislike of what he had to do.

MacGregor and I then had a busy hour and a half of it putting charges of guncotton into the holes which though, as we afterwards found, they did not kill very many of these below, yet wounded many and from the dust and smoke produced terrible thirst, and reduced the garrison to a most pitiable condition. Meanwhile they continued to fire from unlooked-for places, and several men fell, and you may imagine that lighting fuses and dropping charges in such circumstances was not very pleasant or even very glorious work.

Having used up all their explosives, the sappers returned to camp, where Wolseley congratulated the force on what they had done, although Commeline realised it was at a higher cost than in his previous battle. He also describes the pathetic state to which the Pedi were reduced.

We had been fighting for seven hours and our casualties are very heavy, probably 200 is under the mark as the Swazis lost a great number. Almost all the wounds having been inflicted at close quarters, they are as a rule serious and probably the death roll will yet be considerably swelled. As a battle Ulundi could not be compared to this one where we were the attackers, whereas in the former the Zulus attacked our square and were beaten off in half an hour. Our casualties there also were not more than about half what they were yesterday. The infantry who were left to hold the Koppie during the night had a lively time of it, firing going on almost all night, and at one time it sounded in camp like quite a brisk engagement. However at dawn the niggers begged to be allowed to surrender themselves, and 200 of them came out in the most awful state, covered with dust and dirt, half dead from thirst and many of them terribly wounded.

There was much difficulty in guarding the prisoners from the fury of the Swazis, who spare neither sex nor age and laughed at us for protecting men who had been firing on us all day. They are fine fellows to fight, but deficient in the gentler virtues. They are now engaged in harrying the surrounding country, driving off cattle and burning towns, for which purpose we shall probably remain here a few days more. I for one have had enough campaigning for the present and all will be glad to settle down near some sort of civilisation for a time. Secocoeni is not yet caught, though he is supposed to be in a cave close by. His capture would probably finish the war at once. At any rate he has received a taste of the white man's power, which will deter him for many a long day from trying conclusions with us again. There is no doubt from all the prisoners say that he did not believe we could take the Fighting Koppie, and now red coats are sitting on its summit, overlooking a heap of blackened ruins which is all that remains of his famous town.

The blatant racism, and innate belief in the superiority and rightness of the European cause, as military might proved too much for traditional African societies to contend with, runs through not only Commeline's letter but also those from every African campaign. The natural bravery in battle of the Zulu or the Sudanese dervish is given a measure of professional respect, but they remain 'Kaffirs' or 'niggers'. It is quite evident from the letters that once they became 'the enemy' in a military confrontation with imperial forces, the fate of such African nations would be sealed sooner or later, and they would be absorbed into a new order. We find the same note of stark aggressiveness in a letter written by Garnet Wolseley just after the defeat of Sekhukhune, which he had directed and masterminded.

Being Wolseley, there is also more than a dash of self-glorification; he was writing to an influential Member of Parliament, and includes a pat on the back for the short-service young soldier whose appearance in the ranks came from Cardwell's army reforms – supported, naturally, by Wolseley. This is how he sums up his Sekhukhune venture (incidentally, referring to the Pedi as 'Basutos').

We have just had a nice little campaign here, and although perhaps I ought not to say so it was carefully planned and thought out beforehand, and everything went off without a hitch. It began on the 20th November; on the 28th Sikukuni's town was assaulted and taken. The success was eagerly and vigorously followed up, and the result was that on the 2nd December the chief and nearly every surviving member of his family were prisoners in my camp.[4] His sons were killed, as well as most of his uncles, brothers, and other relations. The result of the action has been as follows – our loss in white men killed and wounded about 50, in natives about 500; of the enemy's loss I can say nothing, we killed large numbers of them, but as the fighting extended over many miles of country it is impossible to estimate their loss. Every tribe in the Lulu Mountains was engaged, and they all tell us now that their loss was very heavy; most of their principal chiefs were also killed.

Far and near this victory has borne fruit, and I hope we shall now be able next year to collect a considerable revenue from the natives. All the tribes in the Lulu Mountains have surrendered their arms. Some of them I am sending to other localities, whilst the most peaceably disposed I shall allow to remain on their own land. I am establishing two large mission stations in the mountains, and I expect great things from them as these Basutos, unlike the Zulus, take quickly and naturally to civilisation, ploughs, breeches, and singing of psalms. In one or two generations more they will all be Christians. In all I think I may describe the campaign as sharp, short, and decisive.

I wish you could have seen our young soldiers charge the key of the enemy's position on the 28th. I think those most opposed to the employment of young men would have been convinced that when fighting is to be done, young men are the best. This action is the first our men have fought in South Africa where we attacked,

4. Sekhukhune in captivity was described by an eye-witness: 'The chief, who had a wretched worn-out look, sat on a box in the centre of the waggon with a skin round him. His appearance was hardly up to expectation, for he was supposed to be the cleverest native in South Africa.' General Sir Richard Harrison, *Recollections of a life in the British Army during the latter half of the nineteenth century*, (London: Murray, 1908), page 228.

as in Zululand we always awaited in laager or in a more or less entrenched square the enemy's assaults.

Faith in Wolseley's general powers of judgment is undermined when we read, towards the end of this same letter, his opinion that the Transvaal Boers (then in an early state of unrest) were 'too great cowards to fight'. Not long before, when he arrived at Pretoria on 27 September 1879 to begin operations against Sekhukhune, Wolseley had announced in public 'the Vaal would run back on its course rather than the British nation retreat from any step they had deliberately taken', i.e. the annexation of the Transvaal. Yet only a year after Wolseley wrote with such self-satisfaction of his defeat of Sekhukhune the British army was on the brink of a series of traumatic disasters, when its troops ventured to attack Boer positions. By then the Boers were more than ready to fight for an independent Transvaal.

FIVE

'Desperate Hard Fighting':

THE FIRST ANGLO-BOER WAR, 1880–81

'I hope it will not be long', Major-General Sir George Pomeroy Colley wrote in February 1881, 'before I have force enough to terminate this hateful war.' The Transvaal War (so called by the British newspapers, more accurately the First Anglo-Boer War) was short, sharp, and disastrous for the British army. The shooting went on for barely three months after the 'rebellious' Boers proclaimed a republic on 16 December 1880, but during that time the troops suffered in four costly engagements, two of them outright defeats in battle. Majuba (the worst of them) was added to the recent and shameful memories of Isandlwana (in Zululand) and Maiwand (in Afghanistan). When the newspaper correspondents arrived at last, the campaign was virtually over. Because this war was so scantily reported in the press, and so thoroughly covered up afterwards, it is doubly interesting to read the letters of soldiers who were there – the rank-and-file men as well as officers, some of whom are already familiar from their letters written during the Anglo-Zulu War.

The conflict came about because the Transvaalers (whose republic had been annexed in 1877) reasonably expected Gladstone to give them back their independence. His Liberal government made no decision through 1880, reducing the British garrisons while continuing to levy taxes, until the Boers lost patience and took unilateral action. Long after the fighting had broken out at Bronkhorstspruit in December 1880, the Cabinet was divided between Whigs who wished to crush the Boers and Radicals who wanted to make concessions to them. To the last, a stream of ambiguous instructions went from the Colonial Secretary, Lord Kimberley, to the general in command, who had more than his fair share of practical problems. Colley, a key figure in the shaping of events, is still something of an enigma. As a young officer he fought in the China War of 1860, helping in the destruction of the Summer

Palace at Peking. 'Many parts of it were really beautiful,' he says in one of his stylish letters, 'and it grieved me having to burn it down.' Sensitive though he was, he helped himself to some splendid silken robes from the Imperial wardrobe. The Chinese gave Colley his only real experience of independent military command, for during the next twenty years his career ran through a series of staff appointments. He succeeded brilliantly in all of them, as witnessed by what he did in the Ashanti campaign of 1873–74 (page 44).

By the time he faced the Transvaal Boers in open rebellion he was a respected member of the 'Wolseley Ring' of senior officers. Nor was he a stranger to South Africa and its peoples. He had spent several years on duty there before 1880, when he was appointed Governor of Natal and Commander-in-Chief. The country was familiar to him, with all its difficulties, and he knew personally Kruger, Joubert, and Pretorius, the Boer leaders, fully understanding their resentment against annexation by Britain. Militarily speaking, Colley was out on a limb in his first command of a fighting force. At his disposal were some 1,800 troops dispersed in garrison posts throughout the Transvaal, all besieged by the Boers. He had another 1,800 men with him in Natal, about 1,000 of whom could be deployed in action. The Boers were opposing him with 2,000 armed burghers at the Transvaal-Natal border, but in all they could call out some 7,000 men on commando against the British. They were all mounted marksmen, whereas Colley had no regular cavalry and few field-guns. Outnumbered, far less mobile than his enemy, all his supplies and ammunition had to be manhandled up-country with painful slowness over appalling roads. The ox-drawn waggons made poor time when the going was good, but by January the endless rainstorms turned the tracks into quagmires. Whenever the convoys came to a river, floodwaters made the drifts impassable for days on end.

Compared with the newspaper coverage of wars in Zululand or Afghanistan in 1879–80, the British press gave scant attention to the military (as distinct from the political) character of the 'Transvaal War' that erupted after Bronkhorstspruit. There were cogent reasons for this, related to the local circumstances of the conflict. In particular, the reporters and correspondents were unable to reach the Transvaal-Natal border in time to cover the early fighting. The first newspaperman to arrive at the front, T. F. Carter of the *Natal Times*, took a week to ride 120 miles on horseback. It poured with rain every day, the drifts were difficult, and he was just too late to report the opening battle at Laing's Nek on 28 January 1881.

Setting as it did the pattern of defeat for the relieving column commanded by HE Major-General Sir George Pomeroy Colley, it is a pity Laing's Nek was not witnessed by an experienced war correspondent, home or colonial.

Colley's objective was to force his way into the Transvaal to relieve the British garrisons bottled up at Pretoria and six other towns. The effective sealing off by the burgher commandos of the capital, and of so many troops scattered through the Transvaal, also made it virtually impossible to put together a coherent story for the reading public in Britain. Another factor was the brevity of the campaign: by the time the reporters arrived, it had entered the tortuous phase of peace negotiation. Melton Prior the war artist (his whisky tucked away in boxes labelled 'Drawing materials', as in the Anglo-Zulu War), struggled up-country through thunderstorms, floods and mud, but sketches did not appear in the *Illustrated London News* until 5 March, when the fighting was over. Even then, they were not from Prior's pen: his later drawing of the Majuba battle-scene had to be based on the eye-witness description by John Cameron, the London *Standard* reporter whose despatches were the most widely read by dismayed patriots at home.

Another veteran of Zululand, C. E. Fripp, came out to see what was happening, but none of his sketches appeared in the *Graphic* until 23 April. His drawing of the summit of Majuba was done on 24 March, nearly a month after the battle, and was published on 21 May. The *Daily Telegraph* did not print a detailed account of 'The Fight at Amajuba', sent by its controversial Fenian correspondent Arthur Aylward, until 15 April. He pulled no punches: 'Our troops were out-numbered, flanked, driven back at all points by an enemy that had on two occasions shown the stuff they were made of, and hurled down the mountain side more like sheep than anything else I can compare them to.' No doubt all this could not have been printed earlier than it was, because the assassination of the Tsar and the death of Disraeli had overshadowed all other news, but there was also an over-riding sense of unease at home about bad news from the Transvaal.

This was compounded of shame at yet another military disaster, and of doubts shared beyond Liberal circles that Britain should be at war with the Boers. Both attitudes are reflected in verses that appeared in *Punch*, first 'A Military Ode' to the British infantry:

> Britannia needs instructors
> To teach her boys to shoot,

Fixed targets and mere red-tape drill
Have borne but bitter fruit,
Our blunders are a standing joke,
The scandal of our Isle,
And the Boer loud doth roar,
Whilst our foreign critics smile,
Whilst the Teuton guffaws loud and long,
And our foreign critics smile.

Then one of the verses of a poem about Majuba and Colley concluded:

Today we must praise the slain heroes he led,
We'll portion the blame on the morrow.
'Tis scarcely disgrace to such foemen to fall,
'Tis pity such foemen are foemen at all!

Given that the war was far from fully reported, it follows that letters written home by soldiers on the spot would be especially informative, as indeed they are for most of the Victorian campaigns. Again, however, the circumstances of the conflict, and the small number of troops employed, conspire to keep the letters to a disappointingly low tally.

Among the original letters that have been traced are a few from Percival Scrope Marling, then a young subaltern in the 3rd Battalion of the 60th Rifles, later the King's Royal Rifle Corps. It was a unit that had fought in the Zulu War, from the battle of Gingindlovu onwards, and so still contained a fair proportion of seasoned campaigners, to stiffen the younger recruits, when fighting broke out with the Boers. As against his surviving letters, Marling tells us far more about the war in his autobiography, published in 1931 with the title *Rifleman and Hussar*. The book is heavily dependent on the diaries he kept, and unfortunately Marling does not always clearly distinguish between direct quotation from his diaries and comment added much later in time, presumably when drafting his book. The letters are often simply an alternative version of what he wrote in his diary, naturally enough, but his book is a spirited record of a young man's approach to African warfare. Marling won the Victoria Cross in the Sudan a few years later, and fought the Boers again between 1899 and 1902.

He tells how the 3/60th Rifles marched up-country from Pietermaritzburg, singing 'My Grandfather's Clock' to the accompaniment of two whistles and a drum played on a canteen with two sticks. They reached the British camp at Mount Prospect on 26 January 1881, and were plunged immediately into the fighting at Laing's Nek on 28 January. With H Company, of which he was second-in-command, Marling advanced to the foot of the ridge in skirmishing order, to support the left flank of the attack, where they sheltered behind a low stone wall. From that forward position he saw the whole desperate business. So steep were the slopes that the horses of the mounted infantry were soon blown, as were those of the 58th Regiment, whose CO and Adjutant (Hingeston and Monk) had to ride up on horseback because Colonel Deane and his staff did so. Deane took command out of the hands of the regimental officers, the 58th 'were hustled up without being extended', and failed to carry the heights. Deane and three other mounted staff officers were killed; the only survivor of the staff who rode up Laing's Nek was Major Edward Essex (75th Regiment), whose charmed life had brought him safely from the slaughterhouse at Isandlwana, two years previously.

Marling's narrative may be set aside for a moment to turn to some soldiers' letters about Laing's Nek. One named combatant's account has come to light from a newspaper source, written by Lance-Sergeant W. J. Morris of the 58th. He wrote on 30 January to his mother at Northampton, describing how his regiment, carrying seventy rounds of ammunition and two pounds of biscuit and bully beef per man, were ready for action on 27 January. Torrential rain caused the attack to be postponed to the 28th, when he was roused at 3 a.m. and formed up in column at 6 a.m. in bright sunshine. Having marched to within 2,000 yards of the Boer entrenchments on the ridge, the six field-guns fired three or four rounds apiece, their shells bursting out of sight behind the crest. This performance was repeated by the three rocket tubes of the Naval Brigade. After an hour had elapsed, Brownlow's mounted force attacked the slopes in skirmishing order on the right; they met strong opposition and were forced to retire, although (according to Morris) only four men had been killed and a dozen horses knocked over. Then, as the mounted troops were retiring, five companies of the 58th skirmished ahead under a very heavy cross fire from the Boers.

> Before we got half way up the hill many of us were mowed down one by one. We got up to the top, when we opened fire, and kept it up for some time till the order was given to fix bayonets and prepare to charge . . . We charged the hill, but could not hold it, as we had no support. The Boers were only about thirty yards

away when we reached the top, and they were advancing on us in hundreds. Colonel Deane was shot in the arm. He afterwards got off his horse and used his revolver, and he had not fired many shots when he received the second shot and fell backwards. Someone then said, 'Retire men, as they are too strong for us.' As we were retiring we lost several men under a deadly cross fire. How the remaining few escaped was quite a miracle.

Morris then relates how the regimental colours (never again taken into action by a British regiment) were barely saved from capture by the determination of Sergeant Bridgestock, who scrambled them away on horseback and eventually on foot. The remnant of the 58th, which suffered thirty-four per cent casualties in killed and wounded out of a strength of 503 attacking officers and men, marched back to where the field ambulances were parked.

A flag of truce was hoisted and taken up to the Boers, asking permission to bring the wounded and bury the dead, but they would not let us touch them till they had taken all their arms away from them, and when we went up the groans of the wounded were something fearful. In a horrible state we brought all the wounded into camp that day. I am sorry to say our loss is most of the officers and non-commissioned officers, as it appears the Boers were dead nuts on them . . . I must also tell you we were bringing in the wounded at twelve o'clock at night, and the groans in hospital were shocking. We are not going to attack that hill until we get reinforcements, and then we will pepper them for what they have done.

One can say perhaps that indirectly Majuba was to be the reinforced second attack on the Boer positions at Laing's Nek, but the peppering then certainly did not go as Morris had hoped. One letter from an unnamed officer, possibly Marling, was published in *The Citizen*, a weekly paper at Gloucester. Written at Camp Mount Pleasant on 2 February, it adds fresh detail to this unreported struggle.

I write to give you a short account of the fight we had with the Boers last Friday, January 28, and in which I am sorry to say we were repulsed. Of course you will have seen the account of it in the papers long before this reaches you; but I thought perhaps you might like to hear in my own words, my first experience of a battle. We should have attacked the Boers on Thursday, only it rained the whole day, and there was such a mist that it was impossible. We always have to sleep in our clothes now, to be ready at a moment's notice.

We got to within about 1½ miles of the enemy, about 9.30 a.m., when the first shot was fired from our 9-pounders. Then a company of the 60th Rifles was sent on in skirmishing order, with orders to get within 1,200 yards of the enemy, and commence firing when they saw an opportunity; they advanced over some of the worst ground I ever saw – across a kind of ravine, and through a mealie-field, till they got to the foot of the hill – one thousand yards from the enemy; here they got under cover of a low stone wall from three to four feet high, about 600 yards in advance of any of the other troops, except, perhaps, the cavalry. Then the Naval Brigade came up with the rocket tubes, and began firing rockets. All this time our guns behind had been firing shot and shell to try and dislodge the Boers from their position behind the crest of the hill, but, of course, I couldn't tell with what effect. Then the 100 mounted men were ordered to charge up a hill on the right. This they did in the most plucky way, in spite of the hill being like the side of a house. When they got to the top they found the Boers intrenched, and a tremendous fire greeting them, they had to retire with the loss of nineteen killed, wounded and missing. One man actually jumped his horse into the Boer intrenchment, and cut a man down; but he was shot dead the next moment. Two of the officers had great shaves; they both had their horses shot under them. One officer had a knife he carried tied to a belt round his waist shot to atoms and another bullet went under his arm and through his coat without hitting him. Another had the handle of his sword shot away. They were about six yards from the Boers, who potted at them as they ran down the hill for half a mile.

The 58th was then ordered to advance and make an attack on the right front, this they did, led by Col. Deane and three other staff officers, all mounted. Their men were hustled up at a tremendous pace, without even being extended in skirmishing order, up a hill tremendously steep, and over very rough ground; and the consequence was when they got near the top they were so blown they could hardly move; some of them couldn't even lift their rifles; and there was about 120 yards between their head and tail. A tremendous fire met them about 200 yards from the top. They got up to about 50 yards from the top of the hill and there they stood, simply falling just like you cut down corn. It was a regular butchery. The Boers were quite fresh, and had the advantage of position and shooting down hill.

The fighting of 28 January was also witnessed by a non-combatant NCO, Henry Coombs, a sergeant in the Army Hospital Corps. He wrote to his friends in Sheffield, telling them of the repulse of the 58th.

> The British troops had to retreat, beaten; but, oh, what a retreat it was, they were nothing but marks for the enemy. The Boers were frightened to leave their position, and when out of range all firing ceased . . . I shall not forget to my dying day the whizz of those bullets past my head, and to see those men shot down as though they were dogs. It was pitiful, but only what we expect in war. I was on the field dressing wounded, and could see it all, and we had a large amount of wounded to dress and carry away. We had 40 blacks carrying the wounded off the field. I kept with the doctor all the time, and many a time we thought we were done for, but we escaped all right, and it took us till eight p.m. to clear the field of wounded men.

Whether we accept 8 p.m. or midnight (according to Morris, and the discrepancy may mean the difference between carrying the last wounded soldier off the battlefield and installing the last of the casualties in the hospital tents) as bringing the day to a close, Laing's Nek set a pattern of extreme hardship for the wounded men that was to be repeated in the other engagements of this drastic war. Marling of the 3/60th Rifles noted in his diary for 29 January, 'All night we could hear the wretched wounded groaning and crying out.' He was not impressed with Colley, who had spoken to the demoralised survivors, taking all the blame on himself. 'It is an extraordinary thing he made such a mess of it,' wrote Marling in a later comment. 'As our old man [i.e. the CO of the 3/60th] said, "You don't win a battle by making speeches or writing despatches",' and it was soon the turn of Marling's regiment to be put on the rack at Schuinshoogte. This engagement is better known to English readers as Ingogo Heights.

The scene for another sharp conflict, then, at least as wretched for the men involved as most of the fights against the Zulu two years previously, is set by Sergeant Coombs:

> On the morning of the 8th February, the native runner came into camp [i.e. Mount Prospect], saying that the Boers had nearly caught him and had taken two of our men prisoners. Some 20 wounded were sent away this same morning, and it was feared that they would harm them, or perhaps steal the ambulances. Sir G. Colley took part of the force out to clear the road, when, after he had gone four miles, the Boer army appeared in force, and a battle ensued.

Coombs tells how Colley was ambushed after crossing the double drift at the Ingogo river, on the road to Newcastle, and it seems from his letter that he was present at, and survived, the British defensive fight on the Schuinshoogte slopes. For a more realistic picture of this sanguinary confrontation, however, we should turn to Lieutenant P. S. Marling of the 3/60th Rifles.

He says that whereas the purpose of Colley's sortie was to safeguard the road for the mails between Newcastle and Mount Prospect, the telegraph had not been cut and was still working. A fight was patently not expected, because Colley did not bother to take along a water cart, and ordered dinner in camp for his men at 3.30 p.m. In intense heat, five companies of the 60th marched out, with thirty mounted men (again under Major Brownlow), two 9-pounder and two 7-pounder guns of the Royal Artillery. The latter pair, together with K Company to which Marling had been transferred since Laing's Nek, very fortunately for him, did not cross the Ingogo but stayed on the north bank, guarding the drifts. Suddenly, at about 11.30 a.m., he heard such firing from the main force ahead across the river that he knew 'desperate hard fighting was going on'. He heard all about it from Lieutenant Francis Beaumont, who lay hidden behind a rock for four hours; 'a very little fellow' who had coxed the Oxford University Eight for three years, Beaumont came through unhurt.

At the outset the Boers shot nearly all the horses of the mounted troops and artillery, there being no cover for them on the bare plateau of Schuinshoogte; one of the horrors later in the day was the trampling of wounded men by wounded horses, galloping over the battlefield. By about 2.30 p.m., pinned down by merciless fire and sustaining heavy casualties, Colley thought the encircling Boers were about to rush his position on the left flank. He sent one of his staff officers to ask Colonel Ashburnham to advance a company of the 3/60th to cover this threat. Only I Company was in reserve, and Ashburnham pleaded that only half of it should be sent, but the staff officer insisted on taking the whole company, and leading it into position himself. He was Captain J. C. MacGregor, of the Royal Engineers, who had served in the Zulu War and at the taking of Sekhukhune's stronghold.

Many of the soldiers of I Company were young recruits, recently joining their regiment, and MacGregor led them, riding his horse, to a position within fifty yards of the Boers. 'There is no doubt that he took them farther than he should have done. Captain MacGregor was himself killed, it was inevitable, considering the mark he presented,' says Marling. A letter written by Lieutenant B. M. Hamilton, 15th Regiment, who was Colley's ADC (and brother-in-law), taking part in the fight, adds more detail: 'Poor MacGregor had gone with one of the companies of the 60th to show them where to post themselves, but, unluckily for him and the whole company with him, he took them too far below the brow and they got detached from the rest of our line, and being on the side of the hill the Boers could see them from the top of the one opposite.'

Only nine men of I Company came through unscathed, including Lieutenant Beaumont, the diminutive Oxford cox; the remaining fifty-six were killed or wounded, decimated at least in part through MacGregor's ineptitude. Colley knew the full story, of course, but to read his despatch one would think otherwise. It is a sad reflection on the Major-General's powers of judgment and lack of realism. This is what he wrote about MacGregor, his Assistant Military Secretary: '. . . a most promising officer, who would certainly have risen to distinction if spared, of soldierly bearing, of distinguished ability, and possessing in an eminent degree all the most valuable qualifications of a Staff Officer. He was killed early in the engagement, while pointing out the ground to Lieutenant Garrett, of the 60th, as the latter brought his company into action.'

Fine words, but empty of meaning in terms of what happened at Schuinshoogte, and far from telling the full story. As the afternoon wore on, thunder and lightning began to accentuate the sporadic firing from either side, and it started to rain heavily just before 5 p.m. – so heavily that, in Marling's words, 'all the old hands say it was worse than anything they had in Zululand'. The Boers, who were being reinforced steadily, then (at about 5.30) showed a white flag. Bugles sounded 'Cease fire', but the Boers simply used this as an opportunity to advance, firing, on the silent 9-pounder guns, attempting to take them as trophies. Two officers and thirteen men of the Artillery were killed or wounded, out of a total gunner strength of twenty-seven; the guns belonged to N/5 Battery, part of which was wiped out at Isandlwana, while the wounded officer, Lieutenant C. S. B. Parsons, RA, had been out with Lord Chelmsford's force on 22 January 1879 when the camp was taken by the Zulu.

At Schuinshoogte, the rainstorm continued as darkness fell, and the shooting stopped at last. Most of the wounded were collected together in one spot, getting immediate attention from Surgeon M'Gann and his orderlies, but when Colley decided to quit the battlefield at 9 p.m., it was clear that the wounded would have to be left where they lay. The only horses fit for work were two for each gun and two for one of the ammunition limbers; the other limber was also left behind when Colley, his staff, and the survivors (in the case of the 3/60th, only 103 out of the 217 actively engaged) plodded off into the darkness. Bad as it was for the wounded, there were still hazards ahead for those returning to Mount Prospect, as Lieutenant Bruce Hamilton wrote to his sister, Lady Colley:

> About 9 o'clock we marched off in a hollow square, guns in the centre, and remainder of Mounted Infantry Rifles in skirmishing order all round. When we left the hill we all expected a real hand-to-hand fight before we should be able to cross the river, and if the Boers had occupied the drift I don't know how we should have been able to cross, with the water so high from the rain . . . You ask me if Sir G. was in danger that day. He was, and more danger than I hope he will be in again.

At the Ingogo, danger came from the river itself. When they crossed it on the morning of 8 February, the soldiers splashed across with the water barely above their ankles. Now, after the rainstorm, the Ingogo was almost up to their armpits, and they had to link arms to get across. Despite this precaution, and no doubt because of their exhaustion after a hard day at Schuinshoogte (when none of the troops had anything to eat, and only a canteen of water apiece), six unfortunate men of the 3/60th lost their footing and were swept away by the current. Perhaps the most tragic postscript of all came the next day, when Lieutenant E. O. H. Wilkinson met his death. Having survived the fight, he went back alone to the battlefield on the 9 February to do what he could for the wounded left there, but on his way home again to Mount Prospect he too was drowned in the Ingogo.

His body was not recovered until the 18th, five miles below the drifts, and he was buried on the 20th. In the auction of his effects the next day – proof positive of how down-to-earth the military had to be – Marling (who calls him 'Peter') bought Wilkinson's soapbox and suit of flannel pyjamas. He had served as adjutant of the 3/60th since the Zulu War, from which he wrote (for his housemaster at Eton) an excellent account of the battle of Gingindlovu, before he was invalided home through sickness. His remains lie in the Mount Prospect Military Cemetery, next to three officer casualties of Schuinshoogte – Captain C. Greer, RA, in command of Colley's artillery, Lieutenant O'Connell, and Lieutenant Garrett of the ill-fated I Company, 3/60th.

Marling's company did not get involved in the fighting, but he had an exhausting time of it. K Company went on outlying picquet at 5.30 p.m. on Monday, 7 February. Coming back to camp at 7 the next morning, they marched out an hour later towards Schuinshoogte, and remained on post guarding the Ingogo drifts until Colley's remnant force had made its way back to Mount Prospect. They did not return themselves, escorting the long-suffering wounded, until the afternoon after the engagement. 'These men and myself only got a cup of tea from 6 p.m. Monday till 4 p.m. Wednesday. We were hungry.' Such are the incidental hardships of war. Nor was the miserable saga of Schuinshoogte yet brought to a conclusion. On 12 February, at Colley's personal order and in pouring rain, a party of soldiers went out under a flag of truce to exhume the bodies of the officers killed five days previously.

Vultures by the score covered the battlefield, feeding on the dead horses and the men, who had been buried hastily in three huge pits, scattered over half-a-mile of ground. 'The men would dig for quarter of an hour,' says Marling of this disgusting work, 'and then be violently sick. To show how fierce the fight had been, one helmet had five bullet holes in it, and many had two or three.' Only Lieutenant Maurice O'Connell was recognisable. Marling could see no sense in this business, but perhaps Colley was sensitive still to the criticisms made of Lord Chelmsford in leaving the dead at Isandlwana unburied for so long. Morale was at a low ebb after Schuinshoogte. One veteran officer voiced his opinion that Colley ought not to be trusted with a corporal's guard on active service, and Marling wrote in his diary (10 February): 'The General telegraphed home the fight at Ingogo was a success – we certainly did pass the mails through to Newcastle and remained on the field of battle, but one or two more Pyrrhic victories like that and we shan't have any army left at all. As it is, we are not more than 700 strong at the most now, not much of a force to advance in an enemy's country as large as the whole of the United Kingdom.'

Colley was powerless, having lost his entire staff except for the indestructible Major Essex (acting as Brigade-Major) and his personal ADC, Hamilton. Nor was it only a case of depressed morale, at this stage of the fighting, due to Colley's incurring heavy casualties in mismanaged actions. There was also the sense of insecurity because of the low numbers of men he left to defend the base camp at Mount Prospect. It was held by only 200 soldiers, some of them barely effective, during Laing's Nek, while no more than 150 men defended it when Colley was so hotly engaged with the Boers at Schuinshoogte. The camp was truly vulnerable to attack on 8–9 February, but perhaps Colley was willing to gamble on his knowledge that the Boers were always hesitant to attack a prepared and fortified position.

So, finally, to Majuba. At the very time that the Boers were securing their total success, Marling was writing a letter in camp. He had seen Colley's mixed force set out on the night of 26 February:

> Fortunately the night was very dark and there was no moon. At 9.30 off they marched with 3 days' rations of biscuits and intrenched themselves on a hill to our left front [Majuba]. Directly it was light the Boers discovered what had happened and our troops have been engaged since about 5.30 a.m. this morning, firing is still going on as I write. *12 noon*. A message has just come in to say that poor Romilly, commander of the Naval Brigade, is seriously wounded. I never saw such a wonderful thing as the Heliograph . . . Very heavy firing is going on at this minute.

The first hint of the magnitude of the débâcle came at about 2 p.m. when a wounded sailor reached Mount Prospect with news that the troops had been driven off the mountain. 'He said it had taken him five bloody hours to get up Majuba, but he only touched the ground five bloody times on the way down.' The summary of events on the summit given by Colonel Herbert Stewart (who was Chief of Staff to Colley) deserves more quotation than it gets:

> There was a complete panic in the front line; they retired and, the reserves being advanced at the same time, the greatest confusion resulted. The line then retired behind a ledge of rocks, but it was impossible to get the men steady and to fire properly, notwithstanding the exertions of the officers. The line at last broke and fled. Sir G. Colley was retiring slowly, the last of everyone, waving a handkerchief when he was shot.

Again, as at Schuinshoogte, it was the wounded who fully experienced the horrors of war. Surgeon Edward Mahon, of the Naval Brigade, narrowly escaped being shot down while attending the wounds of Commander Romilly, RN, then carried him to where the other casualties lay:

> When about half way across we were surrounded by Boers, who were with great difficulty prevented from shooting the Commander as he lay, they being under the idea that he was either Sir

Garnet Wolseley or Sir Evelyn Wood . . . I had all the wounded, 36 in number, placed on one spot near the well, and luckily we found blankets and just enough waterproof sheets to cover them all. All we had to give them was water and a little opium, the Boers having taken all our brandy. It now commenced to rain heavily, and continued to do so without intermission during the whole night, which much aggravated the sufferings of the wounded. It also became bitterly cold towards morning.

A word here about the marksmanship of the 92nd, known as the best shooting corps in the army when they fought at Kandahar in Afghanistan, in September 1880. Afterwards they went to Calcutta en route for a home posting, and so did no musketry practice. Ordered to South Africa in January 1881, they did no shooting during the three weeks' voyage. Nor did they do any while in South Africa, so when they fired on Majuba it was the first time for six months, and they found themselves 'exchanging shots with men who kill a buck every day of their lives'.[1]

As all this was going on the Boers kept close watch on half-a-dozen British garrisons stranded in townships scattered through the Transvaal. Nearest to Colley's camp at Mount Prospect was Wakkerstroom, held by two companies of the 58th. Boer patrols cut the telegraph and captured the mail carts, so from early January the troops were out of touch with Natal, except when Zulu runners managed to break the cordon. Among the letters smuggled out was a report on the siege by Colour-Sergeant M. G. O'Callaghan, who had fought at Ulundi and had written home an interesting letter about it. The enemy mounted several surprise attacks against the makeshift fortifications:

> On the 13th January, as our men were working around the fort, strengthening it, a strong body of Boers got under cover of the Koppie to the north-east of the camp, and poured a volley in amongst our tents. I was sitting writing, and a bullet whistled through it and grazed the stripes on my arm. The tents were soon down and our men in the fort, the Boers still firing rapidly on us; but very soon a few well-directed shots sent them to the right about. No doubt if they had the proper elevation a great many of us would be killed or wounded. We could not form any estimate of the Boers' strength.

1. Ian Hamilton, *The fighting of the future* (Murray: London, 1885), page 30.

O'Callaghan hoped that when General Colley marched to relieve Wakkerstroom, he would bring a strong force and proceed with caution, because there were places along the road 'where a few hundred men could make a stand against an army corps, and you may be sure the Boers will now fight like rats in a hole, for they know their cowardly and treacherous acts have committed them beyond redemption'. This indeed happened at Laing's Nek, and later on O'Callaghan wrote at length about it, 'for there being no war correspondents from any of the home papers at the battle, I feel sure the accounts I send will be interesting to all at home'. Two of his closest friends in the 58th were killed there, one of them the band sergeant: 'I loved him as a brother, an excellent soldier and musician.' Nevertheless, despite all the bloodshed and to the disgust of the military, the Boers won back their liberty. 'If we made peace now,' wrote Marling, 'we ought to be ashamed of ourselves.' Kruger, Joubert and Pretorius accepted the offer of a Royal Commission 'to consider the giving back of the Transvaal, subject to British suzerainty, a Resident at Capital, and provisions for guarding native interests'. Evelyn Wood, handling negotiations on the spot, says the Boers attributed their success to the intervention of the Almighty, especially when the British broke the sabbath at Majuba. It must be clear to all, however, simply from these soldiers' letters, that they were not facing the most efficient of military machines. From the British standpoint, the fiasco leading up to Majuba was to have once again its parallel in their defeats during 'Black Week', in December 1899, at the opening of the second war with the Boers.

The risk of Anglo-Boer conflict was close to danger point sooner than that, in fact within a few years of Majuba. It marked the origins of what became the British protectorate of Bechuanaland, now the independent state of Botswana. To pre-empt the appearance of new Boer republics to the west of the Transvaal, it was thought necessary to assert British interests in the region. This would guarantee scope for any extension northwards of Cape influence, and set the scene for the expansionism of Cecil Rhodes in pursuit of a 'Cape to Cairo' line of territorial rights under British protection. The confrontation arose in 1884, very much in the context of what is generally known as the Scramble for Africa, by which various European states had managed to control virtually the entire continent by 1900. Bechuanaland was secured without a fight, because when the Boers saw that Britain was sending out a strong force to oppose them, they backed down. One feature of this episode was the recruiting of a new contingent of young Britons by the Cape government; one wonders if the intention was also to attract fresh colonists to the country, in the hope they would stay in South Africa when the trouble was over.

This impression is supported by the appeal that was clearly made to young men of the prosperous classes. At any rate, the magazines of several public schools print letters under such headings as 'To South Africa with the Bechuanaland Expedition', in which old boys of the school tell of their adventures after sailing out to the Cape in November 1884. According to *The Cliftonian* 'the whole corps is composed entirely of sons of gentlemen', and, if only for the sake of completeness, we shall read one of these letters. The writer reached Cape Town on 26 December 1884, and then travelled inland by train to Langford, where the railway stopped not far from the Orange river. Evidently a keen horseman, he wrote in the first and second weeks of January 1885.

There are about 3,000 men in camp; the Royal Scots, Engineers, Artillery, Carrington's, and ourselves. We are called the First Mounted Rifles. They have got all the horses here, but they are not all served out yet; they are pretty good, but most of them small. There are a good many bad buck-jumpers among them. The place would not be bad if it were not for the sandstorms, we always have one at dinner time. It is the middle of summer here and frightfully hot in the daytime, but at night quite cool. We have very little time to ourselves, directly you settle down to do anything you are turned out to do fatigue duty. The stable work takes up a good deal of time, but I like that very well.

We have heard very little news from the front, but General Warren came into camp yesterday, so perhaps we shall hear something. Two troops go on to Kimberley tomorrow. Hurricane sandstorms come down on us now and then, sweeping down a whole row of tents. Reveille sounds at four o'clock, and parade is at half-past. The early parade consists of skirmishing, for which the ground is very well suited. You have to lie down behind a bush and fire, and then run along on all fours to another bush, you may not stand up at all. They serve us out coffee before each parade, 6.30 breakfast. The morning is taken up with the horses and fatigue duty. Dinner at 12.30. They serve us out one-and-a-half pounds of bread and one pound of meat a day.

What I dislike is that they have no method about putting men on fatigue. If they want twenty men, a sergeant is sent round the camp and tells the first twenty he sees; so that you may be put on again directly you are dismissed, or if you are lucky you do not get any all day. Last Friday night I was on picquet duty. I was put on for two hours, but the sergeant went to sleep in the guard tent and I was on for nearly five. We are about 80 miles from Kimberley, which is our next point. I like the life very much indeed, barring the sandstorms, but I believe there is grass up at Kimberley; I have not seen a blade since I left England.

The camp is very much smaller [11 January] than it was a week ago. Most of the Scots have gone to the front, also the Artillery and most of Carrington's Horse. A, B and C troops of our corps have gone on for Barkly West, and our troops go tomorrow if possible. Barkly is about 100 miles from here, six days' march. Horses are coming in every day, and directly a troop is served with horses they start on the march and, as many of the men have not been on a horse before, the start is a sight to be seen. We have not had any news from the front to be relied upon, but the general opinion is there will be fighting. A great many reports go about camp about the Boers recruiting and getting arms and ammunition ready, but you hear such contradictory reports that you can believe nothing. They say in the Cape papers that if there is any fighting at all there will be a long war which, if the English are successful, will end in the annexation of the Transvaal. They say the Transvaal Boers will certainly support those in Bechuanaland.

It is just as well that the rumours and paper-talk proved to be groundless, and that the eager young trooper did not have to ride into action against the redoubtable Boers. As he wrote his letter, British troops were committed in force in the Sudan, attempting to rescue General Gordon from Khartoum. There had been intermittent fighting against the Mahdi's dervish army for more than a year, as well as military activity in Burma, so another battlefront in South Africa might have posed problems for the War Office and the Treasury. Campaigns were cropping up thick and fast: within a year of its disastrous experience against the Boers at Majuba, the British army embarked on a fresh endeavour in Egypt, and it is in this direction we must now turn our attention.

SIX

'I Can't Write about it Any More':

WOLSELEY IN EGYPT, 1882

The war with the Boers in 1880–81 was unique among Victorian campaigns in any part of the globe, not simply so far as Africa was concerned, in that the long-suffering soldiers were not awarded a campaign medal or clasp. Given that it was an affair best forgotten, perhaps it is not surprising there was no formal commemoration of it. Even so, the omission was resented in the ranks, for plenty of letters refer to the sense of pleasure a campaign medal gave to the soldier as decoration for his uniform, if only to flaunt before his family and friends. It could secure him a few rounds of drinks in his local pub at home, and if times got hard he could pawn it: each medal was one ounce of solid silver. As it happens, regiments engaged against the Boers went on to fight in Egypt in 1882, and the Egyptian campaign was as prolific of medals and decorations for all and sundry as the struggle with the Boers had been meagre. Most of the vast army of ordinary servicemen had two medals, one from the British government and the other, a bronze star, from the Khedive of Egypt, in whose name the campaign was fought. Officers galore were promoted and received Companionships of the Bath, and it was as if the floodgates had opened on what was at last an unmitigatedly successful feat of British arms.

It began on 11 July 1882 with the bombardment of Egyptian fortifications at Alexandria by a powerful squadron of the Royal Navy. This 'most important naval action in which England has been engaged within the last 25 years' packed the newspapers with reports and comments: it had a surprising amount in common with the Falklands operations of 1982. 'The ball was opened by the firing of an empty shell from the *Alexandra*,' wrote the *Western Morning News* correspondent. 'A few anxious moments elapsed during which, as you may imagine, our hearts beat high with expectancy, and then we were gratified with a reply from the forts.'

The underlying cause of the shelling of Alexandria's defences was

British concern to retain indirect control of the Suez Canal, so vital to communications with the Indian Empire. Early in 1882 the government of Egypt was taken over by Ourabi Pasha, a soldier, minister and patriot who would be regarded today much as Colonel Nasser, who was acclaimed as a national hero in the 1950s. Ourabi wished to secure more independence for Egypt, and he could raise an army of 60,000 troops with 300 field-guns. Pressures had been brought against the European business community in Egypt, 90,000 of them and mainly British or French, most of whom fled the country as riots, burning and massacre of Christians broke out in Alexandria on 11 June.

This happened under the noses of British warships already in the harbour; there followed a period of negotiation, accompanied by preparations for a military expedition to Egypt to restore stability and order. Ourabi announced his intention of resisting by arms any attempt to land British troops, and his men began strengthening the forts that guarded the harbour at Alexandria. He was asked to stop these efforts by Vice-Admiral Sir Beauchamp Seymour, the naval commander, as the last British refugees sought shelter on P & O liners offshore. Ourabi (known at the time as Arabi, and soon in the papers as 'Orrible Pasha) assured him that the defensive work had been halted, but searchlights on board HMS *Alexandra* showed otherwise. This was an early military use of what they called 'the electric light', one of several pieces of new weaponry being tried out by the navy, just as missile systems were used for the first time under battle conditions in the South Atlantic.

An ultimatum was sent to Ourabi on Monday, 10 July 1882, giving him twenty-four hours to surrender the forts for dismantling; if he did not comply, the navy would bombard them into submission. No reply having been received, at 7 a.m. the next day (a month after the killing of the British nationals) the shelling began. It was a strong force that cut loose on the Egyptians – eight ironclad warships and five gunboats, sixty-six guns in all. Never before had British ironclads been in action. They were so called because of their steel armour plating; on the *Invincible* (6,000 tons and forerunner of the aircraft carrier of the same name that served off the Falklands) there was 8-inch armour. It stood her in good stead because the gunners in Fort Mexs found her range and plastered her with shells, but only half-a-dozen penetrated her hull. She would have been sunk without her plating, and suffered only a few casualties. She was a broadside ship and carried heavy armament of ten 10-inch guns, also in their maiden conflict. The biggest vessels were much more awe-spiring: *Inflexible*, a turret-ship of 11,400 tons had four 16-inch guns, while the *Téméraire* was armed with four 11-inch and four 10-inch guns. Such massive rifled ordnance had never before been battle-tested, not even against a land target as at Alexandria, nor had the revolving and fixed turrets, mechanical carriages, or loading gear. They did well, but against the forts and in shallow water the little gunboats, quicker to manoeuvre, did even better service.

After this opening blast, within three weeks a large British force of 25,000 troops was quickly mobilised, shipped out, and put ashore in Egypt to crush Ourabi and restore order. They were commanded by that military darling of the time, Sir Garnet Wolseley – 'The Modern Major-General' of the song in *The Pirates of Penzance*. After the main force landed at Ismailia on the Suez Canal (which Ourabi unwisely left undamaged), columns of soldiers slowly fought their way through the sandy waste towards Cairo. Wolseley gambled and won on the poor fighting quality of the Egyptians, but along the line his men paid a high price in discomfort. For a fortnight they had to survive on little more than biscuit and water from the so-called Sweetwater Canal, without tents or medical supplies. Hundreds were invalided home before Wolseley managed to organise his supplies and transport. A series of victories, however, did much to restore the image of the British soldier, dented in recent years by defeats at the hands of Zulu, Afghans and Boers. There was a sneaking feeling that the opposition should have been tougher to merit all the pride in crushing it. The slaughter of so many Egyptians was deplored by some correspondents – 'the butchering of miserable, pitiful creatures', as one put it. Letters written home by so many of the soldiers tend to bear this out, while at the same time showing it was by no means a one-sided contest and most of those at the sharp end of the fighting earned their campaign medals the hard way, through discomfort as much as danger.

Operations began quietly enough when the first contingents were landed amid the devastation of Alexandria, which would be the main port of supply. We can sample the early atmosphere of this war in a letter from Lance-Corporal John Clough, of the 1st King's Shropshire Light Infantry. He was one of three men from the small town of Welshpool serving in Egypt, and on 24 August he wrote, in pencil, to his aunt at Bowling Green Lane: he was then at Ramleh Camp.

We landed here on Monday last, the 21st of August, and as soon as we got off board ship we had to march through the town of Alexandria, and it was an awful sight to see the houses all blown up and burnt to pieces for miles. We had to march three miles through the town and then we rode some miles by train up to the front. As soon as we got there the shots were flying over our heads, but none of them hurt any of us and our artillery opened fire on them and they soon stopped. They have not shown fight since. We expect to start on them tomorrow, so I will be able to tell you more the next time I write.

They very near clemmed [i.e. exhausted] us the first days. We only had one meal and that was breakfast, and we had nothing till the next morning and that was about 9 a.m. We had to sleep in the open field all night on the sand, without a blanket or anything, so you see how we are served here, but I don't think it will last long. We have a good many soldiers here, and everything is awfully dear. They charge sixpence for a glass of ale and we cannot get anything to eat for money, and as for writing paper and stamps they are out of the question altogether. English stamps are no good here, so we have to send our letters without stamps at all. It is a shame to see how the property is destroyed here, thousands of pounds worth, and all belonging to English people, and they killed all the English they could.

The buoyant Percy Marling, whose accounts of fighting the Boers the previous year we have already seen, was again in action in Egypt with the 3/60th, King's Royal Rifle Corps. It was no accident that so many of his letters have survived, as we learn from what his grandfather told his mother on 31 July 1882. 'I think Percy has expressed the wish that his letters home should as much as possible be kept together, that in the future he may if mindful be able to refer to them. The early letters of great men are in after life of the highest value, and as we hope Percy is not going to be a very small one, I think all his letters should be well taken care of.' He did indeed make good use of them later when writing his autobiography. In 1882 Marling reached Port Said on 20 August and sailed on at once to Ismailia in HMS *Euphrates*.

I expect tonight will be the last time we shall have what the Yankees call a good square meal for some time. We are able to take no kit on shore with us, except for what we stand in. We have two companies on guard tonight on deck in case the Bedouin fire at the ship from the banks of the Suez Canal. The Duke of Connaught is out here and very busy, he seems a very good fellow. We have absolutely no transport whatever. Sir Garnet is in great form and has certainly not let the grass grow under his feet.

On 10 September Marling could tell his family of his share in the first battle of the campaign at Kassassin.

My darling Mother,
We had a great fight yesterday and you will be glad to hear in the first place that we repulsed the enemy and in the second that I am all right. The enemy advanced to attack the camp about 6 a.m. and got quite close before anyone noticed them, which was very neglectful on the part of our Scouts.

Our camp is bounded on the right by the railway and no sooner had we crossed the embankment than the enemy opened on us with his big guns at about 2,500 yards' range, and we had a very nasty time of it for about an hour and a half. The shells fell all round us and a splinter from one of them sent the sand and pebbles all over my legs but without doing any damage happily.

Our camp suffered very much from the shells and Holbeck my captain had his tent blown to bits by one and a lot of his kit destroyed. Fortunately I had moved out of the tent the night before to go to another Company for a few days, so none of my things were hurt. We gradually advanced by short rushes of from 50 to 100 yards, and then came under musketry fire, first of all a few stray bullets and then as we got nearer and nearer a perfect hailstorm of them. Some of them came most unpleasantly close and whistled past our ears or tore up the sand at one's feet, in a manner that would have rejoiced the heart of any insurance company from whom you derived an annuity.

We kept up a tremendous musketry fire on them and kept advancing steadily, and about 11 o'clock they began retiring and were all out of sight in an hour. The casualties in our regiment were 2 killed and 31 wounded. Some of the latter however only very slightly. The heat was intense and several of the men had sunstroke. We got back to camp about 3.30 p.m., thoroughly done up. I forgot to say we captured an enormous quantity of small arm ammunition, about 40,000 rounds (Arabi's troops all use Remington rifles) and three guns, but I don't know of what size.

The Egyptian dead and wounded looked ghastly as we passed them in our advance, all covered with blood with their dusky faces upturned in the blazing sun. After they began to retire one fellow jumped up in front of us about 200 yards and ran right along in front of the whole line, I should think he ran 600 yards, and it certainly took 30 or 40 shots before he was hit, I felt quite sorry for the poor beggar. It was really quite like rabbit shooting. We got three or four prisoners. Their big guns made the most

"VICI"!!!

*A victorious Sir Garnet Wolseley lords it over his stricken opponent,
Ourabi Pasha, after the Egyptian campaign of 1882.*

splendid practice at us. I had about six shots with a rifle myself. The artist to the *Graphic* has just come in and asked me to try and make a sketch of our tent being blown up for him to copy and send home. I've been trying but have not made much of a job of it. I think the big fight to take Tel-el-Kebir will be the day after tomorrow. Goodbye now dearest Mumseh, with best love to all at home and the Park.

As Marling rightly guessed, 13 September 1882 was to be the day of the final confrontation at Tel-el-Kebir, where Ourabi had 20,000 men and sixty guns in strong fortifications across the road to Cairo. Against him Wolseley brought 13,000 troops and a similar amount of artillery, marching them in silence for six miles through the night of 12–13 September so as to attack at dawn, a daring enterprise by the standards of that time. Taken by surprise, the Egyptians had to face the cold steel of a bayonet charge. It proved to be the nastiest battle in terms of total carnage yet experienced by imperial troops in Africa. The Sudanese battalions of Ourabi's army offered desperate resistance, but the majority of hapless *fellahin* were cruelly punished by the British at Tel-el-Kebir, with much unnecessary killing when they broke: an exultant pursuit is the ugliest face of war; it had revealed itself after Khambula and Ulundi in the Zulu War. All this comes out in the letters, which we shall sample from a range of newspapers and other sources as they cover the entire campaign in Egypt, culminating in Tel-el-Kebir. We must begin with the kilted men of the Highland regiments, whose exploits always hit the headlines with a special appeal for jingoistic Victorians. They had a harsh rôle to play at Tel-el-Kebir.

Spencer Ewart, a young lieutenant in the Cameron Highlanders, was in the thick of it. He tells his father how they 'moved slowly and silently across the plain, not a sound could be heard but the slow tramp of the men. It was getting near daylight and I was beginning to get uneasy that we were late, when there was a flash of a rifle in front of me, followed by all the Egyptian bugles blowing the alarm'. With the enemy now aroused, the Camerons had to close with them as quickly as possible.

We all ran cheering as hard as we could towards the earthworks, stumbling into holes in the darkness. It was a distance of 400 yards, and I was dead beat when I fell into their trench, a great deep place. I opened fire with my revolver to clear the way. It was a fearful sight, the Camerons bayoneted everyone. From the first line of works they fled to the second, but we drove them out of that and pell mell into their camp. At the far end I found Colonel Leith, who led us magnificently, sitting on a hillock with a piper playing the 'Gathering'.

All this was achieved at some cost, the four regiments of the Highland Brigade suffering the heaviest casualties – 231 killed, wounded and missing out of 460 in all at Tel-el-Kebir. 'When we were all together again,' writes Ewart, 'we found we had lost 13 killed, and 3 officers and 34 men wounded. Blackburn was shot through the thigh, MacDougall through the ankle, and Malcolm got a sabre cut over the head and a bayonet through his arm; he fought well and killed several with his claymore. We lay down till 3 in the afternoon in Arabi's tents.'

Another vivid glimpse of the Scottish attack and hand-to-hand fighting comes from a sergeant of the Black Watch, whose letter was printed in many of the newspapers. 'The 42nd charged over the last fifty yards like tigers, sprang into the trenches while the bullets were whirring, whizzing and pinging like as many bees when they are casting. The pipes struck up, while all the time as far as we could see to the front, right and left was a sheet of flame from the enemy's rifles and cannon.'

About two dozen men were wounded before the Black Watch reached the front-line trench, which was extremely deep and wide in their sector. They jumped in, only to be faced with an embankment fourteen feet high. More were shot trying to scale this obstacle, but the sergeant and a handful of other soldiers cut steps in the earth with their bayonets, clambered up, and gained a footing on the summit. They quickly cleared the Egyptians from their position, 'Lord Kennedy splitting them at a terrific pace', so allowing more soldiers to climb in.

> Then up they came in swarms, wheeling to right and left, bayoneting or shooting every man. Sergeant-Major M'Neil ran his sword through six in rapid succession, then he got wounded in the thigh. I shot the man with a revolver who did it. M'Neil fell, but rose and led on for a minute, but got shot again in the stomach and groin, fell fatally wounded. We charged on at a six-gun battery which was mowing down the 72nd Highlanders, bayoneted over 100 men who defended themselves well, three minutes did it all.

Behind these words lie some of the sharpest fighting that cost the Black Watch fifty-six casualties. Peter Harkin, a private in the Highland Light Infantry, tells his mother how he plodded through the loose sand towards the battle position. 'We halted when we had gone about six miles and rested for two hours; we partook of some rum. Then we advanced to face the enemy. You could have heard a pin drop when we were marching. I was just passing that remark to a comrade that I thought there would be no fighting when suddenly two shells were fired from the enemy.' The Highland Light Infantry had marched fourteen miles in all that day, on the scantiest of rations, and had the misfortune to run against some of Ourabi's strongest fortifications. 'The enemy soon put a heavy fire on us,' writes Harkin, 'both from big guns and rifles; shot and shell were flying over our heads and on both sides of us. The shouting of our men as they got wounded was something heart-rending. I thought every moment I would be launched into eternity. I can't write about it any more.'

By far the heaviest casualties of the entire British attack were in the Highland Brigade, and the Highland Light Infantry lost more men than any other Scottish regiment – seventy-four killed and wounded, by grim coincidence, in the 74th Foot. Fighting alongside them were the Cameron Highlanders, and Sergeant Charles Riley of F Company wrote to tell a friend at home how it had gone with them. On the march to Tel-el-Kebir, he says, 'I have had nothing to lie on only the bare ground, nothing to cover ourselves with, and in the kilt, too.' At first light on 13 September, 'when we got within 300 yards of Arabi's position they saw us, and opened fire on us. Then the bullets flew round my head; my right-hand man was shot through the heart and died at once. As soon as they opened fire we fixed bayonets, and with a good ringing British cheer we charged the trenches, and in about half-hour's time you could see nothing but dead Egyptians, and the rest flying for their lives. We drove them out at last and captured all their guns, ammunition, and six months' provisions.'

Sergeant Riley says he had two or three narrow escapes; his helmet was shot off – 'so it could not be any nearer than that' – and the Camerons suffered sixty-one casualties on the day, most of them wounded. It was a somewhat different story with the Scots Guards, who were also present at the battle, but in reserve. Brigaded with the Grenadiers and Coldstreams, they were commanded by no less a personage than the Queen's son, the Duke of Connaught and Strathearn. In fact the Household troops were well represented in Egypt, for the 1st and 2nd Life Guards formed part of the cavalry force: they had not fought overseas since the Crimean War. C. B. Balfour was a subaltern with the Scots Guards, their pipes playing 'Hieland Laddie' when they sailed for Egypt and again when they were the first to march into Cairo after Ourabi's defeat. In between, Balfour had some uncomfortable times in the desert. 'The first few days here, when men came in to the doctor suffering from diarrhoea, all he could say was "My good man, I have got nothing to give you. You must rub your stomach." Had we fought an action on the day we expected, there was no provision for the wounded, not a single stretcher on the field.'

At Tel-el-Kebir the Guards had to sit it out in support, under fire from the Egyptian artillery.

> The horizon was lit up with flashes just like summer lightning, with a continuous crackle like the rumpling of several *Times* newspapers. But the Egyptians made such a poor showing no support was required by the first line. The whole thing was just like a drill in Hyde Park (if such a thing could be done at night) with nobody throwing stones and letting off squibs all round . . . Thank heavens, we only stayed at Tel-el-Kebir two days. The canal was filthy and the camp stinking. There were about 3,000 Arabs lying dead around, of whom they buried what they could, making the prisoners work at it. The wounded in the trenches were all in by the evening of the 13th. I went round and gave water to some, for which they were very grateful. Some of the dead had their legs blown off, one I saw with the whole lower part of his face gone. Where the Highlanders came in they were lying in heaps, I believe, and where our shell burst, too . . . Out here the people we all envied are the Highlanders, who with pipes playing and one long continued howl were first into the entrenchments and the camp.

The aftermath also shocked an officer of Engineers who went out to make a sketch-map of the earthworks:

> Words cannot describe the horrors in the lines, the fearful stench, the corpses of the Egyptians all unburied and covered with masses of flies, which flew up into your face the moment you approached, even two of the Marines not yet buried, and one or two wounded Egyptians still living under the broiling sun (over 115° in the shade), the dead horses, mules and camels, the wreck of camp tents, arms, etc., abandoned by the Egyptians, the returned fugitives and Bedouin robbers prowling about all through the ruin, and even stripping the corpses of their clothes. It was necessary to keep a ready revolver for these fellows.

A soldier from Oxford saw it all, serving as a signaller (using the heliograph) with the Mounted Infantry. Writing home from Cairo after the fighting was over, he says: 'We had a rough time of it from the time we left Ismailia until we arrived here. We had nothing to eat after leaving Ismailia until the second night after we got to Mahsama, except a few biscuits we happened to have with us. Mahsama was enough to give anyone the cholera. You could see Egyptians lying dead all over the place, and the stink was cruel.' He saw more action at Kassassin, where Ourabi's troops attacked at night: 'We were just making a cup of tea when the devils attacked the camp. We were sent out with the Guards to signal, and that kept us out all night. I was just in rear of them when they made that charge by moonlight, so I had a good view of it.' On to Tel-el-Kebir, where he fought with the cavalry on the flank of the main British assault. 'It was a fine sight,' he says of the battle, 'although you could not help feeling a bit strange to see the poor devils lying about all over the ground dead and wounded, some with heads and some without.' Much of this damage was done by the Bengal Cavalry, with whom his unit was brigaded. 'The Indian cavalry we had were the boys to knock them about; there was no taking prisoners with them. Where they charged I should think there were about 500 found dead. I saw a wounded Egyptian fire at one of them and miss him, and the next minute he was minus his head. It was the cleanest cut I ever saw. He galloped at him, and with one blow he cut his head clean off, and it rolled about 20 yards.'

At the other end of the scale from this bloodthirstiness was the experience of another Oxford soldier, serving as a stretcher-bearer with one of the field hospitals. He did a ten-mile march to Kassassin in the scorching sun. 'We had not marched far before a great many fell out, and had to be carried into camp. I fainted twice myself, and had to be brought in by ambulance, but we had some biscuits and laid down, we were soon alright.' He had a busy time at Tel-el-Kebir, 'a fight which none who were engaged in it will ever forget. The cannonballs were dropping left and right of us, and once we were in a very critical position. We were carrying in a wounded officer, and had just got him on the stretcher when a shell burst close to us, wounded the two men with me and killed a horse, so I had a narrow escape.' Afterwards the scene of carnage in the Egyptian entrenchments horrified him. 'There were about 1,200 killed, and quite as many wounded. I was carrying wounded men all day, and up early the next morning fetching in wounded Arabs, and yesterday it was like a butcher's shop here, cutting off arms and legs by the dozen. I am quite knocked up, so that I went sick this morning, and have got a few hours' rest, but there are lots of wounded lying about yet.'

A Plymouth battalion of Royal Marine Light Infantry went through the whole campaign and fought at all five engagements. Sailing from Cyprus in the *Tamar*, the Marines were among the first arrivals at Alexandria, on July 17. Soon they found themselves in the fighting at Kassassin as described by one of their officers, whose letter appeared in a contemporary edition of *The Western Morning News*. 'We had an awful time of it yesterday. I was on outpost duty the night before, and, on coming in, the Assembly sounded so we all went out to repel an attack on our camp. At about 6 a.m. we commenced, and fought the whole day until 4 p.m. We drove them back steadily and though retreating they kept up a very heavy fire both from artillery and infantry on us. The heat was something awful, and of course we had no shade.' In this run-up to Tel-el-Kebir, the Royal Marines suffered twenty-five casualties in bearing the brunt of the attack, but 'The General congratulated Colonel Jones on the field on the way the Marines had behaved. I was close by and heard him. Altogether we drove them about seven miles from the camp, so we had a good 12 miles marching ourselves, and that on an empty stomach is no joke.'

A gunner in the Royal Marine Artillery had to abandon his breakfast too as the Egyptians attacked in three lines: 'We were thrown out in skirmishing order, and advanced. The enemy opened fire on us, that was something dreadful, but they did not keep it up long, as our infantry kept advancing as steady as if on parade at home. The main body came up, halted, and put volleys into them like steam, and they fell on the field like rotten sheep. Still, the ordinary rations are not sufficient for a fighting man who has to march through heavy sands and fight in the bargain.'

So to the decisive battle at Tel-el-Kebir. This was foreseen by Sergeant James Caine of the Marines when he said: 'We intend marching to some place about ten miles further up the country, where we expect to have a very warm reception. It is estimated that about 22,000 Egyptian troops are there well entrenched.' What happened there on 13 September, is described by Colonel H. S. Jones, in command of the Marines. 'After a weary tramp we found ourselves just as dawn began to break out about 1,200 yards in front of the entrenchments, but the stars having failed us we had to make a change in front. Whilst this was being done the enemy opened fire on us with shell and musketry. It was a grand sight to see our fine fellows making their way against a hellish fire across that flat desert.' When they were a hundred yards from the Egyptians the Marines fixed bayonets and ran at them.

The whole line of ramparts seemed in a blaze, but, nothing daunted, our men gave a cheer and dashed into the ditch and scrambled up the parapet – Heaven only knows how. I managed to dig my sword into the sand, and made a lever of it by which to pull myself up. Then a regular hand-to-hand fight took place, in which our bayonets played an important part. It did not last long, the enemy soon fled, and then a scene of carnage ensued. It took me a long time to get the men in hand again.

The 2nd York and Lancaster Regiment were at Kassassin, as described by Private Edward Brown. He wrote a letter to his father on 15 September, and it was published in the *Sheffield Daily Telegraph* a few weeks later.

The first time we met the enemy [he says], we were going up the railway; there were rushes growing on both sides, as soon as we got out of them they fired on us, so we opened out and skirmished for about 300 yards. We dug trenches and afterwards fired upon them for about eight hours till dark at night. There were but our regiment (the old 84th), the 46th and a few Marines to face them, but they were cowards – they didn't stand their ground; as soon as we shouted they were off.

Ted Brown must have been a sporting man, judging from the way he recounted his experience at Tel-el-Kebir. 'I shan't forget the Doncaster Leger day so long as I live. About five o'clock that morning we advanced towards the Egyptians and got within fifty yards of them, when we fixed bayonets and charged them in the trenches, which were about ten feet deep. Our company did not fire until we got up to them; then we shot them down like rain falling.'

While the British infantry made their frontal assault on Ourabi's entrenchments, regiments of cavalry waited on the flanks to follow up the Egyptians if and when they broke and ran. This duly happened, and a glimpse of what took place appears in a letter from a trooper in the 7th Dragoon Guards. As they charged the retreating enemy, he writes, 'I had not the heart to cut dozens down that I might have done, for they fell on their knees and held up their rifles for mercy. But I could not help cutting some down, because they fired on us up to the last'. He goes on:

One of the enemy was laid on his face, and as a man of the 4th Dragoon Guards rode past him he rose up and fired at him, and I just caught him as he galloped by and cut him from his shoulder to the middle of his back. But the best fellows for fighting are the Indian troops. They cut heads off as if they were cabbages and the head fell in many cases eight foot away from the body. The battle only lasted two hours, and the whole time we were butchering them on the flanks as they tried to run away.

He was writing from Cairo after it was all over, billeted in the Khedive's palace with the officer to whom he was orderly. After the battle they did a forced march – '76 miles in 36 hours, not so bad, for I had nothing to eat for three days but two biscuits, until I got in here last night, nearly dead. We captured Arabi Pasha, he is a fine-looking fellow; we are all thoroughly knocked up, but we shall soon be home now. I am only a mile from the great Pyramids.'

Quite a few letters from soldiers were printed in the *Western Mail*, one of the earliest written by a corporal of the Grenadier Guards, John Davies, when he was not far from Alexandria. 'Our camp is now situated about four miles from the enemy's; also our outposts are within one mile of Arabi Pasha's camp. Our outpost had a brush with him last night in skirmishing order. We soon made him flee to his trenches. We have got the electric light on him by night, and can see every movement he makes.' Corporal Davies then lapsed into rather an amusing purple passage, something rare in the plain, unvarnished style generally used by the Victorian soldier. 'When we all go at him, we Scotch, English and Welsh will show Arabi that we are soldiers who will stain the massive plains of Egypt with our blood for the sake of the peace and honour of our country. We shall make a dash at him, and soon make short work of him.' The war was reported very fully in the *Mail*, both as to the general situation and as it related to matters of local interest. One of the best accounts, however, of what it was like to be at Tel-el-Kebir comes from Viscount Fielding, who wrote to his parents, Lord and Lady Denbigh. He was a lieutenant in the Royal Artillery, serving with N/2 Battery and like everyone else in the British attack had to march on the enemy through the 'dark as Egypt's night' of 12–13 September.

'We saw the first faint streak of dawn behind us, then suddenly, when it was first getting light, there were two shots and immediately afterwards a furious rifle fire began along a line which seemed to go right across our front for nearly a mile. Then for the first time we heard the ping of bullets all round us. It was a trying time for all, standing there with the air literally full of bullets.' The battery also came under shell fire before advancing towards the entrenchments.

There they lost one of the field-guns in crossing the trenches, but pressed on through the debris of the Highlanders' attack.

> We found the enemy bolting in every direction across the plain, but they were pegging away hard at us from lines to our left front. After giving them a few rounds they began to run, so we galloped after them coming into action every 300 or 400 yards. It was a most exciting chevy, as we were quite by ourselves. We drove the enemy out of two or three redoubts where they tried to stand, assisted by the 42nd [Black Watch], who ran along the other side of the trenches, and got so close to the Egyptians sometimes that we fired several rounds of case shot at about 200 yards, with great effect.

Later the Viscount was able to shell the railway trains in which Ourabi and his staff escaped from the battlefield, and then occupied the Pasha's 'nice-looking tent' in the captured camp.

Although they could not know it, many of the soldiers who had it much their own way against the Egyptians were soon to face an infinitely more aggressive and dangerous opponent in the Sudan. Compared even to Tel-el-Kebir their experiences of war against the followers of the Mahdi would prove to be as different as going up Snowdon is from climbing the north face of the Eiger, and just about as exhausting. After their easy victories against Ourabi's army, and a year or so of garrison duty in Egypt, they were thrown in at the deep end of close combat with the fiercest warriors in Africa. The Black Watch was one regiment to go through this ordeal. They set out for Suez, en route for the Sudan, on 15 February 1884; their train stopped at Tel-el-Kebir, where they got out to inspect the new cemetery for their comrades who fell in 1882. The men took the red feathers from the regimental hackles on their helmets, and placed bunches of them at the head of each grave. 'Looking at these from the train as we passed,' one soldier wrote, 'they seemed like some bright-hued flowers lighting up the scene.'[1] They were also an omen of what lay ahead for the soldiers of the Black Watch.

1. James Grant, *Cassell's History of the War in the Soudan* (London: Cassell, 1886), volume 2, page 135.

SEVEN

'The Pluckiest Fellows I've Ever Seen':

CONFLICT IN THE SUDAN, 1884–85

The curtain went up in 1883 on a protracted drama that featured in due course the death of General Gordon in Khartoum and the crushing of the Khalifa Abdullahi's army at Omdurman in 1898. The scene was set in the Sudan, one of the harshest of African territories, most of it rock, sand, thorns, flies and crushing heat, relieved only by the thin thread of the river Nile. Why, then, should a small force of British soldiers find itself, at the outset of 1884, fighting for its life against as redoubtable a warrior nation as Africa could offer, firing the first shots of a prolonged imperial involvement? The answer lies in the entanglement with Egyptian affairs that followed the war of 1882.

After the defeat of Ourabi Pasha, Gladstone's government assumed responsibility for Egypt, chiefly because of the need to have control of the Suez Canal as a lifeline to British India and the Far East. But this also meant that Britain inherited the problems of Sudan province, hitherto a dependency of Egypt and exploited by the corrupt regime of the Khedive. In some quarters contact with the Sudan was welcomed because it gave fresh opportunity to stamp out the slave trade that flourished there. But whether the motivation of British influence was to be humanitarian or merely the necessary business of collecting taxes from the Sudanese, it was drastically overshadowed by the appearance in 1881 of Muhammad Ahmad al-Mahdi. A charismatic warrior-priest, best known simply as the Mahdi, he was accepted by the Sudanese as 'the Successor to the Prophet of God' and led them in explosive revolt against the Egyptians. It was a religious rather than a political movement, the Mahdi raising the cry for a holy war or *jihad*, reminiscent in some ways of the fundamentalist revolution in Islamic countries in our own time.

By the early 1880s the British had gained a great deal of experience in dealing with 'rebels' of various sorts in Africa, but the

Mahdi was to prove too much for them. When imperial forces eventually had to be advanced against the Mahdi's followers, they were hated both as agents of Egyptian oppression and as unbelievers. Initially the Khedive's army was stiffened with a corps of British officers, and then sent on the offensive into the Sudan. Disaster followed disaster. Late in 1883 Hicks Pasha and his 10,000 soldiers were annihilated: when this shocking news was reported in the House of Lords it was compared with the extinction of Pharoah's host in the Red Sea. Things became still more serious when a provincial chief, Uthman Digna (the newspapers called him Osman Digna), went over to the Mahdi and led his large army to besiege Egyptian forts on the coastlands of the Red Sea.

Uthman's attack on garrisons close to Suakin, the only seaport in the Sudan, posed a serious threat to British interests. So another expedition was sent there to check him, commanded this time by Baker Pasha. On 5 February 1884 these unwilling champions advanced in square formation, hoping to inflict a first clear defeat on the Mahdist loyalists. Baker had over 3,000 well-armed troops, and felt perfectly confident of success. But at the opening confrontation with the Sudanese, who were fewer in number, the Egyptians threw down their rifles and ran for it: massacre followed, ninety-six officers and 2,225 men were killed. Four Krupp field-guns and two Gatling machine-guns were taken by Uthman's warriors, at that stage mostly carrying swords and spears, and the Remington rifles of the slain Egyptians were gratefully looted.

The upshot at home was that not even Gladstone could afford to stand idly by while British columns and fortresses fell at the hands of what was seen as another 'savage' power. Quite apart from the necessities of Egyptian politics and Suez Canal strategies, it was bad for national morale and international self-respect. Therefore by 28 February 1884 an army of 3,000 British disembarked near Suakin. Most of them, including the Black Watch who placed their red hackles on their comrades' graves at Tel-el-Kebir, were veterans who had tasted victory in Egypt in 1882. Their first taste of action against the Mahdi, then, was more or less in the wings: their task was to break Uthman's siege of Tokar and so generally assert imperial force of arms in the eastern Sudan. Commanding them was Lieutenant-General Sir Gerald Graham, whose leadership of a brigade in Egypt had resulted in a knighthood for his services, and there were some famous names, such as Redvers Buller, among his subordinates.

No time was lost in bringing the Mahdists to battle, if only because they were camped around the fresh water sources needed by the British. Indeed, some of the soldiers could scarcely have recovered their breath from coming ashore, before they were fighting for their lives. 1884 was a leap year, and on 29 February a pitched battle of ferocity was fought at the wells of El Teb, within sight of where the remains of Baker Pasha's shattered column still lay unburied on the face of the desert. As Graham's men moved forward to attack Uthman Digna's entrenched position, many of them must have been reminded once again of what happened at Tel-el-Kebir. In reality it was a totally different experience: the British advanced in square formation, rather than in line, and it is as well they did so because 6,000 Sudanese swordsmen and spearmen charged home against them. Perhaps the shock of having to face up to this onslaught of cold steel was heightened by the remembrance of easier fighting in Egypt. At any rate, the sense of shock is there in the soldiers' letters written afterwards to their families at home.

Percy Marling was there, adding to his recent encounters with Boers and Egyptians, but this time satisfying his social pedigree by fighting from horseback, serving with the squad of 3/60th Rifles that made up the Mounted Infantry. Marling scribbled a few hasty lines to his father after El Teb. 'I have been in a good many actions now, but it was one of the hottest I have seen. We attacked the entrenchments in a four-deep square, with mounted infantry and cavalry on the flanks.' He describes how the fighting Hadendowa tribesmen charged to the attack, running and bounding with religious fervour right up to the square: one of them leapt inside before he was bayoneted. 'I must say they are the pluckiest fellows I've ever seen. At the beginning of the battle I was sent to occupy a small hillock and had a very warm 30 minutes, just getting away in time before we were surrounded by a lot of brutes on camels.'

After Uthman's trenches and rifle-pits were captured, there was an ugly episode of killing the enemy wounded, something that was to happen time and again in the Sudan, causing a furore of protest from liberal and humanitarian quarters at home. The troops on the spot justified it because of the dangerous nature of the wounded Mahdists. 'We shot or bayoneted all wounded because it wasn't safe to leave them, as they speared or knifed everyone they could reach.' Marling explains how the fifth Sudanese pulled out of a heap of bodies shammed dead and then tried to stab a Highlander before being shot; 'the next three had bullets put into them as they were pulled out'; the ninth seemed to be dead, 'but he suddenly jumped up and ran off amid a flurry of shots, one of which wounded one of our soldiers'. Marling pursued him on his pony for a mile before capturing him – 'he fell exhausted, picked a piece of mimosa from a bush and held it out as a token of surrender' – the one and only prisoner taken at El Teb. The British buried 2,010 Mahdists, or 'dervishes' as they were usually but not wholly accurately called in the press.

Fighting ashore in a Naval Brigade, as they so often did in these distant wars, were 400 marines and 150 sailors from HMS *Hecla*, *Dryad*, *Briton*, and *Euryalus*. Lieutenant Walter Almack, one of *Briton*'s officers, wrote home after El Teb. He had served over twenty years but saw no action in the face of the enemy before landing in the Sudan, to find himself that same day plunged into some desperate fighting. He commanded the left half-battery of Gatling machine-guns, opening fire at 900 yards. Advancing with the square he saw the deadly volleys of the infantrymen 'mowing down the Arabs directly they sprang up to charge. We had the good fortune to be in the very thick of it the whole time. The right half-battery did not fire much till just at the end of the day, but it was more trying for them to stand quiet and be shot at.'

An excellent letter from a bluejacket of *Briton*'s contingent outlines the pattern of battle; he had arrived from Bombay only a few hours before the forward movement was made.

> The pipers of the 42nd and 75th Highlanders played some of their old stirring war marches as the force moved over the rough ground; but when the mounted scouts turned back there was a dead silence for some time. The moment for action had arrived, and orders were awaited with eagerness. The black faces and glittering spears and swords could be seen in the distance, and several rounds of shell were fired at a range of about 800 yards. When it was resolved to turn the enemy's position it was at once seen that there was some hot work cut out for the Naval Brigade, as the movement to the right, with the object of taking the rebels in the rear, very much altered the original formation. The Arabs, nearly naked and yelling fearfully, came on for the Black Watch, behind whom were most of the bluejackets, with terrible impetuosity, their object being to break the ranks and then do their bloody work in the mêlée. Most of them were tall broadchested fellows, with the fierce glare of wild beasts in their black eyes.
>
> The Gatlings played fearful havoc among them, and when at length Admiral Hewett, sword in hand, rushed forward and ordered the left-half battery to charge a point of the defences that was doing deadly work on the Brigade as well as on the Black

Watch, the tars followed the admiral with a ringing cheer. Some of the rebels planted themselves firmly at weak points of their defences, and there used their great heavy swords with dreadful effect until shot down or bayoneted by the Highlanders. Again and again the Arabs rushed on, but only to fall under the hail of bullets, or the stabs and slashes of bayonet and sword. The whole force kept well together, and fought its way right through the rebel position.

There was plenty of close-quarters fighting for others in the Naval Brigade. Although wounded in the side, Captain A. K. Wilson of *Hecla* defended his guns in single combat, saving many of his men's lives. At one time he was armed only with the hilt of his broken sword, and received the Victoria Cross for his bravery. The Marines were hard pressed, especially the company under Lieutenant Frederick White, who was ordered to charge the left-hand redoubt of Uthman's earthworks. He was attacked by two 'dervishes', one on each side of him; he tried to cut one down with his sword, but Private J. H. Birtwistle had to run up to help him, forced his bayonet through the man, and when it broke off clubbed his rifle and killed him. The other assailant was checked by Private F. Yerbury who caught him by his long frizzed-out hair, spinning him round and round so he could not use his spear, and he was shot by Sergeant-Major J. Hirst. By contrast with all this and much more blood-and-thunder stuff reported in the papers under 'The Soudan War', they also printed a letter from someone on the P & O transport ships, carrying a regiment from Aden to Suakin. 'I found in conversation with the officers,' he says, 'that though delighted at the prospect of active service their sympathies were with those they were going to fight against. One of them remarked that a man had to live some time in Egypt to be able to appreciate the vile oppression of the Khedive's government, an oppression which more than justified the revolt of the Mahdi and his Sudanese.'

The attack at El Teb, with a British casualty list of no more than thirty killed and 150 wounded, was rated a successful action, and gave rise to an unjustified sense of optimism about warfare in the Sudan which was very soon to be deflated. El Teb nevertheless taught the British commanders a few valuable military lessons. Clearly the Sudanese skills in attack put them on the level of being irregular cavalry and therefore they had to be met in the open, as if they were mounted men, and faced with a tight square formation. Unlike the Zulu, the Mahdists did not attack in heavy masses, but in loose and extended order. This made them more difficult targets for young British soldiers whose marksmanship with their Martini-Henry rifles was not always of the best. After El Teb an order was read to the troops saying that on no account should they open fire until the enemy were within a range of 300 yards. General Graham also had an order for his cavalry: they were not to take any offensive action until the Sudanese showed clear signs of wavering. The reason for this was the premature charge at El Teb of the 10th and 19th Hussars, one squadron of which was badly cut up when the Mahdists stood up to them and gave as much as they got: Colonel Barrow, in command of the cavalry, was himself seriously wounded. Little could be done about the feeble amount of artillery at the disposal of the British column, and they were to pay for this weakness. Wolseley had refused to send from Egypt even a single battery of field-guns of the Horse Artillery. All they had were four Krupp guns, and some brass mountain-guns that were carried in sections by camel. These were light calibre and slow to bring into action, and had to be protected by infantry. The deficiency was slightly eased when Admiral Hewett took ashore some guns from his ships: two 9-pounders and eight 7-pounders, together with six Gatling and Gardner machine-guns. They were soon to be put to best use.

In the days following the battle Marling tells how they relaxed and rested on their laurels: Baker Pasha was avenged. 'Yesterday Thornton and I rode out to some villages near here and looted everything we could lay hands on', enjoying that night a great dinner of goat, calf, fowls and whisky. General Graham re-captured the fortress of Tokar on 2 March but evidently wanted to have another crack at the power of the Sudanese. On 11 March (having celebrated his twenty-third birthday on the 6th) Marling and the mounted infantry joined the main force in their *zareba*, before scouting operations on 12 March against Uthman Digna's armed camp near the wells of Tamai. The next day saw a truly bloody encounter at Tamai, a battle typical of what was to follow in the Sudan. Very early on the morning of 13 March Marling and his men were sent forward to reconnoitre the ground and discovered a ravine filled with what he estimated to be 6,000 Mahdists. As he peered over the edge one of his men was shot alongside him; the Sudanese began pouring out of the ravine, but Marling emptied his revolver 'into the brown of them', picked up the wounded man, draped him across his pony, and led him back to safety. For this action he was awarded the Victoria Cross.

The main attack was not going according to plan. On the evening of 12 March Graham moved his men up to within a mile or so of Uthman's position. During the night Sudanese riflemen fired non-stop into the British camp, making sleep impossible, and when dawn broke the troops were far from fresh. Graham then divided the force into two brigades, one commanded by Buller, the other by Davis, each brigade forming its own square and at 8 a.m. they all marched forward in echelon, with about 500 yards between each square. Davis's brigade (with Graham accompanying it) took the lead and soon ran into heavy firing from the Mahdists. Then things began to go terribly wrong with this square: the soldiers saw thousands of Sudanese running to attack the right front corner and fired their volleys too soon; clouds of smoke from their black-powder rifles hid the enemy from view. The Black Watch in the front of the square began charging forward, the 65th (York and Lancaster Regiment) on the right front bent inwards, the Royal Marines on the rear face did not keep up with the rest, the sailors with their Gatling guns were helpless as the infantrymen crowded round them.

The square disintegrated as the Mahdists broke through the gaps, stabbing and slashing at the soldiers who retreated in disarray, leaving the machine-guns to the enemy. Tamai gave rise to disturbing headlines in the British newspapers: 'Great battle with Osman Digna – Enemy's position carried – Desperate fighting – A square broken – British forced back – A critical moment – Guns lost and recaptured – Heavy British losses'. Something of the awful confusion is captured in a letter by 955 Private James Hope of the Black Watch, many of whom were killed and wounded.

> We were then within 100 yards of them, and we kept advancing, but we could not get the square formed, as the marines kept going to the left and then to the right, and that put us out of order. Then we were ordered to charge, a great mistake. I think the enemy were just wanting us to do that. But we charged and we were just rushing to our death, for the smoke from our big guns and the firing on our right completely blinded us, and we could not see more than three yards in front of us, and the enemy were advancing on their hands and knees and cutting our men down like rabbits. Then the marines began to retire, and they got inside the square, and we were all forced to retire and leave the guns. I thought it was going to be another Hicks Pasha affair, but General Graham came riding right up to the front of the square and got about 200 around him, and then the other regiments came rushing up, and were prepared to do or die. Then we began to advance,

we kept up a steady fire and we could see them falling as thick as snow.

We made a rush and once more got our guns. Then you should have heard the cheer, it struck terror into the blacks, and as they were retiring down the ravine we were shooting them down. But when we came to know the truth we were overjoyed to see that the square had retired for if we had gone ten yards further there would not have been one dozen of the Black Watch left to tell the tale, as there was a deep ravine and at the bottom there were thousands of Arabs, and if we had gone ten yards further we would have rushed right over, and those not killed by the fall would have been cut to pieces. I had one narrow escape when the square was retiring. A marine kicked me on the heel as he was running and I fell on my face, and five of the blacks came rushing past me. They must have taken me for dead, for I never got a scratch. I jumped up just in time to save myself for two were running towards me, but I had shot one and bayoneted the other, and got into the square again. We always had plenty of food, but water was always scarce. There is no news of a shift at present, but I hope we get back now, as I am sick of this place.

Another private of the Black Watch wrote precisely of his good fortune at Tamai in perilous circumstances:

They were upon us in masses in a minute. I had only fired one round when it came to a hand-to-hand fight. My right-hand man was killed by my side, my left-hand one fell wounded by a spear thrust from a huge Arab over six feet in height. I thrust my bayonet into this fellow up to the hilt, and in trying to get it out his body fell on me and knocked me down, and striking my head against a stone I was stunned and became insensible. How long I remained so I do not know, but on coming to my senses found a heavy weight on me. It was the dead body of this Arab lying across my chest, and the body of a comrade was across my legs and stomach. I raised myself on my elbow, when to my horror and dismay, I saw our chaps in full retreat, and between them and me some hundreds of the enemy.

A dozen of them just round me were engaged in spearing every wounded man of ours they came across. It struck me instantly my only chance of escape was to lie still and feign death. One of the wretches was just then finishing off poor Tom, my comrade. Had they once seen there was life in me I was done for, I felt certain; so I laid quite still, but oh! the agony I suffered no tongue can tell. I silently prayed then as I had never prayed before in my life. They passed over me two or three times, one stepped with his naked foot right on my cheek as I lay with head on the sand. Some 10 or 15 minutes of dreadful suspense followed, till the advancing square came up to where I was lying, and I was saved.

Fortunately through all this the First Brigade's square under Buller fought off its own attacks and remained unbroken, advancing to put in covering fire that helped the re-formation of Davis's square. That accomplished, both of them pressed on over the ridges and ravines to disperse the Mahdists and to capture and burn the Tamai villages. It had been a costly business; the Naval Brigade did not give up its guns without a fight and Lieutenant Walter Almack, who had come through El Teb, did not survive Tamai. Private Thomas Edwards of the Black Watch had charge of two mules loaded with Gatling ammunition for Almack's half-battery, and when the Sudanese broke in found himself surrounded. Almack, Edwards and a bluejacket tried to defend No. 4 gun, but the sailor was quickly speared; Almack used his revolver and sword as best he could before his right arm was almost severed, and he fell over the gun. Edwards tried to cover him, but three dervishes jumped in and killed Almack. Edwards had downed several of them and was wounded himself, but he managed to fight his way back to the confusion of the British line, together with his mules; he was awarded the Victoria Cross.

The heavy British losses of 110 killed and 112 wounded reveal the total decimation that went on at close quarters, because the wounded generally outnumbered those killed by three or four times when firearms were the main weapons used in battle. It was estimated that 2,000 Mahdists were killed out of a total force of 10,000 present at Tamai. The Black Watch suffered most heavily of the British regiments involved. One section of B Company that charged to the brink of the ravine was practically wiped out, with only three survivors, all badly wounded. Marling saw the kilted soldiers suffering 'fearful cuts on their knees from the two-handed swords'; he saw a Black Watch sergeant crawling around a mimosa bush, his face covered with blood; behind him a wounded Sudanese, also on hands and knees, was stabbing at his legs with a spear; he changed direction and met the sergeant face to face, but the Highlander had his finger on the trigger of his rifle and shot him dead. An officer described in a letter how some of his friends used their claymores against the Sudanese swordsmen. 'They pulled the kilts off our men,' he goes on, 'and one of them pulled the green ribbons off my kilt, but I killed him.' He also says how he went round with a spear finishing off the wounded 'after a half-dead Arab sent a spear close to my leg'. One of Marling's men was attacked when giving a drink of water to a wounded Mahdist, so the brutal routine followed at El Teb was repeated at Tamai. Half-a-dozen were found under a tree: 'The men stood 50 yards off and just whanged a volley into them, and went on firing as long as they saw an arm or a leg move.'

By early April, together with most of the expeditionary force, Marling had left these scenes behind and was once more in Egypt, though not for long. Within a year it was back to the Sudan for him and many others, to be locked in dire combat once more with the Mahdists. None of the letters refer to them as 'Fuzzy-Wuzzy', and as Kipling's well-known poem of that name did not appear in the *Scots Observer* until 1890, perhaps it was not much used in the fighting period. The British realised from the outset how much the Mahdists treasured the many flags they carried into battle, and took them as trophies whenever they could. One captured at El Teb was brought home by a midshipman of HMS *Euryalus*, Edward Tyndall-Biscoe, and duly given to Lord Northbrook. More prestigious still was the flag taken at Tamai and presented to Queen Victoria. Lieutenant Wilfrid Lloyd of the Royal Horse Artillery was attached to the force while on leave, and so could return home once the fighting was over. In the last week of March he went along to Windsor Castle with the large red and yellow flag: on one side an Arabic inscription said the Mahdi presented it to the Governor of Tokar, on the other a text from the Koran, 'There is no God but God, and Muhammad is the Prophet of God. Everyone professes the knowledge of God.'

While all this was happening at Suakin, the next chapter unfolded itself at Khartoum, capital of the Sudan. In an attempt to check the Mahdi's rebellion, a new Governor-General was installed there in the person of General Charles Gordon, who had already held that office some years before. Once Gordon was in residence the Mahdist forces clamped a besieging ring round Khartoum and sat back to starve him out. Eventually, after tortuous political manoeuvrings, Gladstone authorised an expedition to go to his relief and bring him out. Wolseley was the obvious choice to command this difficult venture, and he began to move his men partly by boat up the Nile, despite its many cataracts, and partly by a series of short-cuts over the desert southwards. By the last days of 1884 the advance guard had reached the Nile at Korti, and was ready for the final advance on Khartoum.

Camel transport was an essential part of the relief column's effort to cover the long distances through desert country. To this end four Camel Regiments were formed: the Heavy, made up of sections from the Life Guards, Royal Horse Guards, and the Dragoon Guards; the Light, from various Hussar regiments; the Guards, from the footguards of the Household Brigade; and the Mounted Infantry, with units drawn from the various infantry regiments. The camel was quite a challenge for men accustomed to the successful management of horses, as recounted by an officer of the Grenadier Guards while on the march from Wadi Halfa to Dongola. Saddling up was a complicated business, and mounting was far from easy.

> Generally speaking, the camel gets up just as the man gets his foot in the stirrup, and the results are curious. Woe betide if you try to throw your right leg over before the beast is up; you will infallibly come a hideous cropper. The only thing is to stand in the stirrup, let him rise with you, and then get into the seat. The usual day's work begins by reveille at 4.30, sometimes earlier, according to the length of the day's journey which as yet has never exceeded 11 hours, about 30 miles. Breakfasts are finished and everything is packed and finished by 6, and we start in the cool of the morning by leading our beasts four or five miles before mounting. Sitting on top of a camel walking straight on end for eight or nine hours, with only a break of half-an-hour at noon, is a slightly monotonous affair. My own beast, though I love him tenderly, is not blest with swift walking powers, and my conversation during the day is limited to 'Wake up, damn you', occasionally varied by 'Damn you, wake up'.
>
> As for the country, my idea of a desert used to be 'an illimitable waste of burning sand, broken by neither rock nor tree whereon to rest the weary eye'. As yet we have not come across anything of the sort; the ground has been decidedly mountainous, and in fact sometimes so much so that we have had to dismount and lead our animals. We do not see so much of the Nile as you might expect from looking at the map, though as yet we have halted every night except one on the banks, from whence the views are excessively pretty. Sometimes the ground is so strong that one really pities the podgy, soft-looking feet of our camels, but they knock their toes against the sharp stones with the greatest unconcern. I have also had practical experience that their feet are not soft, by a violent kick I received from the hind-leg of a camel, who thought himself insulted by my examining his headstall in the dark. Altogether he is an overrated beast: my experience thus far is that he gets a sore back after four days or less, does not go more

141

than five consecutive days without water, and his walking certainly never exceeds two-and-a-half miles per hour.

If the use of camels posed their own peculiar problems, so did the use of boats for those who took to the waters of the Nile. An infantry captain had set off in a hurry with three companies of his regiment, each company being transported in a sailing boat or *dhahabiyah* – he calls it a 'dahabeeah', travelling upstream from the First Cataract. He describes it all in a letter of 15 November 1884, when sailing 100 miles south of Aswan, under the flag of Thomas Cook from whom the military had hired them.

> This native boat is rather a large one, about 60 or 70 feet in length, and has at its stern a small deck-house containing eight small cabins; of these I and my subaltern have two, one as an ante-room, the other as a boudoir. Another we use as a pantry and two others as kitchens for our servants. Between this suite and the remainder are a pair of doors, and this effectually shuts us out from the men. When we first came on board we thought we should be very comfortable, but the first night dispelled this illusion. We found the whole place simply swarming with bugs. The misery they inflicted on us that night makes me shudder to recall, they swarmed over our bodies, and hardly left a square inch without a bite. At 12 o'clock, after killing over a hundred of them, we could stand it no longer, but sallied out on a small ledge which projects from the end of the ship. Here suspended, like Mahomet's coffin 'twixt sky and earth, we slept till morning, keeping up continuously a desperate though ineffectual warfare against the vermin which swarmed in myriads, only less in number than those in the cabin.
>
> The next day we had the whole ship thoroughly scrubbed and soaked with lye and water, which has made it much cleaner and in some degree diminished the vermin. Luckily now we are, owing to a happy thought, quite comfortable. We happen to be towing at the stern a small gig, one of twelve allowed for the Staff. This has all its paraphernalia inside it, so we rigged up a bed with some planks along the seats, put up the awning, and are now as luxurious as possible. The only objection against it is that the boat is towed at some distance from the stern, and it requires rather a difficult gymnastic performance to reach it.

All these and many more strenuous efforts were to be in vain so far as the rescue of Gordon was concerned. Wolseley's expedition was split into two columns: one followed the Nile on its wide eastwards loop past Berber, the other under Sir Herbert Stewart set out on a march directly across the desert southwards to Metemmeh. With this second force went the intrepid Percy Marling, again serving with the Mounted Infantry, and in a remarkable letter he describes how they all nearly came to grief at the end of the march. On 17 January the Mahdist forces attacked them at Abu Klea wells, the Baggara horsemen and spearmen again breaking the square. Although beaten off they came on again at Abu Kru on 19 January, and Marling reveals what a shattering experience all this was for the British troops before they reached the Nile, only to hear of Gordon's death on 26 January.

On board steamer on the Nile near Gubat, 8 miles the Khartoum side of Shendy, 90 miles from Khartoum January 28th 1885, Tuesday, 11 a.m.

My dearest Father,
I hope the two letters I sent off three days ago to tell you of my safety will have reached you. I also sent you a telegram but as it had to go nearly 200 miles by camel first, the odds are rather against your getting it. We had an awful week of it, three fights in five days, the first two desperate ones, the last quite nasty enough for the most bloodthirsty amongst us. Out of a total of 1,700 that left Gakdul we have lost 305 killed and wounded. As I told you we got near Abu Klea wells about 1 p.m. on Friday, January 16th and found the niggers in force about 56 miles the Gakdul side of the wells. We made a *zareba* and encamped for that night, and were shot at the whole night through, so with that and constant alarm and having to stand to our arms for two hours before dawn you may imagine we get precious little sleep; three men, some horses and several camels were hit.

Just as we were trying to get a little breakfast the order came to move off, poor Gough our CO was hit in the head, fortunately by a spent bullet. We advanced for about 1½ miles in square, the enemy slowly retreating in front of us with a lot of flags, and we could see another large force move to our left but out of shot. All the hills round were lined with their sharpshooters who gave us a lot of trouble. A message came in from our scouts to say that the niggers had all gone, we could only see their flags sticking as we thought in the ground, when suddenly as though out of the ground about 3,000 niggers jumped up and rushed on the square. Our skirmishers prevented us firing at first, and they only got back to the square about 250 yards in front of the niggers, who came on to the left front where the MI [Mounted Infantry] were, but we gave them such a warm reception that they wheeled off to where the heavy cavalry stood. These were very unsteady and fired wildly, and when the niggers came close up they gave, and the niggers broke into the square, right on to the rear rank of the front face.

I had to turn my rear rank about, so that our men were fighting back to back, shooting in front and sticking behind. For about 10 minutes it was touch and go, but we beat them off and every nigger who got inside was killed. Our loss was very heavy, 9 officers and 66 men killed, 9 officers and 72 men wounded. I was all but shot by one of our sergeants who put his rifle over my shoulder and fired bang off close to my right ear. By the time we got the square reformed it was 3 p.m., when we advanced. I was sent out in front in command of the skirmishers. Poor old Moses, my pony, was shot dead under the general at the very beginning.

We pushed on another four miles and got to the wells of Abu Klea just at sunset. They were just a collection of about 20 holes (some of them choked up) in the sand, from about 8 to 20 feet deep, with about a foot of the dirtiest, filthiest water at the bottom. I should think I drank a bucket of it all the same. One's work for the day was not over yet, as at 8 p.m. I had to start back with 300 men to bring up our 8,000 camels, stores, wounded, etc., from the *zareba* six miles back. I don't think I ever felt so dead beat, we had had nothing to eat all day, and next to no sleep the night before. We got back to the *zareba* about midnight and I got a mouthful of grub and cup of tea, and started to load up. The men were at it all night and we started back for the wells about 7 a.m., each man leading three camels behind his own, and the native drivers about 10 each, besides this we had some wounded.

The column was about a mile long with an advance guard the same, if only 100 niggers had come they would have played Old Harry with the lot of us. I never knew such a long 6 miles. We repassed the battlefield on our right, where our dead were still lying unburied, and came across a lot of wounded niggers whom we shot at once. I got some breakfast and lunch, and all started again at 3.30 p.m. for the Nile, leaving 100 of the 35th Regiment to hold the wells and protect our wounded. We had to leave all our dead on the field, amongst them old Burnaby, who was killed trying to rally the heavies. Some of the wounds were ghastly, men literally nearly cut to ribbons. We marched the whole night without intermission till 9 a.m. the following morning, one of the worst nights I ever had, I was continually falling asleep on my camel. Everything got mixed up, commissariat, mounted infantry, artillery, Guards and Marines, and the whole time of the rearguard was occupied in picking up men who had fallen off their camels asleep. One man in the Guards was lost altogether and strayed into Metemmeh and was killed.

Our way was through a lot of dense scrub which made it worse.

I should think that night march we lost nearly 800 camels. Morning found us about five miles from the river, with dense masses of the enemy all along our front and flanks, and our supply of water running short. We made a laager with all the camels tied down in the centre, and a small parapet of the saddles and biscuit boxes outside. The niggers started shooting at once and hit no end of our men. I had three of my own men hit in a very short time, one a Lance-Corporal, Howard by name, almost as I was speaking to him, and the other two (one is since dead) just in front of me. Poor Herbert Stewart, the General, was badly wounded in the groin about midday, I went up to say good-bye to him and he shook hands and wished me luck, but he evidently thought it was nearly all up. Poor Sankey Herbert, his private secretary, was shot dead too, also Cameron the correspondent.

However I was so utterly tired out that in spite of the firing I lay down behind a camel and fell fast asleep for nearly an hour. About 2 p.m. we got the welcome order to form up outside in square to force our way to the water. It was a regular forlorn hope but our only chance. We moved off, some 1,300 men with about 20 camels in the centre. We marched oh so slowly, constantly moving to the right or left to get open ground and stopping altogether to keep the square together. I should think we took two hours to do as many miles. All this time the niggers were potting at us as hard as ever. The Guards and Marines formed the front force, and the Mounted Infantry the left. Every minute the firing was getting hotter and hotter, and our men were falling fast every second. Hore and I were together in the left-front corner when a bullet came right between us and hit a marine in front of us in the head, killing him dead.

At last, just as it was getting sunset, the niggers charged in two columns. I don't think I ever felt so glad as when I saw their flags appear over the crest of the hill, bearing down on us. They came straight on to our left face and left front, but not one of them got within 40 yards of the square. It was now we began to feel the want of a general, as Sir Charles Wilson, RE, who was the senior officer, knows nothing of drill and is besides an awful old woman, and Boscawen, a Lieut.-Colonel in the Guards, though a very good fellow has very little experience and was utterly unfit to take the command, in what really was a most difficult and dangerous position. After we had repulsed the niggers he actually wanted to march the front face of the square away to water in the river two miles off, and the other three sides to go back to the *zareba*, although the enemy's cavalry were threatening us some 500 yards to the rear. The front face had actually marched off 100 yards from the remainder, but everyone shouted 'Halt', and Johnny Campbell went and expostulated with old Wilson, and used such awful language that it was stopped and we all went on together.

I shall never forget when we got to the top of a slight rise and saw the Nile glistening below us in the dim moonlight, we reached it about 8 o'clock. I had such a drink of muddy water, ate a small piece of bully and biscuit, and as soon as the square sentries were arranged fell asleep. Our wounded had an awfully bad time of it, most of them lying on the ground without any covering at all. The doctors did all they could, but of course they had next to no appliances with them. I woke about 1 a.m. when there was a bit of an alarm, bitterly cold with my teeth chattering so I could hardly speak. Sewell, our adjutant, most kindly lent me one of his blankets, and three of us (Hore, Payne, and myself) all got under it and crouched close up to one another for warmth.

Up at daybreak and occupied a village on high ground about 4 miles from Metemmeh, there we left our wounded and 100 men of the Sussex Regiment, and started back to the *zareba* to fetch the rest of our wounded and all the camels; on our way we saw a lot of niggers above Metemmeh, and had a good deal of shooting at them. We got to the *zareba* about noon and found to our great relief that it was alright. Poor fellows, they gave us such a cheer when we arrived. We started back in square with the general and Hon Crutchley of the Guards on stretchers in the centre, and all the camels in a bunch on our right rear. However the enemy did not venture to attack us and we got back to our village just before dark, and started to water the camels at once. They had been 8 days without water and nearly 4 without food, and in that time had marched close on 80 miles carrying heavy loads.

That night we got our first square meal for I don't know how long, and I had a bit of a wash, the first time I had touched water since we left Gakdul nearly a week before, except when four of us sponged our faces over at Abu Klea, out of the lid of my canteen, which I gave to my camel to drink afterwards. Reveille at 4 a.m. and paraded in the dark to attack Metemmeh but found it too strong, all the houses loopholed and full of sharpshooters and two big guns. The whole business too was disgracefully mismanaged, so we had to give it up with a loss on our side of one killed and 11 wounded. We have only three small guns with us and next to no ammunition for them, and one Gatling which is of course no good for bombarding.

Whilst we were in front of Metemmeh four of Gordon's steamers appeared most opportunely, they had been waiting near an island some little way off for five months, expecting us, and hearing the firing came down. We got back to our village and moved down here to be close to the water. That night I was on outlying picquet so had a pretty wakeful night of it, it was bitterly cold too. Next day we were occupied in entrenching ourselves, and in the evening I had a bathe, not at all before I wanted it, and shaved off my nine days' beard. You would scarcely have recognised me, I was such a dirty-looking scarecrow. Next day I was on fatigue from 6 a.m. till one, but was so seedy I had to lie down about noon. At dark we sent back a convoy to Gakdul of 1,000 camels, with about 300 men, with which I was to have gone but the doctor said I was to remain here; I could hardly stand, I had such frightful pains in my stomach, our medic said I had probably got a lot of mud and sand in my tum–tum caused by the bad water, and dosed me accordingly. However I am quite fit again now.

We have heard nothing of the convoy since it left over a week ago, and in fact have not had any communication with the outer world since we left Korti three weeks ago. As to what is going on four miles anywhere away from this we are as ignorant as unborn babes, our last newspaper is nearly two months old, I think December 3rd is the last one we have. At present we are sitting here watching the niggers in Metemmeh just like two cats. Two of Gordon's steamers have gone back to Metemmeh and Sir Charles Wilson with them and 20 men of the Sussex Regiment. Now that poor Stewart is wounded we want a lead badly, I only wish Wolseley or Buller were up here. Don't imagine this has been written all at once, I began two days ago and go on with it at odd times whenever I have a moment to spare.

At present I am writing by moonlight; you can easily read print by it, it is so clear. There will be very few things soon I shan't have turned my hand to, I am in charge of one of Gordon's steamers and eight boats we have captured from the niggers, besides 150 of Gordon's troops, Bashibazouks, Turks and Egyptians, about the most finished collection of scoundrels I have seen. I'm going to bed now, save the mark, on the ground five yards from the water, *sub Jove frigido*, so good night, I can hear the tom-toms still going in Metemmeh.

Percy Marling penned those closing words on 30 January 1885, and spent the next day chopping more wood for the steamer's boilers in preparation for an expedition upstream on the Nile. By the time he resumed his running letter on 1 February this plan had to be abandoned because of disastrous news. Marling could no longer complain of not knowing what was happening, and the realities of the British position sparked off some heart-searching and reflection:

Everything is knocked on the head; this morning Stuart-Wortley, who had been sent up to Khartoum with Sir Charles Wilson a week ago, reappeared in a small boat with the news that

Letter from Lt. P. S. Marling, 3/60th Rifles, to his father, reporting the fall of Khartoum and uncertainty as to General Gordon's fate.

Khartoum had fallen about four days ago and was in the hands of the Mahdi. Both steamers were wrecked coming down from Khartoum. They got up to Tuti Island and found it in the possession of the enemy, and also saw that the Egyptian flag was not flying on the top of Government House. The niggers fired rifles and guns at them, the steamers had to return. Between here and Khartoum there is a cataract, almost impossible at this time of year, one steamer was wrecked at the top and the other at the bottom. Sir Charles Wilson, two other officers, and 20 men of the 35th Regiment and 200 of Gordon's troops are now on an island about 35 miles from here, in great straits. We have only two steamers left here and one of them is going up to try and get them off.

Altogether things are looking about as bad as they can. We cannot find out for certain if Gordon is alive or not. We had one bit of luck yesterday, our convoy arrived from Gakdul with some more grub and lots of ammunition. Last night for the first time for over a week I went to bed without feeling hungry. For the whole of the last week I have felt as empty as possible, as there was literally not enough to eat. In England people can have no idea of what an awfully hard time we have had up here. In our march from Gakdul which took eight days we did not get 16 hours' sleep, 3 pints of water per day, and for the last four days next to nothing to eat, besides continual fighting.

I have looked death in the face pretty often now, but I don't think I ever realised how near it was till these last three weeks. I'm afraid I am usually rather thoughtless about serious matters, but it does make one think when you see your friends, and men one has been speaking with but a second before, shot or stabbed down by one's very side. As long as I live I shall never forget those five awful days from Abu Klea to here. When the square moved out for the second fight I honestly did not think we should come back, but it was our only chance as we were bound to get the water that night. Our camels had been 8 days without water and nearly 4 without food, and the 19th Hussars' ponies 56 hours without a single drop. During the week I only took my boots off once and that for two hours in the middle of Abu Klea wells after the first battle.

Poor old Gordon, after holding his own so gallantly all these months, to be beaten just as help was literally within a few yards of him, it does seem so sad. They say, but of course nothing is certain yet, that one of his Egyptian pashas who commanded the Sudanese troops treacherously opened the gates of the town to the Mahdi by night, and let in the enemy. We are sending back a convoy of sick and wounded tonight to Korti, and I shall send this by them. Smith has been busy building me a hut of *dhurra* stalks the last two days. One of my own men, Wareham, died from the effects of his wound, I buried him myself with a party of ten men and read as much of the burial service as I could over him, by the light of the lantern.

Everyone here is literally in rags, both officers and men, and the latters' boots are in the most shameful state. I enclose you some of Gordon's paper money that he issued in Khartoum, it is worth 20 piastres, 5 piastres go to a shilling. Please keep this letter, but whatever you do do *not* send it to the papers. I hope it will reach you, I only wish I could come with it. Heaven knows when and how this business will end. Goodbye now my dear, dear Father, best love to the mother and the boys.

Other letters paint the same picture of extreme discomfort and danger. Corporal F. H. Middleton writes to his brother in Egypt about Abu Klea; he was serving in one of the camel regiments, promoted to sergeant for what he did, and as darkness was falling when he wrote on 1 February 1885 he says 'really must abbreviate, so please excuse'. This is his pithy cameo of Abu Klea:

Forced enemy to charge, our scouts rather late getting in square, should have gone round to rear but forced their way in the front face, nearly humbugged the whole arrangement. Cavalry on left face of square, Horse Guards, etc., made awkward infantrymen, all their officers got killed, and men were nearly having mincemeat made of the lot of us. Thanks to B Company camels, to Mr. Burleigh [*Daily Telegraph*] and to Lord Beresford, or we should all have been members of the large majority by now. The B Company camels got outside square, and having been killed formed a nice defence against enemy's cavalry. Mr. Burleigh went outside square by himself and cheered the men on. Lord Beresford took Gardner gun and turned that organ straight down face of square. After scrimmage was over we had plenty to do. Frightful sight after smoke cleared away. Wounded men, dead men, dead camels, all of a heap. After clearing all wounded marched into wells, stayed all night.

Among the heavy cavalry that buckled at Abu Klea was Lieutenant Charles Hibbert of the 2nd Dragoon Guards, the Queen's Bays. He survived that trauma and had better things to say of the action at Abu Kru on 19 January, and its aftermath.

Our squadron leader was wounded at the commencement and my captain was in the laager disabled by gout, so I was the senior

"TOO LATE!"

Telegram, Thursday Morning, Feb. 5.—"Khartoum taken by the MAHDI. General GORDON's fate uncertain."

Early reports seemed to say that Gordon was safe at Khartoum, but the relieving columns failed to reach him in time, and Gordon had been killed by the dervishes.

officer in the squadron [Blues and Bays]. At last the enemy charged the left and front faces of the square, but not one of them got within 150 yards. We then marched down to the river and drank it nearly dry out of our helmets. Under arms all night in the bitter cold and nothing to eat. Next morning half the force went to bring up the camels, and the rest of us fortified the village. I saw a cow running about, so took a rifle and shot it and we made some stew, the first thing any of us had, barring a few bits of biscuits, since the previous Friday morning. Next day we went out to reconnoitre Metemmeh. It is a big sand town a mile long and all loopholed. As we advanced they fired on us with three guns, but did very little damage.

Suddenly we saw the Khedival flags of some steamers coming down the river. They came right abreast of us and landed, and it turned out to be Gordon's four steamers which had been on the look-out for us ever since September. We shelled the town a bit and then retired, and established ourselves strongly on the river. We have indeed had a very rough week of it. In the heavy division we lost 25 per cent killed and wounded. The bravery of the enemy is simply wonderful, and the worst of it is they are such good shots, people say as good as the Boers. We hope Buller will arrive to take command in a day or two, when all will go well. People of experience say it has been about the hardest job of modern days, and only men could have stood it.

Hibbert's laconic words sum up the Sudan conflict very well, but it was by no means the end of the story. If Gordon's death was a source of perturbation in domestic and imperial politics, it also struck a resonant chord in the nation's emotions. The exact circumstances of how he died are difficult to reconstruct. In order to sustain British aspirations in the Sudan, it was turned into the myth of a martyr's end, with Gordon in white offering no resistance as he was speared by Mahdist soldiers. It is more likely he was shot, possibly while actively defending himself. Doubts were present from the first news of the fall of Khartoum and the uncertain fate of Gordon. *Punch* at once published a sketch captioned 'At Last!' with Gordon welcoming the British expedition. The following week (on 14 February 1885) *Punch* had to print the real version as Victory shielded her eyes from the sight of dervish warriors dashing into Khartoum: 'Too Late!'

EIGHT

'It Looked As If the Whole of Africa Was Coming at Us':

THE MAHDI AND THE KHALIFA, 1885–98

More fighting was to take place before the British army finally relinquished its attempt to reach Khartoum and turned its back on the Sudan. This was due to the way Wolseley had divided his forces. As we have seen, he went with the main expedition upstream along the Nile, reaching Korti on 26 December 1884. There he sent Stewart's 'desert column' on a direct route to Metemmeh, cutting across the great loop of the Nile's course, so as to make a rendezvous with Gordon's river steamers. It was this force we found taking the wells at Gakdul without opposition, but running into serious conflict at the wells of Abu Klea, and eventually failing to reach Khartoum in time to save Gordon. The letters have shown how arduous an experience it was for those men, who then had to march back across the same 200 miles of desert, returning to Korti on 7 March 1885.

While this was happening, the main section of Wolseley's army had left Korti in December to follow a longer and slower route along the Nile. The 'river column' commanded by Major-General W. Earle made steady progress with its flotillas of river boats and marching columns. They met little opposition, but when news of Gordon's death reached them it brought them to a halt for a few days. Continuing to advance southwards, they discovered that the jubilant Mahdists were confronting them at Kirbekan with the evident intention of bringing Earle to battle. In the engagement that came on 10 February the British fought with greater tactical success than elsewhere during the Sudan campaign, though Earle himself was killed. An eye-witness account of Kirbekan, which the newspapers were quick to hail as 'a brilliant action', appears in a captain's letter; he served with the ubiquitous Black Watch.

There was a general advance up river on the 9th of February and on that evening we bivouacked about a mile and a half from the enemy's position, with the 38th, Egyptian Camel Scouts, and the Hussars. I was on outpost duty, and could see plainly many men dressed in white moving about among the hills on the left bank of the river in our front. They were evidently in a very strong position, and they exchanged a few shots with our Hussar Scouts. On the morning of the 10th we were roused at 5 a.m. and our regiment, dressed in the kilt, had breakfast and paraded with the 38th. At 7 a.m. we advanced in column of half battalion, the 38th leading, and wound our way through the rocky ground until we gained the rear of the left of the enemy's position. We could see some of the enemy crowning the ridges as we passed round his left flank, but he took no notice of us.

As we advanced along the rear of the high position which he has taken among the rocks, a fire from their Remingtons was directed on our columns. Nevertheless, we advanced steadily till we reached the front, when the 38th were wheeled to the left. The 42nd [Black Watch] went a little farther, and General Earle came and told Colonel Bayly to send two companies to occupy the high rocks facing the river. A Company, under my command, and C Company advanced by sections. We saw no enemy between us and the river, but a few unarmed men were running up the banks. The General then came up to me and said he was afraid they had given us the slip on this side.

Earle then made some sensible readjustments to his plan of attack, helped by the news that the British cavalry had overrun the Sudanese camp, capturing many banners and cattle. He redeployed the two companies of Black Watch, with a third reserve company, and sent them to extend the line held by the 38th, who were suffering hot rifle fire, right down to the water's edge.

We formed and advanced in line over about 300 yards of open ground, the three companies marching as steadily as if on parade, notwithstanding the heavy fire directed on us. Here we lost three or four men. When we gained the left of the 38th the General came up and ordered my company and C Company to advance up the river and enfilade the enemy. We quickly obeyed and in a short time were busy at the enemy, and got him fairly in flank. Colour-Sergeant Tweedie killed six of the enemy one after the other. After we had made the rebels keep their heads very low indeed, the 'cease firing' sounded, and A, C, E and one company of the 38th were ordered to form line on the river bank preparatory to charging the position. Just as we received the word

'Charge!', had gained the top of the bank and were about to rush, the enemy charged out with their flags and spears right down towards B Company, under Lord Alexander Kennedy; but they were nearly all shot dead, and the others were shot as they tried to swim the river.

When we gained our former station on the rocks it was evident the enemy were on the move. We saw them charging about from rock to rock, and bowled them over as they tried to escape to the river. One, quite white, was killed as he tried to cross the river, he must have been a European. Then a rush was made up a gully by a number of the enemy, who sought to escape by the rear, and we poured volley after volley into them, and those who escaped our fire were shot by Marriott's Egyptian Camel Corps higher up the valley, but not before they killed two of the Egyptians, who fought very well. We now had fairly driven the enemy out of his well-chosen and very strong position, and had time to look about us. To my sorrow I heard that General Earle had been killed, and Colonel Coveny of ours was also dead. I saw Colonel Wauchope was wounded in the shoulder, and Lieutenant Kennedy in the side; our loss was 1 officer and 4 men killed, 2 officers and 15 men wounded [i.e. in the Black Watch].

It was tragic that Earle should be killed after leading such a successful operation, with so few casualties, and according to the letter-writer it happened quite fortuitously after the Mahdist left position was captured.

The rebels had made a stone house with loopholes and a thatched roof in a hollow of their position. Our men killed several men coming out of this house, and had seen others enter. The roof of the house was on fire, and I believe ammunition was exploding inside. Some of my men told the General some rebels were inside, but he advanced to the house when he was immediately shot through the head from a loophole, and the man who shot him threw his Remington out of the hole. The General fell quite dead. In the evening I went over the captured position, and I counted 105 dead bodies of the enemy. The 42nd fought with coolness and gallantry throughout this severe action, which commenced at 8 a.m. and ended at 11.40 a.m., and were commanded by our veteran Colonel Green.

We had a most determined enemy against us. They were excellent shots, had Remingtons, and plenty of ammunition, and were in a very strong position. Major Slade was with my company during most of the day, and was as usual foremost in the fray, and killed a man with his sword. He fought with us at Teb and Tamai, and when the fight began yesterday he stuck one of our red hackles in his helmet and directed the movements of the enfilading party. The position on the high hill was carried by the 38th at 12.50 noon, and from our position I could see the enemy fire till the 38th went close up to them. They then threw themselves on to the bayonets, spear in hand, fighting till the last. We were all sorry to hear the 38th lost their colonel, Eyre; I understand their loss was 1 officer killed and 2 wounded, 3 men killed, 21 wounded. I consider the total loss of the enemy was about 1,200 including about 250 killed in the position and in the river [i.e. where the Black Watch was engaged].

Kirbekan, well handled though it was, achieved very little because on 24 February the river column also received orders to pull back to Korti, as part of the British withdrawal to Egypt. While these various abortive operations were happening along the Nile, however, yet another British force (also under Wolseley's over-all command) had been fighting from Suakin on the Red Sea. It was a return to familiar ground for its leader, Major-General Sir Gerald Graham, whose memories of Teb and Tamai, with all the dangers and bloodshed of the previous year, must have been fresh in his mind. Nor was he to be disappointed in 1885. The plan, optimistic in the extreme, was that Graham's column should build a railway from Suakin to Berber, the nearest point on the Nile, over a distance of just under 300 miles. This time his command included Indian troops and even some Australian volunteers, supplementing the Canadian boatmen who helped Wolseley on the Nile in a show of imperial solidarity. Graham planned to pitch his base camp at Hasheen, a short day's march inland from the port.

The advance inland began on 20 March 1885, when the troops marched from Suakin in the familiar square formation. This precaution was forced on them because Graham knew that Uthman Digna, his old adversary, was not far away with an armed host. Early on the morning of 22 March one of his subordinates, General McNeill, set out from Suakin to construct a series of fortified redoubts as well as camps of the usual *zareba* type, protected by a fence of thorn trees, but his troops were surprised by the Mahdists in a savage attack. This is known as the battle of Tofrek and, given the general paucity of letters from the Sudan campaigns, we are fortunate to have a splendid account of it written by a corporal of the Royal Engineers. Stylistically and as a piece of reporting Frederick Warde Bennett's letter deserves quoting in full: he had served in the Egyptian war with 24th Field Company, RE, and wrote from Hasheen on 27 March 1885. Bennett addressed the letter to his sister and brother-in-law and friends, who lived at Deddington in Oxfordshire.

I know you will be glad to hear from me after what has happened here. We had a splendid voyage out, stayed at Port Said to coal, and had to wait for orders at Suez. After leaving there we had about 700 miles to go up the Red Sea. I kept a good look-out, but did not see any chariot wheels knocking about. We arrived at Suakin on the 6th of March, a very quick voyage considering our stoppages, and that we were only allowed to go five miles an hour through the Canal. There is more water than when I was through it last time, and great improvements along the banks. All English vessels homeward bound were stopped to allow the Transports to get along, so we had lots of cheering from them. I did not cheer much myself going out, but thought if all's well, and I return home safely again, my lung powers will not be wanting. We commenced disembarking as soon as we arrived at Suakin, and had the ship cleared by dinner-time next day, and then marched about four miles into the desert, which is nothing but sand, and pitched camp.

We have the shipping and town behind us, and high hills all along our front, about six miles away. Signs were not wanting to show that we should not remain idle long, for the first night our gunboats opened fire and all stood to arms, expecting an attack, but it was no go. Things went on like this for a week or so. We kept constantly hearing of our scouts and advanced picquets having a dash at them, and a sentry or two being dropped upon and butchered, till last Thursday[1] General Graham ordered an advance to the hills on the following morning, and away we started at 4 a.m. A good battle was fought, but it did not fall to our lot to fire a shot, it was the cavalry and artillery's day.[2] It looked like once being made very warm for us, and we had only just time to get a couple of the artillery guns into a small redoubt that we had been making on the two hills, when they poured shot into the enemy, every shot except the first telling; and we could see the rebels leap into the air and fall, never to rise again. The position gained, 'Home' was the next order.

We left one regiment and a part of the 17th Company, RE, to garrison the place. Great disappointment was felt amongst the infantry and our people that we had not a chance to have an exchange, Martini v Remington, but we hoped for better luck

1. 19 March 1885.
2. 20 March 1885.

next time. The next day we heard that another move would be made on Sunday[3], and on that day nearly every available man in camp was out, all looking remarkably smart. The same old grin was on the face of the Bengalis, as at the last affair[4] [20 March]. No one could imagine for a moment that this day would end so disastrously for the 24th Company, RE. A great many of our dearest friends fell in the battle, including our Sergeant-Major, one of the best men I ever wish to know. Altogether 18 of our Company were killed. No Company of Engineers has lost so many since the Crimea, and may God grant that no other will share the same fate.

Many of the poor fellows were killed while running to get their arms, they being at work cutting down trees, bush, etc., when the alarm was given, and however the rest reached the square will ever remain a mystery. I will not attempt to give you much of a description of the affair, for it baffles anything I could ever imagine. Our company was divided into four sections; two were out working as I have stated, and the other two were inside the *zareba* which was nearly finished. A few of the mess had commenced dinner thinking all was right, no warning was given and what few cavalry we had were still out, when all of a sudden a terrible yell was heard and kept up, and in another minute our camels and horses were being forced into the square. All was confusion for a few seconds, men tumbling over one another, almost fighting for their arms.

Soon squares were formed and eventually one square, and up went a good British cheer. The first thing was to kill all the camels of our own, as this was the only possible chance of saving ourselves. The Gardner guns dare not fire for fear of killing our own people. After another lapse of a few seconds to allow all to get back that could, we opened fire on all sides, and what followed will never be forgotten by anyone present. On came those brave rebels, time after time, only to meet certain death, and after two hours' hard fighting, hundreds of them were lying dead close up to the *zareba*, and I believe one or two were actually killed inside. Nothing was done that night, but the next morning we collected our dead and buried them. I had a very unpleasant task to perform, viz. to sew them up in blankets just as they fell. Horses and ropes were then brought out and the enemy's dead were all dragged together, and burned and buried. It is not all clean yet, so you can imagine what it's like to have to stop here; 1,500 dead bodies were counted just round the *zareba*, besides the number that were 'potted' in the bushes.

3. 22 March 1885.
4. Among the Indian Contingent was the 17th Bengal Infantry.

However I escaped I don't know, but I was fortunate enough to be inside the *zareba* when the alarm was given, and so owe my life, perhaps, to that cause. A great many of our men tried to escape in the bush when they found their retreat cut off, but were brutally stabbed. After that was seen, very few of the enemy's wounded stood much chance. These Arabs trust to the spear, assegai, and two-edged sword, which they used with both hands. One of our company cut a rebel clean in two with one of these swords. He's a big, powerful fellow called 'Knobbler', and having stabbed the rebel the sword fell from his grasp. 'Knobbler' picks it up, the rebel makes an attempt to rise again, with the result I have just mentioned. The General moved about quite calm, and our Colonel was on his knee firing buckshot from a double breech-loader during the battle. He has got the VC already, and I expect to see his name prominently over this affair. Tamai is our next place, and I believe Monday or Tuesday will settle that, and then I believe we retire into summer quarters and wait for the winter. With fond love to all, believe me, your loving brother, Fred Warde Bennett.

P.S. We are not short of Tobacco this time, the Commissariat supply us with it at 1s. and 1s. 4d. per pound.

After Tofrek the course of events ran differently from the soldiers' expectation. On 2 April part of the force pushed on to Tamai and finding it deserted Graham simply burnt it, as he had done once before in 1884. Military activities then came to an end, orders to evacuate the Sudan were carried out by the middle of May; stubbornly, an armed presence was kept at the port of Suakin. Not long afterwards, on 22 June 1885, the Mahdi died at Omdurman on the left bank of the Nile, immediately downstream of Khartoum. His passing brought no interruption to the militant fervour of the Mahdia, which continued to be a dominating force in the politics of the region down to the last year of the nineteenth century. Already before the death of Gordon the Mahdi had named his successor, the Khalifa Abdullahi, an early and unswerving supporter. The Khalifa commanded the Black Flag *raya* or division of the Mahdist army, composed mostly of Baggara horsemen but later including most of the *jihadiyya* (riflemen) and artillery. He had also taken a daughter of the Mahdi as one of his wives. The Khalifa's name was to become as ominously familiar in British political and military circles as that of the Mahdi.

Throughout the later 1880s intermittent fighting flared in the borderlands between Egypt and the Sudan. At first all went in favour of the Khalifa, but from about 1889 the tide began to turn. In August of that year his army under Abdal Rahman al-Najumi was routed with the loss of many generals at Toski, just within the Egyptian boundary, and the Khalifa's long-standing threat to invade Egypt and take Cairo itself lost its credibility. He was suffering other losses from British pressures at Suakin, and from a third campaign he was waging against the Coptic Christians in Ethiopia. The Sudan was afflicted with a Biblical succession of famine and plagues of locusts and mice. Gradually the balance of strength began to slip away from the Mahdist state, while the Egyptian army under a new and more able set of British commanders gained fresh confidence. Positive arguments for a renewed attack on the Khalifa were also being urged in Britain. Vengeance for the defeats inflicted before and after the death of Gordon was one of them. Humanitarian feelings were aroused by propagandist accounts of Sudanese repression and cruelty, as in Alfred Milner's book *England in Egypt*. Even more to the point, the Conservative ministry that displaced the Liberals in 1895 was concerned about French claims to territory in the Sudan. This fear was well justified and it was decided to take action against the Khalifa so as to forestall France. Other political factors were also at work: they might not have moved Gladstone, who had resigned as Prime Minister in 1894, but Lord Salisbury was very willing to respond to them.

Preparations began in 1896 with the requisitioning of Thomas Cook's pleasure steamers on the lower Nile. An army of 10,000 Egyptian soldiers moved to the Sudanese border under the command of Major-General Sir Herbert Kitchener, whose name became even more familiar to the world at large than Wolseley's was in his day. Kitchener was a ruthless and efficient soldier who epitomises the aggressiveness of military imperialism, both for what he was to do in the Sudan and for his share in the war against the Boers in South Africa between 1899 and 1902. He also had at his disposal more powerful and destructive forms of armament, notably in the Maxim machine-gun and heavier lyddite shells for his artillery. Nor did Kitchener intend to make undue haste in the business of defeating the Khalifa. Gradually and with great care he followed the Nile upstream, his flotilla of river gunboats negotiating the succession of five cataracts that break the Nile's flow between Aswan and Berber. Hundreds of smaller boats had to do the same, carrying huge supplies of food, forage, ammunition, medical supplies and the rest of an army's everyday needs. Kitchener's advance was a masterpiece of logistical planning.

Serious opposition did not materialise until the early months of 1898. By then Kitchener was Sirdar in command of an Anglo-Egyptian army composed of one brigade of British regulars and three brigades of Egyptians and Sudanese troops. At the beginning of April the newspapers started reporting the first clash of arms. On 6 April the Sirdar's columns advanced eight miles after a reconnoitring force under General Hunter was nearly outflanked and surrounded by the Mahdists; danger was averted by the fire of Maxim batteries and the Egyptian cavalry, which twice charged the enemy – a token of the new order of things. Not far ahead lay the entrenched position of a large body of dervishes, reputed to be 16,000 strong, commanded by the Amir Mahmud was Ahmad, one of the most devoted but least competent of the Khalifa's generals. On the evening of 7 April Kitchener struck camp and marched to within five miles of Mahmud's entrenchments, then bivouacked for a short while. At one in the morning he advanced again until he was within 500 yards of the Sudanese *zareba*.

At 6 a.m. on Good Friday, 8 April 1898, the battle of the Atbara began with the Sirdar's artillery blasting its gunfire from both flanks, enfilading the *zareba* with deadly effect. The Maxims then opened up, first forcing the groups of enemy horsemen out of the scrub in which they were sheltering, and later spraying their bullets into the trenches. At 7.30 the infantry were ordered to rush the trenches, and although the Sudanese held their own fire until the Anglo-Egyptians came in close range they were quite soon driven back to the river. Headlines at home proclaimed this 'Great Battle in the Soudan. British Victory. Three thousand Killed', in blatant self-satisfaction at a successful move to avenge Gordon. The usual chilling calculation of casualties showed how at the Atbara the Sudanese lost during the battle and in the cavalry pursuit following not less than 3,000 men killed. Against that the Sirdar's roll was seventy-four killed and 453 wounded. Ten guns were captured, while a hundred banners, those symbols of Mahdist allegiance and rank, were carried away as trophies: several may be seen on display in the museums of Highland regiments who fought at the Atbara.[5] On 13 April the Sirdar entered Berber at the head of a victory parade, the captured Amir Mahmud being pushed along in the humiliation of chains and halter, in parody of a Roman triumph.

The ordinary soldier's experience of battle at the Atbara is well

5. Douglas Johnson, 'A note on Mahdist flags', *Soldiers of the Queen*, volume IV, No. 14, pages 7–15.

"WELL DONE, ALL!"

ATBARA, APRIL 8, 1898

Kitchener after his victory over the Mahdists at the Atbara in April 1898,
his face set towards the greater confrontation at Omdurman later in the year.

portrayed by a sergeant of the Seaforth Highlanders. In a letter written by Tom Christian to his brother (who lived at Wheatley near Oxford) we can sense the confident mood that permeated the Sirdar's fighting men.

To continue from my last letter, we left Assouan on 3rd March, took boats till we got to a cataract, then marched, or rode on camels (in kilts) for 14 or 16 miles at night, falling over rocks and down ditches, half asleep. Train from Wady Halfa across the Nubian Desert to railhead, about 70 miles above Abu Hamed; boats to Kenur Camp which was reached on the 16th. Stayed at Kenur till Sunday morning, 20th, when we marched to meet Mahmud. He retreated along the north bank of the Atbara; we followed day by day, to Hudi, where there was a night alarm, and a private of ours ran on another man's bayonet (our first casualty). On to Ras Hudi, 21st March, stayed there till 4th April, then to Adabar. On 6th to Umbedia, and next day, Thursday, marched at night to attack Mahmud, who had been reinforced by Ali Digna [Uthman's brother], and lots of spearmen. Each brigade slept in a square – one British, one Egyptian, two Soudanese. The latter are splendid-looking men, 5 ft 10 in to 6 ft high, and quite anxious to fight the Dervishes, who have carried off their relations into slavery. We fortified all our camps by making a *zareba* of thorn bushes, etc., 5 ft high and 7 ft thick, with the back resting on the Atbara, to ensure plenty of water for the animals, for we had hundreds of camels, mules, horses and donkeys. We laid down, April 7, with fixed bayonets and all our clothes and belts on, only allowed to take off our helmets. One section of 25 men of each company stood up two hours at a time, besides two sentries close up to the hedge with loaded rifles; our *zareba* was about two miles long.

Sleep was almost impossible, for the howling of dogs and hyenas over dead camels. We (the British Brigade) had circled round in the desert and encamped on left of Mahmud's position. Soudanese on right, Egyptians in centre, and another Egyptian Brigade over the river to cut off the retreat. Well, to come to the Good Friday fight. Spies had told our General the enemy had pits, trenches, wire and everything up to explosive bullets for our reception; that riflemen stayed in the pits and fired up in the air as long as they heard bullets firing near them. We advanced in this way: Camerons in line, front rank firing as hard as possible; near rank with blankets in hand, to pull holes in the *zareba*; Lincolns, Seaforths and Warwicks in column to rush through the holes and go for everything in front till they reached the river. The Artillery and machine guns gave them 1¾ hours' shells as hard as they could load and fire. Then we went up the sloping, gravelly ground, with bullets glancing off in all directions, but mostly overhead, for they never thought we'd have cheek enough to come close in ten minutes – which we thought years!

When we reached the *zareba* we found the Camerons firing for all they were worth, and men falling all round us. Then we rushed through, and the Dervishes made a feeble stand and after staring in amazement bolted for the river, everyone mixed up in a mob after them; but we found in the pits men were chained to logs and were firing in our rear, so lots of our fellows went back and bayoneted them all, for most of the killed were shot from behind. When we who did go on reached the river bank, which was 20 feet high, we found thousands flying across the dry, sandy bed to the other side, but not 20 in 100 reached it, for 6,000 rifles were firing after them as quick as possible. 'Cease fire!' was sounded, and we came back to get a few trophies, but the camel drivers had lifted them all, except some spears. Mahmud was found in a pit, given up by a Soudanese woman who was captured during one of the Dervishes' raids, and her brother was fighting in one of the Soudanese regiments. The two officers in my company were put out of action, Captain Baillie shot in the knee, and Lieutenant Gore killed. One man, Devlin, died of his wounds, all in F Company.

After the fight we marched out into the desert to escape the smell of the camels, donkeys and dead Dervishes, lying thick. Coming back I saw our Colonel having his arm bandaged, and stretchers and doctors pretty busy. Twas only then I realised what I had been through. Just then I was warned to take my section, fully armed, to escort a water party down to the river, to fill bottles and camp kettles for dinner and tea. The sight in the riverbed was awful, for camp followers were stripping the best-dressed among the slain. By the swords and coats there must have been many chiefs killed. There were numbers of standards in the camp, but the reserve got most of them for our orders were to drive the enemy on and not allow them to gather in force, because then they charge with swords and spears, and it's no joke to meet them. But the boot was on the other leg this time; it was we who charged. It was as good as a circus once we got inside the *zareba*. There were two small trenches, which made some of us fall, and that did us a good turn, for the bullets were flying thick just there, and I'm sure many owed their lives to falling down; then in towards the centre there was a deep, wide trench, filled with spearmen, but they went with the mob.

We marched back at five that Good Friday evening about 10 miles; rested a day, then on again at midnight for 12½ miles; then again 18 miles to this place, Darmali, a large deserted mud-hut town on the east bank of the Nile, south of Berber. We had to clean it out a good bit, heaps of straw, rushes, bones, dead camels, etc. We are living all right now, more rations every day, for the transport is quite safe from Berber, and not under a strong escort as it was on the Atbara. We get coffee at 6 a.m., tea and biscuits at 8, dinner boiled with pumpkins and all sorts of vegetables at 12.45, tea and biscuits at 4.15, as again tea or coffee at 7; and if it turns cold at night, rum at 9. The heat is so intense in the day; if we lie down we leave a wet patch on the ground, and then at night, with all our clothes on and two blankets for three men, we wake up cold and see the moon like a frosty night; next day the sun will burn the boots on our feet.

I don't know if we'll stay here till autumn, or go back to Wadi Halfa, Aswan, or Cairo, till the Nile rises to let the gunboats get up to Khartoum. The Nile rises 25 feet at Assouan in the season, so you may guess there's a very small stream just now, but it's such a breadth! about 150 yards across, and in some places wider. You'd hardly recognise us as Highlanders, some with boots, no spats, no hose; some no kilts, wearing trews borrowed from anywhere, belts brown, buttons sand colour; nearly all with beards, for we don't shave. Will you send me some papers describing the battle, if you have any left, and an illustrated one, too, if you can? I am quite well in every respect, and eager for another fight.

Tom Christian fought again a few months later at the battle of Omdurman, where the Sudanese lost their independence through the total defeat of the Khalifa. With the Atbara behind them, the Anglo-Egyptian expedition continued their unrelenting progress along the Nile to Khartoum, passing the relics left behind by Wolseley's soldiers thirteen years earlier. By 1 September 1898, with a force of more than 20,000 men, Kitchener could see the dome of the Mahdi's tomb rising over the roofs of Omdurman. In front of the town ranged the Khalifa's army of 50,000 warriors, stretched in line for four miles across the desert. The inevitable and bloody conflict that came the next day is known to the Sudanese as Karari; indeed, the British newspapers began their reporting of events by calling it 'Kerreri', where the dervishes were determined to fight. Major Ismat Zulfo has written an excellent analysis of the battle of Omdurman, the strategy adopted by the Khalifa and his generals.[6] A plan to obstruct Kitchener's advance at the Sabaluqa gorge was abandoned because the Mahdist army could not be supplied so far

6. I. H. Zulfo, *Karari. The Sudanese account of the battle of Omdurman*, translated by Peter Clark (London: Frederick Warne, 1980).

from Omdurman, despite the advantages of the scheme which would have neutralised the British gunboats.

Zulfo also shows that a better mode of attack was suggested for Omdurman by Uthman Digna, that old adversary of the British army. He would have made a night attack on Kitchener's *zareba*, but the idea was set aside due to dissension among the generals. On the day, the Sudanese hoped to develop a three-part tactic, enticing the Anglo-Egyptians into enfilading fire from the hills, attacking them then with the Black Flag main army, following this with a separate attack in the flank. Instead on 2 September their hold on the high ground was lost at the critical time, and their timing of their manoeuvres became confused; nor did they allow for the devastating fire-power of Kitchener's men, artillery, machine-guns, and rifle. We may begin to picture what Omdurman was like for the ordinary British soldier by returning to Tom Christian of the Seaforth Highlanders. He told the story in a letter written after he had returned to Cairo with his victorious comrades, on 15 September.

To give you a short account of our last advance. We left Darmali on the 14th August, took boats to Wadi Hamed, camped till 25th, then marched by easy stages as far as Egina – built the usual *zareba*, and made preparations for a rest and tea, when in came a lot of scouts, camel corps, etc., with the news that the Khalifa was advancing. So we put on our things again, and marched out of the village to a great sandy plain, facing Omdurman, about one mile from Egina, made another *zareba*, fetched nearly all our baggage from the village, then had tea, and waited to be attacked.

About 10.45 p.m., Thursday, I was up with twelve men watching (each company doing the same two hours at a time), when firing broke out from a hill about a mile away, for a few minutes, and shortly after we were told spies had come in with word that the Khalifa was going to attack us at dawn. So we all charged our magazines seven rounds, and were ready at 3.45 a.m., Friday [2 September]. When daylight made things plain, we saw as far as sight reached the great plain covered with white jebba-clad dervishes, banners flying and drums beating – a splendid sight!

We were ordered to kneel down, but could see through the *zareba* as they came on. It looked as if the whole of Africa was coming at us, for their front extended for miles. When they advanced to about two thousand yards the guns opened on them, and they commenced a terrific fire, but we heard no familiar whistle of their bullets yet. When they came to 1,300 yards we fixed bayonets and rose, firing section volleys, each volley aiming just below a flag. We fired 97 volleys right off. Each time a flag fell, up it came again, and we heard them all singing, but the only word we really distinguished was 'Allah'!

At last the greater part of the dervishes swung round to our right to attack the Egyptians, but some of them had got into a dry watercourse in front of us, and they caused all, or nearly all our casualties. After a while a battery of Egyptian artillery took up our ground and shelled them out. Then the British Division made a forward movement, and went half left as if to go into Omdurman. After going about a mile, climbing up over the left shoulder of the hill, we heard heavy firing on the right, so we had to right form up in support of the Egyptians, and then saw the dervishes making their last stand round the Khalifa's black flag. Could not help admiring their courage, for they were hemmed in by two brigades in line, firing volleys as fast as they could load. We did not have to fire, but simply support the others who did.

I have seen a lot of pictures of this, but all are wrong in showing Omdurman – it could not be seen as plainly as in the pictures, for there were two risings on the plain which almost hid it. Once we saw two men alone charge with drawn swords against a whole Egyptian regiment. Also saw the two men who held up the Khalifa's black flag until they fell riddled. After this we marched over the field, formed to the left, and then on to Omdurman; halted for dinner, then on again right into the centre of the town, which is a tremendous size. A good thing they came out to meet us, for if we had attacked them in the town I quite believe we should have lost half our force. Mud huts were dotted about all over the place, then a space of about fifty or a hundred yards. Inside were large walls in squares, surrounding a number of better-built huts – walls 20 feet high and 12 feet thick, with stones mixed up with the mud.

We camped, or rather slept, as we were in ranks till Saturday morning, when we marched back to a nice rising ground north of the town. On Sunday another man of my company died of wounds, making two of ours killed. A party of all regiments went to Khartoum (while we were burying our late comrade), where the flags were hoisted, and a memorial service held. Monday morning we marched round to Mahdi's tomb and back. Tuesday afternoon we left Omdurman for here, where we arrived to come through again without a scratch, but I hope we shall have no more Soudan marches; lots of fellows were quite knocked up days before the fight, but struggled on till the end. Talk about rough ground! South of Metemmeh it is awful! However, I am feeling well, though very thin. We are expecting the other half-battalion in shortly, so then we shall be settled down for a bit, I hope.[7]

For a lucid and almost conversational profile of Omdurman we cannot do better than to read a letter by Colour-Sergeant Edward Fraley of the Rifle Brigade. A day or two after the battle he wrote a brief account of how things had gone with him, but that letter did not reach his father, who lived at Neath in South Wales. So he wrote again from Crete on 5 October 1898 to meet his father's request for a full description. Fraley admitted the limitations of such personal reporting: 'like the correspondents who were there one can only describe what one actually sees, and there may be a dozen different things occurring at the same time and one can only describe perhaps one of them which actually comes under one's notice'. Despite his good sense in appreciating the narrowness of one man's view of battle, Fraley writes with a graphic, personal style of what he saw, so that the immediacy of his experience comes across very vividly. The letter is offered here without any tidying up of Ted Fraley's rather free-and-easy punctuation, and just as he wrote it.

I'll start from the night before the fight, we'd had a pretty good march and came through a village called Kerreri, which they expected to find occupied, or rather a position just in front a very good one too, that would have taken a lot of fighting to take but thank Goodness it was not occupied, so it saved us the trouble, we went in and got into camp about 1 or 2 as near as I can guess and we were allotted our different positions for pitching camp, we always formed a Zariba everynight, everyone was tired as usual we'd got our blanket shelters pitched (these were 4 blankets sewn together, for shelter from the sun, they afforded cover for 8, at retreat they were lowered, and we slept on them) and the cooks started cooking.

We'd been in camp about an hour when the order came. Pack up shelters and get dressed, meaning our equipment on, and after a little waiting away we went again, of course we guessed something was up, I suppose we went about a mile or so perhaps less and then we formed up in line on our left the Nile (good old Nile always looked for it at the end of a march) . . . well we heard they were coming on and stuck there for some time but they did not come, then we fell out and went to a small deserted village just

7. An excellent account of this campaign, making wide use of soldiers' letters from all ranks in the expeditionary force, is Philip Ziegler, *Omdurman* (London: Collins, 1973).

in front of us and got stuff and made a zariba all along the line the Zariba is made with some very prickly trees small ones and I shouldn't like to walk through them with my trousers off . . .

We laid down again and had another snatch of sleep and about 4.15 a.m. Reveille we had some Tea and biscuits then took up position at the Zariba again and the Lancers went out, we waited some time and bye and bye it went round they're coming and sure enough we could see the Lancers slowly retiring and hear them shooting, about 6 or 6.30 we could see them swarming over the hills in front there were thousands with their banners flying and covering the same extent of ground that we did, they waited until they got some way down the hill then the guns next to us started firing, they started with one shot to find the range and all the Officers were watching with their glasses . . . then they all opened fire and if anyone had to face a hail of lead those Dervishes did, but still they came on and as they got closer the shells simply made lanes and empty spaces in their ranks where a minute before they were as thick as bees, then the Infantry opened fire, and what a din, but no smoke.

At this time they cleared away from the left where we were apparently they thought it was rather warm and they do not like the Gunboats which I forgot to mention before were on the left as well and they all seemed to be making for our right where the Egyptians and Soudanese and 1st Brigade were, and then our Brigade had a decent old double we had to move to the right in support and halted about 20 yards in rear of the fighting line, gradually the fire got less and less and then we could see them in scattered groups and bodies making for the hills and retiring to our right, the big guns still worrying them whenever a body got together, everybody then had a bit of a breather and they went around and got a list of the casualties . . .

We then formed up in order for march and advanced through the battlefield to make for Omdurman of the sights I shall not say anything but it was bad enough on the left where we were but it must have been awful on the right where most of them had been killed and our troops had a lot more casualties through wounded Dervishes having a last shot or prod with their swords or spears, need I say when this happened they did not live long . . . at 1 p.m. we halted just outside Omdurman for 3 hours for a feed and rest, and when we got our things off you ought to seen [sic] the troops making for the Nile, talk about drinking, why everyone had a rare old drink . . . we fell in again at 4.15 p.m. and then went through Omdurman as we went through the people came out, and extended in their way a welcome, offering our troops water, I don't think they had much else to give away, the women made a sort of screaming noise and laughed all over their ugly faces, of all the stinking places Oh Omdurman, it is built of nothing but mud huts . . .

Eventually we got through this town of smells past the Mahdi's tomb and halted for the night, it was dark now no moon about 7 or 8 after putting out pickets etc. we got a small drop of water about a half cupful each it had to be shared out, and it had to do for meat as well as drink, because it was thick enough with mud and we got nothing to eat, but we had an issue of rum about 2 table spoonful each, and we simply laid down where we were not particular whether there was a little stone under ones right shoulder blade or whether the ground was softer in one place or another, I had a mess tin for my pillow and it was soft as down, I slept like a top and I didn't hear of anyone who couldn't sleep that night, we'd had a pretty long day of it . . .

As to the little things & big that occurred during the fight there is no doubt about it the Dervishes are very brave to stick it like they did was wonderful, we saw one case during the fight, some of the Dervishes were under cover halted under a small rising in the ground but four a few paces apart came on carrying a banner, first one dropped, then the fellow carrying the flag, another picked it up and still came on, when the two left almost dropped together, they marched straight to death right enough. The Maxims too did awful execution. The Maxim Det nearest to us Irish Fuslrs, I heard the Captain say steady now men, cease fire and wait till they come over the rise, pointing it out about 650 or 750 yards away as they came over he said now, traversing fire commence and as the guns went from right to left they simply fell down in a line, just the same as if they had been to told to lie down, some of the bodies they saw afterwards had been hit with bullets five and six times in a line across their bodies before they fell.

What surprised me most was the behaviour of our own troops but it seemed just as if we were on a Field day at Aldershot, everyone cool, talking, and when not firing having a smoke, and the officers had to tell them to lie down because they would stand or kneel to see what was going on, the firing, volleys, were splendid, they fired one rank at a time and when the rifles got very hot and the men tired they relieved each other and the fellows just finished would clean out their rifles and sit down and have a few whiffs until they were wanted again, of course there were the poor chaps wounded or killed who dropped now and again, then one would call Stretcher, up came the stretcher party, look at his wound if wounded do him up roughly then carry him off, there was not the slightest fuss about the whole thing . . .

One of our men was sitting up just lighting his pipe, all at once there was a whizz and he looked surprised, and stopped puffing, he took his pipe out and said to the Cr. Sgt. who was near him

Sergt. I think I'm hit. He said are you where he said in the knee, right enough they slit his trousers up and found the bullet had gone clean through just above his knee and they took him off quietly. There are a lot of different things I could write of but Dear Father and Mother when I look at the paper I've used already, I think I must leave off and wait until I see you. I hope please God it will not be long, then I can spin you some yarns, the 21st Lancers did splendid work and worked like slaves, so did the Egyptians & Soudanese in fact everyone did well too considering, As for Genl. Kitchener he is a splendid fellow and a wonderful man.

As might be expected, the newspapers printed many letters from men who were at Omdurman, which became an event of national celebration. Most of them say how impressed the soldiers were when they saw the Khalifa's army coming to the attack. Lieutenant H. V. Fison of the Northumberland Fusiliers writes: 'At 7 a.m. we caught sight of the enemy, and after the fight all of us said it was the finest sight we should ever see in our lives. The Dervishes came on 60,000 strong, their line extended over four-and-a-half miles. The whole way along their front were huge banners, carried on poles, with the Khalifa's black banner in the middle.' Before the troops advanced, says Fison, orders were given by Kitchener that 'all wounded Dervishes passed over had to be bayoneted, and it was absolutely necessary to do this, as if one was passed over alive he would turn round and shoot at you, which event often happened'. It is difficult to digest the fact that more than 11,000 Sudanese were killed in this action, with more besides when Omdurman was captured. 'I rode out yesterday to see the battlefield,' Fison writes, 'but have no inclination to go again.' Fison, whose father was Member of Parliament for Doncaster, caught enteric fever (typhoid) at Omdurman and died on 5 October.

One of the most publicised incidents was the cavalry charge made by the 21st Lancers at Khor Abu Sunt, its dash and colour striking a romantic chord with the British public. In reality the Lancers ran into near-disaster when they suddenly found themselves on the brink of a ravine filled with Sudanese. A prosaic and decidedly unfeeling vignette of all this comes from a Lancer's letter; Private Rawding wrote to his parents at Newark:

The next day we had to fight from six in the morning till five o'clock at night before we slaughtered the Dervishes. We charged about 3,000 of them, there were only three squadrons of us, so it was ten to one. Lieutenant Grenfell was cut to pieces, 24 others being killed and 45 wounded. We killed over 600, wounded and every thing, but they did not live long when we went round giving them a poke. You know we lost over 60 horses in the charge. Some had their tails cut off, some had broken legs, and in the Grey Squadron you could see nothing but blood. All the Dervishes were armed with Remington rifles, served for the purpose of this affair; they get them from a French company. They are not very good shots, they killed our chaps when they got in amongst them.

One chap who was riding next to me hit me on the back of my hand with the back of his sword. It was only a little mark, but five days after I could not use my hand through blood-poisoning, as the sword was covered with blood, and my hand was dirty. It festered, and I had a funny hand for about three days, but it is healed up now and I am ready for another man-killing job. It is nice to put a sword or a lance through a man; they are just like old hens, they just say 'quar'.

Accompanying the 21st Lancers on this affair was the man who reported it for an admiring public, Winston Spencer Churchill. Soon after it happened Churchill scribbled a letter in pencil to his friend General Sir Ian Hamilton, so we can compare his professional style with the unsophisticated quality of the ordinary soldier's letters. It is headed 'In the train, Sudan Military Railway, 16 September 1898'; Hamilton says it was 'written down red-hot at the time' and is therefore more striking than Churchill's account of Omdurman as given in his book *The River War*.

I had a patrol on 2 September and was I think the first to see the enemy – certainly the first to hear their bullets. Never shall I see such a sight again. At the very least there were 40,000 men, five miles long in lines with great humps and squares at intervals. I can assure you that when I heard them all shouting their warsongs from my coign of vantage on the ridge of Heliograph Hill I and my little patrol felt very lonely and though I never doubted the issue, I was in great awe.

Churchill's charge with a troop of Lancers came when the Sudanese army had been broken by gunfire:

Opposite me they were about 4 deep. But they all fell knocked AOT and we passed through without any sort of shock. One man in my troop fell. He was cut to pieces. Five or six horses were wounded by backhanders, etc. But otherwise – no scathe. Then we emerged into a region of scattered men and personal combats. The troop broke up and disappeared. I pulled into a trot and rode up to individuals firing my pistol in their faces and killing several . . . Then I looked round and saw the Dervish mass reforming. The charge had passed through, knocking over nearly half. These were getting on their legs again and their Emirs were trying to collect them into a hump again. I realised that this mass was about 20 yards away and I looked at them stupidly for what may have been 2 seconds. Then I saw two men get down on their knees and take aim with rifles – and for the first time the danger and peril came home to me. I turned and galloped . . .

I am in great disfavour with the authorities here. Kitchener was furious with Sir E. Wood for sending me out and expressed himself freely. My remarks on the treatment of the wounded – again disgraceful – were reported to him and generally things have been a little unpleasant. He is a great general, but he has yet to be accused of being a great gentleman.

Perhaps the best way to round off these scenes of imperial warfare in the Sudan, and indeed for all the Victorian campaigns in Africa, is to turn to a letter from someone in the Royal Army Medical Corps, whose job it was to make good the ravages of combat. Clement Riding was a sergeant-major in the RAMC stationed at a hospital camp near Berber. He tells his father, a Sheffield chemist, how uncomfortably hot it was, with temperatures climbing to 110°F in the shade.

We have dust storms about every second night. Of course we have no doors or windows, so everything is covered with sand and dust. We had a fearful storm of rain, thunder and lightning a fortnight ago, and the hospital was nearly washed away. All buildings are large and lofty, each holding 60 patients. We had 150, 140 of them from Khartoum wounded, six officers. We have sent 32 to Cairo, and more are going tomorrow. We are actually on the right bank of the Nile, close enough to throw stones into the water.

I have not been into the village as it is too far to walk. We are very much bothered with insects of all kinds, beetles, flies, ants, etc., especially at meal times. They get into our mouths with food and drink. We may leave this place end of September, I hope so as it is too much being in the hot sun all day. I am quite brown, nearly black, you would be surprised to see me in my shirtsleeves, with a solar topee (helmet of pith). We have about eight soldiers in the graveyard here, two buried lately; one fell off the train. Hundreds of our men have left their bones in the Sudan.

Omdurman did not quite settle affairs in the Sudan. The Khalifa was not captured, and over a year went by before spies brought in news of his whereabouts. He was brought to a halt well to the south of Khartoum, and in a dawn attack Kitchener's troops swept to another success. The Khalifa was killed, his eldest son, the nominated successor, taken prisoner. At last Kitchener, the military victor, could hope 'that a brighter era was now opened for the Sudan'.

FINALE:

'A Long and Bloody War Is Before Us'

(W. S. CHURCHILL, 1899).

During the 1890s, small units of imperial troops were quite frequently put on stand-by for active service in various parts of Africa where new territory was coming under the British flag. Enormous tracts of land fell within such colonial expansionism, but it did not mean military confrontation on the old scale of fighting African armies of size and effectiveness, whether they were Ethiopian, Asante, Xhosa, Zulu, Boer, Egyptian or Sudanese. Hints of it appeared here and there, as in Matabeleland or Northern Nigeria, but by and large the later spasms of frontier warfare were waged against African tribal groups of a lesser order of martial power. Equally, the brunt of colonial soldiering was borne not by redcoats but by forces specially formed for the purpose. The British South Africa Company had its own prestigious corps, the BSA Police, to keep order within its vast concessions; it could be augmented by recruiting to provide the Pioneer Column raised in 1890 to open up Rhodesia. There were battalions of native African soldiers, officered by British commissioned and non-commissioned men, to fight in Nigeria, Uganda, Kenya or Nyasaland. It was also policy to draft in Sikh detachments from the Indian Army, notably so in the pacification of East Africa.

Typical of the occasional involvement of imperial troops at this time, given their minor role over-all, was the despatch to Rhodesia in May 1896 of a Mounted Infantry Corps. The battalion had four companies, one composed of men from rifle regiments, two companies coming from the 60th Rifles – with whom Percy Marling fought in the Sudan in 1884 (page 133). Rhodesia was the first campaign to have units trained at the Mounted Infantry School in Aldershot, founded in 1888: the earliest use of mounted infantry went back ten years to the Ninth Frontier War in the Cape and then the Zulu War. The MI sailed to Cape Town, on to Beira in Portuguese East Africa, and then marched inland to Umtali by

27 July 1896.[1] They then began a series of punitive actions against fortified kraals in Mashonaland. Typical of these was the attack on Makoni's stronghold. After a night march the Mounted Infantry struck at dawn on 3 August. The surprise attack echoes the operations against the Pedi nearly twenty years before, as described by Charles Commeline (page 91). The Rifle Company was reinforced by a Maxim machine-gun and two 7-pounder field-guns, representing the new and the traditional armaments in African warfare. After a bombardment there was a fire-fight across the wall surrounding Makoni's kraal, then a bayonet charge that sent the Shona rushing off to the safety of their caves. All the cattle, sheep and goats were driven off by the imperial troops, whose casualties were three killed, four wounded; 200 Shona were killed. Such operations went on until November, within a fifty-mile radius of Salisbury, before the Shona gave in.

The chances of finding letters from such piecemeal encounters, involving at the most a few hundred men, are correspondingly slight when compared with the more prolonged and substantial campaigns covered in this book. One can only surmise with confidence that, where they exist, such letters would share the quality and interest that combatants seemed to bring quite naturally to their narratives of personal experience of battle. The more desperate the circumstances, the more vivid and incisive was the written record. During the first British war against the Boers, for example, the stark defeat at Majuba in the early light of 27 February 1881 is difficult to rival, and it speaks from a letter written afterwards by Captain Thurlow of the 3/60 Rifles.[2]

> Then we saw a redcoat running down the steep slopes in our direction, and then some bluejackets, and then a confused lot of men, Highlanders, sailors, and 58th, and soon the edge of the hill was occupied by the Boers, who poured a tremendous fire into our unfortunate men as they scrambled down the rocks on the mountain-side, knocking them over like rabbits; those that escaped retired on our redoubt, giving their story of their repulse from the mountain and of the General's death. Soon after this we saw a great crowd of Boers on the top of the mountain, and could hear them cheering, and soon they began coming down from both sides, and it was plain enough they intended to attack us in our redoubt; they streamed down the *dongas* and ravines in large numbers.

1. Major-General Sir Stewart Hare, *Animals of the King's Royal Rifle Corps*, volume 4, pages 347–52 (London: John Murray, 1929).
2. *Ibid.* page 27.

Thurlow's company managed to extricate themselves by the skin of their teeth from this menace. His use of the term *donga* for a gully (on par with the Indian soldier's *khud* or *nullah*, necessary words for folds in the terrain that could mean cover for friend or foe) reveals that he already had the experience of fighting the Zulu on their own ground. He was to go on to fight in Egypt and the Sudan over the next few years, as we have found from the letters of one of his comrades, Percy Marling (page 119). Those conflicts epitomise the harsh realities of imperial military life in Africa. Through varying circumstances the soldier was deployed at the inevitable sharp end of acquiring territory or influence in the 'Scramble', a fate shared by the 1890s with his counterparts in the overseas armies of France, Germany, Belgium and Italy. In the case of Tommy Atkins, however, the turning of the nineteenth century was to be over-shadowed by a clash of arms that brought a new kind of frightful-ness to the war-riven continent. Omdurman in 1898 had meant disaster for one of the most remarkable nations in independent Africa: a year later the die was being cast for a struggle between Britain and the Afrikaner republics of the Transvaal and Orange Free State. The shift of scene is crystallised by following the letter Winston Churchill wrote after Omdurman with another written by him from Estcourt in Natal, dated 10 November 1899. It was addressed to Sir Evelyn Wood, whose presence in the Ashanti and Zulu campaigns we have already registered (pages 46, 77), and on whose recommendation Churchill had found himself in the Sudan.

We await troops to advance to the relief of Ladysmith. I have been afraid to try to ride through the lines although it has been done – so I down my heels pending the arrival of an army to clear the way. The present situation here is bad and critical. Ladysmith is blocked completely and all the cavalry but one squadron of irregulars is bottled up within it. We scurried out of Colenso, bounced by a 12-pounder gun, and here we remain at Estcourt, two weak battalions and a few volunteers, in an untenable cup in the hills.

Five days have however passed in safety. Four more will bring reinforcements and change the complexion of affairs. Were the Boers less ambitious they would be more formidable. If they said, 'Let us crush Ladysmith, a month would do it. How can we get a month? Obviously by tearing the railway to pieces as far as Durban (or very nearly).' We have hardly any force to stop them and no cavalry. They could thus delay the concentration for relief.

As soon as they come here we must fly, for we are the

Pietermaritzburg garrison, so that their chance is very evident. But '*qui trop embrasse*', they eye the railway lovingly, they expect to use it themselves *after* they have captured Ladysmith and beaten the relieving army, to supply them on their victorious march to Durban – and so, thank heaven, they leave us alone and the moments are flying very rapidly. It is astonishing how we have underrated these people. The combination of mounted infantry and heavy guns is extremely effective. Our Intelligence Department must look to their laurels. Sir A. Milner told me, 'Far greater numbers than were expected:' A long and bloody war is before us, and the end is by no means as certain as most people imagine.

The Boers have already captured twice as many soldiers as have been hit – not a pretty proportion. They firmly believe they will win and although I do not share that opinion, it must be admitted that it does not sound so unreasonable as it did only a month ago. I think we ought to punish people who surrender troops under their command – and let us say at once 'No exchange of prisoners'.

In a matter of days after writing these lines Churchill was captured by the Boers when they ambushed an armoured train. His perceptive outline of the desperate situation facing the British forces in the opening stages the South African War (which indeed proved to be 'a long and bloody war') encourages the temptation to illustrate its course of events from soldiers' letters. Before it drew to a close in 1902 nearly 500,000 British troops were sent to fight the Boers, and a high proportion of them wrote letters describing their experience. But the temptation to explore this healthy stock of material must be resisted, not simply because to do so in full would unbalance the picture offered in this book, but on the ground that it is a different kind of story, and deserves to be recounted in its own right, some other time. Only one brief insight will be offered here, as a token view of the war's character.

It is chosen to reveal the close relations between people at home in Britain and the troops fighting in South Africa. Although of course there was fierce opposition to the war on moral and economic grounds, led by the Liberal politician Lloyd George, by and large it was a 'popular' war. The degree of involvement on the home front was a forerunner of what followed in both World Wars: the singing of 'Goodbye, Dolly Gray' as battalions sailed for the Cape seems like a rehearsal for 'It's a long way to Tipperary' in 1914. All this emerges in the wartime philanthropy of Sarah Angelina Acland. She was the daughter of Sir Henry Acland, famous as a pioneer of public health, one of the first to combat successfully the scourge of cholera in British cities, and Regius Professor of Medicine in the University of Oxford.

A profile of Angie Acland's life is given in a recent book by 'five historians who happen to be feminists'.[3] She figures in a chapter on 'Victorian spinsters: dutiful daughters, desperate rebels, and the transition to the new women', but the evidence of her letters suggests that the picture of her painted in *Exploring Woman's Past* is not nearly enough complete. It is true that after her mother's death in 1878 Angie was fated to look after her father until he died in 1900. She devoted herself entirely to being Sir Henry's housekeeper and social secretary: she idolised him. The shock of his death was severe, she tells her brother William (she had seven brothers): 'I cannot imagine what I shall do, if I still have to live on. All my interest in life has so entirely gone during the long nursing of Father.'

Yet her other letters reveal that she had plenty of interests of her own, which may explain why she lived until 1925; her expressions of despair owed something to a conventional, self-defensive stance in relation to her brothers and their numerous families. She was an expert photographer, for instance, long before her father's death, and took a well-known picture of him sitting with John Ruskin. More to the point here, she involved herself (again, at the very twilight of Sir Henry's life) in sending letters and parcels on a regular basis to British soldiers at war in South Africa. She took this welfare work seriously, having on her desk a War Office leaflet itemising the kind of comforts needed by the troops. Besides the familiar items like socks and tobacco, it mentions such peculiarities as portable mincing-machines, cholera belts, and worsted night-caps or tam-o'-shanters.

Angie Acland took a more down-to-earth approach in her impressive programme of parcel-sending, as we learn from the letters of delighted recipients. One set of twenty letters is labelled with the title 'A Coward', but he turns out to be someone of quite a different stamp. 1553 Private Archibald Coward was in Natal with F Company of the First Battalion, Rifle Brigade. He wrote his earliest letter to her 'under difficulties' from Estcourt on 8 December 1899; after reaching Durban he had gone by rail to Pietermaritzburg, where the regiment had a week's rest. Another train journey to Mooi river was followed by the march to Estcourt, and they were preparing to

3. Patricia Crawford (ed.), *Exploring Woman's Past* (London: Virago, 1983).

go on to camp at Frere. Coward spent the battle of Colenso, which he describes as a fiasco, safely under cover and not long afterwards had his first parcel from Miss Acland, including a woollen cap, handkerchiefs, pipe, tobacco, a supply of Oxo. He was in some hard fighting at Vaalkranz, as part of the relief of Ladysmith. 'Even as I write the enemy are sniping at us. I am sitting on the veldt, a water-bottle on my knee, puzzling my brain what to say whilst the bullets are whistling over my head.' Another parcel quickly followed, with 'the most important things a campaigner requires' – socks, caps, notepaper and pencils among them. Coward put it all to good use and sent Angie his brass chocolate box, the Christmas gift of Queen Victoria to all her soldiers on active service in South Africa.

By May 1900 he was feeling the cold nights camping in the open at Laing's Nek, but life was brightened by the continuing stream of good things sent from Oxford: cardigan jacket, flannel shirt, the inevitable but hand-knitted socks, a pair of boots that fitted him well, sweets, cigarettes, foot powder. 'We have driven the Boers out of Natal, and our armies are carrying the war to the enemy's country.' Coward marched on to Standerton and Heidelberg, where he stayed until September 1900. 'The inhabitants seem bewildered at our good behaviour, for I fancy they had been led to believe we should play the devil with their property and persons.' Parcels continued to fortify him with tea, rum, chocolate, also bottles of chlorodine and quinine to safeguard his health: 'All of which are very useful and proof of your kindness of heart.'

Archie Coward wrote a touching letter of sympathy when news of Sir Henry Acland's death reached him in the Transvaal. He recalled talking with him at Oxford a year previously: 'The world of Science and Medicine have also lost a great man.' Soldiering with a mobile column then took him far into the wilds for weeks on end, but a letter of 22 January 1901 reveals that he had returned to Natal. Shot and wounded on Boxing Day 1900, he was a patient in the Fourteenth General Hospital at Newcastle, 'bowled over, to use a sporting phrase, on the last lap, but such is the fortune, or rather the misfortune of war'. A Mauser bullet fired by one of Lucas Meyer's horsemen had gone through his hip and groin, and he wondered if he would be able to walk naturally afterwards. 'They took all rifles and equipment from the wounded, I lost everything including letters from both you and Sir Henry, and my pocket ledger.' The Newcastle hospital was staffed with nurses 'both army and civilian', some of whom were very kind, 'although the sister of my ward pays a great deal of attention to flirting with a negligent doctor of the RAMC in charge of my ward. And mark this, delicacies are obtainable but withheld. In fact, rigid and unwarrantable economy are the order of the day. So I cannot say much for one's treatment, personal or otherwise.' Coward's criticisms would have been helpful to Miss Acland, who was involved with official investigations into medical care for the troops in South Africa. Their correspondence shows just how preoccupied she was with her own interests, which included helping Coward's sick mother and his young sister Mary. Archie Coward also emerges as yet another fine letter-writer from the ranks of Queen Victoria's private soldiers.

The 'Old Queen' died while the South African War still had more than a year in which to grind on its grim way towards eventual peace in 1902. By then the conflict lapsed into a series of guerilla operations, with long periods of inaction broken by sudden raids and ambushes. Against this more relaxed background we end with a letter on the lighter side of campaigning in Africa. The mayor of Oxford asked the local newspapers to print a letter sent to him by Mary Green, widow of a colour-sergeant in the Oxfordshire Light Infantry. She had two sons serving with the regiment in South Africa; one of them had written to thank the people at home for sending out comforts at Christmas 1901. Sergeant Ben Green exemplifies the standard of soldiers' literacy achieved by this time, and his remarks reflect the innate patriotism that was typical of most imperial campaigners. He writes from Lace Diamond Mines in the Orange River Colony.

This is Christmas Eve, I cannot hear the muffled rumbling of the water boiling in the copper, nor can I smell the delicious smell of the Christmas puddings as they rise and fall in the bubbling water, neither do I smell the green holly and evergreen as they are being neatly fixed over the tops of the picture-frames, nor gaze with interest at the many decorations adorning a humble home, but I have just come from the Staff Sergeant's tent, where we have been talking of old times. I noticed, too, a bright moon in the sky, and the air is warm, while the mosquitoes pass ever and anon with their aggravating song by one's ear. The camp too, is quiet and the distant report of a sentry's rifle shows that they are on the alert against Boers passing the outpost line.

The moon being so bright that my candle cannot be distinguished on the outside of the Orderly-Room tent, I am able to write to you during the hours that I should be in the land of dreams. First, the Acting Orderly-Room Sergeant having asked me to go to his duty I am once again acting in that capacity, which, as you must know, requires all one's energy. I have no assistants so far, not even an orderly, but I hope to have at least one man to help me before long. You may judge then that I can give but little attention to family affairs for the present, and my letters must necessarily be few and far between as well as meagre at times.

The people of Oxfordshire and Buckinghamshire very kindly contributed to present all the Battalion out here with a Christmas gift; their contributions were so liberal and exceedingly well organised that each one this day received a parcel in which were the following articles: tinned plum duff, tinned cake, sweets, tobacco, pipe, cigarettes, Christmas card, pocket handkerchief, and a sixpenny novelette. All these articles were of the very best class, bought from the Army & Navy Stores. I must certainly admire the spirit of the people of Oxon and Bucks whose generosity I shall not forget, and who instead of raving about refugee camps and rebels, set quietly to work to give the worn soldiers of their counties a little luxury at Christmastime. God bless them all. They are English and I am proud of them. We also received, or will do so tomorrow [Christmas Day] plum duff, tobacco, and one pint of beer, the first for ever so long, as a present from the Field Force Canteen recommended by Lord Kitchener.

Unfortunately, lately I have had a slight touch of dysentery, so will not be able to eat quite so much duff as I would like. I am quietly doctoring myself, and I have no doubt I shall soon be all candle. Dysentery is very prevalent around here, due to bad water. There are no less than 60 cases in the Battalion. Our Provost Sergeant, who messes in the same tent, shot a couple of wild ducks yesterday; we are keeping them for tomorrow, if they will keep. We have commandeered some spuds, so Christmas will not be so very bad. By the way, I should much prefer cuttings out of the *Daily Telegraph* than the *Daily News*, and while thanking you for the latter venture to remark that I am astonished to notice how that sage old paper is degrading itself. No doubt you have also noticed it, and sent me the cuttings that I may also observe it. Very good of you. I somehow thought that is what pro-Boerism would do for it.

The whole sequence of the South African war is depicted in a vast number of soldiers' letters, from the much-publicised sieges of Ladysmith, Mafeking and Kimberley, to the protracted business of guerilla warfare that spluttered on to the bitter end in 1902. Newspaper coverage was on a scale previously unknown, and fifteen correspondents were killed or died of disease. Some time the soldiers' letters will deserve to be brought to light to add their special dimension to this final episode of Victorian warfare in Africa.

The Letter Writers: Sources

Preface

Captain Edward Woodgate, 4th Regiment (The King's Own, Lancaster): Letters in possession of Dr. G. K. Woodgate, St. Peter's College, Oxford.

Major-General Sir Garnet Wolseley: Natal Provincial Archives, Pietermaritzburg; The Sir Evelyn Wood Collection, A 598, III-2-21.

One: 'From the Seat of War': Victorian Soldiers' Letters

Private Robert Waterfield: *The Memoirs of Private Waterfield*, edited by Arthur Swinson and Donald Scott (London: Leo Cooper, 1968), page 110.

Private George Morris, 1st Battalion, 24th Regiment: Regimental Museum, Brecon.

Private Edward Milton, 3rd Light Dragoons, *The Oxford Chronicle*, 25 April 1846.

Sergeant Clifford Mitchell, 13th Light Dragoons: *Jackson's Oxford Journal*, 23 December 1854.

Private Joseph Coulter, Scots Fusilier Guards: *The Weekly News and Chronicle*, 9 December 1854.

Cavalryman (unnamed), Heavy Brigade: *Jackson's Oxford Journal*, 24 February 1855.

Sergeant John Bargus, 63rd Regiment: *Jackson's Oxford Journal*, 30 December 1854.

Corporal (unnamed), 19th Regiment: *Jackson's Oxford Journal*, 3 February 1855.

Sergeant William Saddler, 14th Light Dragoons: *The Oxford Chronicle*, 10 September 1857.

Private Thomas Jackson, 58th Regiment: *The Oxford Chronicle*, 23 August 1879; 12 March 1881.

Sergeant Harry Thomas, 25th Regiment: *The Rugby Advertiser*, 21 May 1879.

Corporal George Howe, 5th Field Company, Royal Engineers: *The Sheffield Daily Telegraph*, 16 April 1881.

Corporal Frederick Bennett, 24th Field Company, Royal Engineers: *The Oxford Times*, 25 April 1885.

Sergeant Thomas Christian, Seaforth Highlanders: *The Oxford Times*, 1 October 1898.

Private (unnamed), 2nd Battalion, Oxfordshire Light Infantry: *The Oxford Chronicle*, 5 February 1898.

Corporal (unnamed), 19th Hussars: *The Oxford Journal*, 2 December 1899.

Corporal W. E. Wicks, Black Watch (42nd Royal Highlanders): *The Oxford Journal*, 23 December 1899.

Lieutenant Charles Commeline, 5th Field Company, Royal Engineers: Gloucestershire Records Office, D 1233, 44.45.

Two: 'I Am Writing this under Great Difficulties': THE CAMPAIGNS IN ABYSSINIA AND ASHANTILAND

Lieutenant Edward Woodgate, 4th Regiment (The King's Own, Lancaster): Diary in the possession of Dr. G. K. Woodgate, St. Peter's College, Oxford.

Officer (unnamed): *The Sheffield Daily Telegraph*, 30 April 1868.

Staff Officer (unnamed): *The Sheffield Daily Telegraph*, 8 May 1868.

Colonel George Pomeroy Colley, Staff Corps: Sir William Butler, *The Life of Sir George Pomeroy Colley (1835–1881)*, (London: John Murray, 1899), pages 95–6, 103, 108.

Colonel Evelyn Wood, Staff Corps: Natal Provincial Archives, Pietermaritzburg; The Sir Evelyn Wood Collection, A 598, I-2-1, I-2-2.

Private George Gilham, 2nd Battalion, Rifle Brigade: E. Milton Small, *Told from the ranks: recollections of service during the Queen's reign by privates and non-commissioned officers of the British Army* (London: Andrew Melrose, 1897), pages 76–86.

THREE: 'It Was Indeed a Slaughter': WARFARE IN THE CAPE COLONY AND ZULULAND, 1877–79

Private Griffith Griffiths, 2nd Battalion, 24th Regiment: Regimental Museum, Brecon.

Private George Morris, 1st Battalion, 24th Regiment: Regimental Museum, Brecon.

Major Redvers Buller, Frontier Light Horse: Natal Provincial Archives, Pietermaritzburg; The Sir Evelyn Wood Collection, A 598, II-2-1.

Lady Florence Dixie: Ibid., A 598, III-2-7.

Corporal George Howe, 5th Field Company, Royal Engineers: *The Sheffield Daily Telegraph*, 5 April 1879; 28 August 1879.

Sergeant (unnamed), 2nd Battalion, 24th Regiment; *The Chatham and Rochester Observer*, 5 April 1879.

Trooper (unnamed), Baker's Horse: letter dated 29 June from 'Flying Column camp', *The Eastern Province Herald*, 18 July 1879.

Captain W. Penn Symons's reconstruction of the events of 22–23 January 1879 is filed in the Archives of the 24th Regiment of Foot [South Wales Borderers] at the Regimental Museum, The Barracks, Brecon. For edited extracts from it, see Frank Emery, *The 24th Regiment in the Zulu War: Isandlwana*, published by the Regimental Association, Brecon, 1981.

Private, 17th Lancers: *The Sheffield Daily Telegraph*, 5 July 1879.

Commandant Friedrich Schermbrücker, Kaffrarian Vanguard: *The Friend of the Free State and Bloemfontein Gazette*, 1 May 1879.

Officer (unnamed), Wood's Swazi Irregulars: *The Friend of the Free State and Bloemfontein Gazette*, 1 May 1879.

Private A. Brett, 13th Light Infantry: *The Portsmouth Times and Naval Gazette*, 10 May 1879.

Private (unnamed), 80th Regiment: *The Sheffield Daily Telegraph*, 17 May 1879.

Major Alfred Walker, 99th Regiment: *The Irish Times*, 23 May 1879.

Sergeant Major Thomas Sharp, 1st Battalion, 1st Regiment, Natal Native Regiment: *The Irish Times*, 15 March 1879.

Driver Elias Tucker, N Battery, 5th Brigade, Royal Artillery: *The Western Morning News*, 28 March 1879.

Colour-Sergeant Anthony Booth, 80th Regiment: Regimental Museum, The Staffordshire Regiment, Lichfield.

Private Henry Jones, 80th Regiment: *The Leicester Herald*, 23 April 1879.

Lieutenant Edward Daubeney, 80th Regiment: *Wilts and Gloucestershire Standard*, 26 April 1879.

Private Edmund Fowler, 90th Light Infantry: *The Wigan Observer and District Advertiser*, 28 April 1879.

Wife of a soldier at Eshowe (unnamed): *The Western Morning News*, 9 April 1879.

Private William McNulty, 1st Battalion, 24th Regiment: *The North Wales Guardian*, 5 April 1879.

Lieutenant-Colonel Henry Fanshawe Davies, Grenadier Guards: County of Hereford and Worcester Record Office, 705. 385, BA 4238-1(i).

A. F. Pickard to Sir Evelyn Wood, from Balmoral Castle, 14 October 1879: Natal Provincial Archives, Pietermaritzburg; The Sir Evelyn Wood Collection, A 598, II-1-6.

FOUR: 'We Have Just Had a Nice Little Campaign Here': THE SOUTHERN FRONTIERS, 1879–81

Trooper (unnamed), Cape Colony Volunteers: *Jackson's Oxford Journal*, 19 September 1846.

Trooper George Money, Cape Mounted Rifles (Artillery): *The Oxford Chronicle*, 14 February 1880.

Lieutenant Charles Commeline, 5th Field Company, Royal Engineers:

Gloucestershire Records Office, D 1233, 44. 45, letter from 'Lulu Valley, Sekukuni Country', begun 23 November and concluded 29 November 1879 at 'Secoecoeni Town'.

Major-General Sir Garnet Wolseley, letter written from Army Headquarters, Pretoria, 22 December 1879: Bodleian Library, Oxford; MS. North d. 36, pages 125–8.

Trooper (unnamed), 1st Mounted Rifles. Bechuanaland Field Force: *The Chronicle*, 14 February 1880.

Five: 'Desperate Hard Fighting': The First Anglo-Boer War, 1880–81

Lieutenant Percy Marling, 3rd Battalion, 60th Regiment (King's Royal Rifle Corps): Gloucestershire Records Office, D 873, C 110; P. S. Marling, *Rifleman and Hussar* (London: John Murray, 1931), pages 40–53.

Lance-Sergeant W. J. Morris, 58th Regiment: *The Northampton Mercury*, 19 March 1881.

Officer (unnamed): *The Citizen* (Gloucester), 19 March 1881.

Sergeant Henry Coombs, Army Hospital Corps: *The Sheffield Daily Telegraph*, 5 April 1881.

Lieutenant B. M. Hamilton, 15th Regiment: Sir William Butler, *The Life of Sir George Pomeroy Colley (1835–1881)*, (London: John Murray, 1899), pages 315, 418–20.

Major-General Sir George Pomeroy Colley: *Ibid.*, page 415.

Colonel Herbert Stewart, Staff Corps: S. G. P. Ward (ed.), 'Majuba, 1881. The diary of Colonel W. D. Wood, 58th Regiment', *Journal of the Society for Army Historical Research*, volume 53, 1975, page 95.

Surgeon Edward Mahon, Royal Navy: *The Army and Navy Gazette*, 7 May 1881.

Colour-Sergeant M. G. O'Callaghan, 58th Regiment: *The Sheffield Daily Telegraph*, 29 March 1881.

Trooper (unnamed), 1st Mounted Rifles, Bechuanaland Field Force: *The Cliftonian*, volume VIII, March 1885, pages 393–5.

Six: 'I Can't Write About It Any More': Wolseley in Egypt, 1882

Lance-Corporal J. J. Clough, 1st Battalion, King's Shropshire Light Infantry: *The Montgomeryshire Express*, 12 September 1882.

S. S. Marling, Esq., Stanley Park, Stroud: Gloucestershire Records Office, D.873, C. 110.

Lieutenant Percy Marling, 3rd Battalion, 60th Regiment (King's Royal Rifle Corps), on board HMS *Euphrates*, Suez Canal, 20 August 1882: Gloucestershire Records Office, D. 873, C. 67; C. 110.

Lieutenant Spencer Ewart, 1st Battalion, Cameron Highlanders, from The New Hotel, Cairo, 18 September 1882: *The Marlburian*, XVII, 1882, pages 163–64.

Sergeant (unnamed), Black Watch, (42nd Royal Highlanders): *The Irish Times*, 9 October 1882; *Manchester Guardian*, 9 October 1882.

Private Peter Harkin, 2nd Battalion, Highland Light Infantry: *Manchester Guardian*, 13 October 1882. The report says he wrote the letter from Cairo 'to his mother, who is an inmate of Hexham Workhouse, at which institution Harkin was brought up'.

Sergeant Charles Riley, 1st Battalion, Cameron Highlanders: *The Sheffield Daily Telegraph*, 5 October 1882.

Lieutenant C. B. Balfour, 1st Battalion, Scots Guards: S. G. P. Ward, 'The Scots Guards in Egypt, 1882: the letters of Lt. C. B. Balfour', *Journal of the Society for Army Historical Research*, 51, 1973, pages 80–104.

Officer of the Royal Engineers (unnamed): *The Marlburian*, volume XVII, 1882, pages 203–204.

Signaller, Mounted Infantry (unnamed): *The Oxford Chronicle*, 'Letter from an Oxonian at Cairo', 7 October 1882.

Stretcher-bearer, Army Hospital Corps (unnamed): *The Oxford Chronicle*, 14 October 1882.

Officer, Royal Marine Light Infantry (unnamed): *The Western Morning News*, 30 September 1882.

Gunner, Royal Marine Artillery (unnamed): 'A Marine's Experiences in Egypt', *The Chorley Guardian*, 30 September 1882.

Sergeant James Caine, Royal Marine Light Infantry: *The Western Mail*, 30 September 1882.

Colonel H. S. Jones, C. B., Royal Marine Light Infantry: *The Western Morning News*, 29 September 1882.

Private Edward Brown, 2nd Battalion, York and Lancaster Regiment: *The Sheffield Daily Telegraph*, 5 October 1882.

Trooper, 7th Dragoon Guards (unnamed): *The Sheffield Daily Telegraph*, 3 October 1882.

Corporal John Davies, 2nd Battalion, Grenadier Guards: 'Letter from a Welsh soldier', *The Western Mail*, 29 August 1882.

Lieutenant the Viscount Fielding, Royal Artillery: *The Manchester Guardian*, 9 October 1882.

SEVEN: 'The Pluckiest Fellows I've Ever Seen': CONFLICT IN THE SUDAN, 1884–85

Lieutenant Percy Marling, 3rd Battalion, 60th Regiment (King's Royal Rifle Corps): Gloucestershire Records Office, D 873, C 110.

Lieutenant Walter Almack, Royal Navy, HMS *Briton*: *The Sheffield Daily Telegraph*, 22 March 1884.

Seaman (unnamed), Royal Navy, HMS *Briton: The Western Morning News*, 31 March 1884.

Officer (unnamed), sailing from Aden to Suakin: *The Sheffield Daily Telegraph*, 18 March 1884.

Private James Hope, Black Watch (42nd Royal Highlanders): *The Edinburgh Evening News*, 4 April 1884.

Private (unnamed), Black Watch (42nd Royal Highlanders): *The Oxford Times*, 19 April 1884.

P. S. Marling, *Rifleman and Hussar* (London: John Murray, 1931), pages 102–19.

Officer (unnamed), Black Watch (42nd Royal Highlanders): *The Edinburgh Evening News*, 7 April 1884.

Officer (unnamed), Grenadier Guards, Camel Corps: *The Army and Navy Gazette*, 20 December 1884.

Officer (unnamed), sailing upstream on the Nile: *The Army and Navy Gazette*, 27 December 1884.

Lieutenant Percy Marling, 3rd Battalion, 60th Regiment (King's Royal Rifle Corps): Gloucestershire Records Office, D. 873, C. 110.

Corporal H. Middleton, Camel Corps: *The Daily Telegraph*, 12 March 1885.

Lieutenant Charles Hibbert, 2nd Dragoon Guards (Queen's Bays): *The Oxford Chronicle*, 7 March 1885.

EIGHT: 'It Looked As If the Whole of Africa Was Coming at Us': THE MAHDI AND THE KHALIFA, 1885–98

Captain (unnamed), Black Watch (42nd Royal Highlanders): *The Daily Telegraph*, 10 March 1885.

Corporal Frederick Bennett, 24th Field Company, Royal Engineers: *The Oxford Times*, 25 April 1885.

Sergeant Thomas Christian, Seaforth Highlanders: *The Oxford Times*, 28 May 1898 and 1 October 1898.

Colour-Sergeant Edward Fraley, 2nd Battalion, The Rifle Brigade: *Transactions of the Neath Antiquarian Society*, 1977, pages 14–19.

Lieutenant H. V. Fison, 1st Battalion, Northumberland Fusiliers: *The Sheffield Daily Telegraph*, 3 October 1898.

Private John Rawding, 21st Lancers: *The Sheffield Daily Telegraph*, 5 October 1898.

Winston Spencer Churchill: Ian Hamilton, *Listening for the drums* (London: Faber and Faber, 1944), pages 243–7.

Sergeant-Major Clement Riding, Royal Army Medical Corps: *The Sheffield Daily Telegraph*, 4 October 1898.

FINALE: 'A Long and Bloody War Is Before Us' (W. S. Churchill, 1899)

W. S. Churchill: Natal Provincial Archives, Pietermaritzburg; The Sir Evelyn Wood Collection, A. 598, V-1-3.

Private Archibald Coward, 1st Battalion, The Rifle Brigade: Bodleian Library, Oxford; MS. Acland d. 148.

Sergeant Benjamin Green, 1st Battalion, Oxfordshire Light Infantry: *The Oxford Journal*, 1 February 1902.

BIBLIOGRAPHY

C. Barnett, *Britain and her Army, 1509–1970* (London, 1979).

Michael Barthorp, *War on the Nile: Britain, Egypt and the Sudan, 1882–1898* (Poole, 1984).

Darrell Bates, *The Abyssinian Difficulty: the Emperor Theodorus and the Magdala Campaign, 1867–68* (Oxford, 1979).

I. F. W. Beckett, *Victoria's Wars* (London, 1974).

E. N. Bennett, *The Downfall of the Dervishes* (Edinburgh, 1899).

Brian Bond (ed.), *Victorian Military Campaigns* (London, 1967).

C. Chenevix-Trench, *Charley Gordon: An Eminent Victorian Reassessed* (London, 1978).

Winston Spencer Churchill, *The River War* (London, 1899, 1900).

Sonia Clarke, *Invasion of Zululand, 1879* (Johannesburg, 1979).

Sonia Clarke, *Zululand at War, 1879* (Johannesburg, 1984).

H. E. Colville, *History of the Soudan Campaign* (London, 1889).

C. C. Eldridge, *Victorian Imperialism* (London, 1978).

Frank Emery, *The Red Soldier: Letters from the Zulu War, 1879* (London, 1977).

Byron Farwell, *Queen Victoria's Little Wars* (London, 1973).

Byron Farwell, *For Queen and Country: A Social history of the Victorian and Edwardian army* (London, 1981).

L. H. Gann and Peter Duignan, *The Rulers of British Africa, 1879–1914* (London, 1978).

Philip Gon, *The Road to Isandlwana* (Johannesburg, 1979).

P. M. Holt, *The Mahdist State in the Sudan* (Oxford, 2nd edition, 1970).

J. Lehmann, *The First Boer War* (London, 1972).

A. Lloyd, *The Drums of Kumasi* (London, 1964).

J. Luvaas, *The Education of an Army, 1815–1940* (London, 1965).

Sir Philip Magnus, *Kitchener: Portrait of an Imperialist* (London, 1958).

Colonel J. F. Maurice, *The Campaign of 1882 in Egypt* (London, 1887, reprinted 1973).

Leigh Maxwell, *The Ashanti Ring: Sir Garnet Wolseley's Campaigns, 1870–1882* (Leo Cooper, in association with Secker and Warburg, London, 1985).

John Milton, *The Edges of War* (Cape Colony), (Johannesburg, 1982).

Donald Morris, *The Washing of the Spears* (London, 1966).

F. Myatt, *The Golden Stool* (London, 1966).

F. Myatt, *The March to Magdala: The Abyssinian War of 1868* (London, 1970).

BIBLIOGRAPHY

A. Nutting, *Gordon: Martyr and Misfit* (London, 1966).

Thomas Pakenham, *The Boer War* (London, 1982).

Adrian Preston (ed.), *In relief of Gordon: Wolseley's Campaign Journal of the Khartoum Relief Expedition, 1884–1885* (London, 1967).

Oliver Ransford, *The Battle of Majuba* (London, 1967).

A. R. Skelley, *The Victorian Army at Home: The recruitment and terms and conditions of the British Regular, 1859–1899* (Montreal, 1977).

A. J. Smithers, *The Kaffir Wars 1779–1877* (London, 1973).

Julian Symons, *England's Pride* (London, 1965).

Philip Ziegler, *Omdurman* (London, 1973).

Index